Hidden *Harmony*

Malinda Cramer's

HIDDEN *Harmony*

Compiled and Edited
by
Joan Cline-McCrary

Divine Science Federation International
Denver, Colorado

Library of Congress Catalog Card Number 90-83266
ISBN 0-9617598-1-X

Cover Photo: Ronald R. Franklin

Published by
Divine Science Federation International
1819 East Fourteenth Avenue
Denver, Colorado 80218

Contents

Acknowledgements

Divine Science Federation International is grateful to those who have made possible the reprinting of the work of Malinda Elliott Cramer. The late Dr. Ruth Fangman Townsend was able to accumulate all except eight of the total 211 issues of *Harmony* Magazine. The remaining issues came from Dr. J. Gordon Melton of the Institute for the Study of American Religion in Santa Barbara, California, (who had access to the missing portions of Volume 1) and from the library at Unity Village, Unity, Missouri (which had access to the missing portions of Volume 2).

Divine Science Federation International also wishes to thank Mrs. Mary Tanton of Cazenovia, Illinois, who provided the Federation with a copy of *God Incarnation -vs- Personal Re-incarnation, Evolution and Karma*. The picture of Mrs. Cramer came from the 1902 edition of *Divine Science and Healing*, a copy of which was given to the Divine Science Federation International by the estate of Mrs. Edith Cross of St. Louis.

The printing of this book, as well as the other recently published Cramer material, is due to the generosity of those who have contributed to the Malinda Cramer Fund. To these contributors, we give our special thanks.

We also wish to thank Meme Baumann, Jeanne Pomranka, and Robin Sheperd for their proof-reading and editorial assistance.

Foreword

The pages of *Harmony* Magazine are brittle now, and yellowed by their 100-year residency in library vaults and back rooms, but their content remains vital and pertinent to today's reader. Moreover, their words reveal the voice of a master teacher. It is the voice of Malinda Elliott Cramer, one of the bright lights of American religious history.

Much of Mrs. Cramer's wisdom was hidden for several generations, lying in various libraries scattered throughout the United States, and by 1980 only Mrs. Cramer's *Divine Science and Healing* — out of a voluminous production for more than eighteen years — remained easily available to the public. Interestingly, the wisdom is available to us, now, only because of the perseverance of the late Dr. Ruth Fangman Townsend, a Unity teacher from San Diego. Because of Dr. Townsend and her associates in Revelation Research, all 6000 pages are now available for research.

Until 1988, this was not the case. Not only had most of Mrs. Cramer's works been shuttled into various libraries, much of her history had been lost. Her entire operation — college, daily healing work, church, as well as her national/international monthly publishing efforts (which served as a focus for numerous satelite movements) — literally went up in smoke with the fire that followed the San Francisco earthquake in April, 1906. And her death in August of that year resulted in her name fading into obscurity as the 20th Century progressed.

Although her husband, Charles L. Cramer, reprinted her monumental work, *Divine Science and Healing*, in 1907, (subsequent editions were undertaken by Divine Science) and although some of her work was reprinted by Nona Brooks during the 1920's, most of her writings passed out of sight. Consequently, the name of Malinda Elliott Cramer has become little more than a footnote in American religious thought.

Yet, Mrs. Cramer was one of the most prolific writers of an entire genre of American religious thought, and, as such, must have influenced untold thousands in the Victorian world, for we still hear her echo in today's spokesmen.

This book, *Hidden Harmony* is just one of several that have been produced recently (or are in production) of the writings of this remarkable lady. Malinda Cramer definitely wielded the written word, and in her hands it was mighty. Furthermore, we can surmise that what we read in *Harmony* was what was heard from her pulpit and lectern. She candidly admitted that although some of her associates had repeatedly urged her to speak "inspirationally" (without notes), she refused to do so, preferring to read from a carefully prepared text — thereby not indulging in what was termed "inspirational speaking."* Consequently, Mrs. Cramer's presentations were constructed to convey a clear teaching.

Happily, her insistence has resulted in her material's remaining in existence these 100 years.

It is from the eighteen volumes of *HARMONY* Magazine that the wisdom of Malinda Cramer emerges. Yet, reading between the lines, one suspects that Mrs. Cramer's understanding far exceeded what we find on the written page. Consequently, this collection is an attempt to try to see some of her "occult" understanding. Thus the title of this collection — *The Hidden Harmony*

The word OCCULT has a connotation in the 1990's that it had not fully acquired by the 1890's. The 19th Century usage of the word was still near Webster's primary definitions — i.e. *occult: not revealed: secret: abtruse, mysterious: not able to be seen or detected.* Even the fourth definition — i.e. *relating to supernatural agencies, their effect, and knowledge of them* — lacked today's connotation of evil and the suspect.

Cramer was one among several who were revealing *the occult* (what had hitherto been hidden) to the Victorian world. She saw things in a different light from those who kept things hidden. She declares it early in her career as she writes in the second issue of *Harmony*:

> *... there is nothing hidden that shall not be revealed; first find the kingdom of heaven, and all knowledge is yours. ... The way is within you all. Therefore, let us make nothing mysterious nor secret; remembering always that Knowledge is Wisdom. He that wisely gives of the tree of knowledge is the heavenly physician.* Harmony l:5 (2)

Mrs. Cramer was unusual among her peers, not for the magazine that accompanied her Home College and the movement that it fostered, but for the fact that she PERSONALLY edited (and did much of the writing) for that magazine. It seems likely that Cramer saw her magazine as important as her teaching and almost as important as her healing work.

Just after the turn of the century an interesting comment appears in *Harmony* regarding Los Angeles. Cramer remarks that "everybody and

---

*One of Cramer's associates (whom she calls a "long-time close friend"), W.J. Colville, was such a speaker. The San Francisco *Chronicle* called Colville "the celebrated inspirational speaker and *improvisatore.*" According to another account, he was reputedly "often quite unconscious" while delivering his address or answering questions.

their relations have been here (to teach the Science), but then left them leaderless." One suspects that Cramer's intent with *Harmony* was to provide the needed leadership. Similar comments are made with regard to the movements in Kansas City and in St. Louis (sometimes by Cramer's students and sometimes by Cramer herself), that although others had broken the virgin ground, it was *Harmony* Magazine — and the subsequent visits by Cramer — that had expanded the "Science" movement in those cities.

All material in this collection (except for *God Incarnation Versus Personal Re-Incarnation, Evolution and Karma*) has been reproduced from the original pages of *Harmony*. The reader may notice some printing difficulties experienced by printers in the 19th Century. A number of the letters are broken. Most likely these were well-used type characters. Furthermore, occasionally the letters "u" and "n" are inverted, and sometimes a letter will be several spaces above or below its line.

Harmony was printed with hand-set type, at least for the first volumes. (Automatic type was first successfully set in January,1889.) The reader may notice the imperfect spacings and uneven lines characteristic of hand-setting. The cost, in today's dollars, to print the first few volumes would likely have been around $15,000 per year. Much of this cost was borne by the Cramers. The churches and centers generated by the Divine Science Movement were not closely held to the mother church as were those connected to Christian Science. Consequently, the cost of the magazine above the income from subscriptions was not spread out over the members of numerous churches. The following comments come from Volume 15, September, 1903, and indicate how the Cramers felt about their magazine.

Joan Cline-McCrary

Special, to the Readers of Harmony.

The editors of HARMONY extend love, gratitude and thanks to all its readers for past co-operation and true appreciation.

The publishing of HARMONY has not been, nor is it, a money-making business. Its continuation from year to year has been due to our love for the good that could be accomplished through its pages. It is a matter of spreading the truth among the people, that they may realize "the more abundant life," and enjoy its freedom. Divine Science is spreading, and is as sure of permanent growth as Truth itself.

Of The Soul

———

BETWEEN the garret and the basement of feeling lies contentment—the middle ground of satisfaction, upon which the Soul does all her permanent work.

The Soul, occupying the middle ground between spirit and body, is spoken of as feminine, because her nature is to produce or bring forth. She acts as a cause for what is more external, namely, body; and she brings forth according to her perception of spirit, *i. e.* principle.

The Soul, struggling against emotion and despair, in her search for peace, gives emotion and despair the only power they can have.

Experience is the Soul's schoolmaster; another master can but point her to experience.

When the Soul is governed by the senses she follows a material career until she sees that there is nothing in it; after which she faces the other way, and, following a spiritual career, finds there is all in it, and the value of her experiences. The lesson she has learned is, that the senses are deceivers ever.

As water seeks its level, and finding it rests, so the Soul continually seeks her source; and, finding it, rests.

————

The Great Lesson To Be Learned

There is but one time, that is Eternity; what IS now, has been and will be. There is but one Life, one Mind, one Law; *whatever is, is forever.*

Be not misled by the appearances of things. Remember Matter is an appearance, and in it you will only find appearances. Like is always found with like; bodies with matter, but principle with Spirit. Sensation and emotion are effects, and are therefore mere appearances belonging to matter; but mind and love are causes, and belong therefore to God. Thought—please pay great attention to thought—belongs to Matter *or* to Spirit, according to whether it is material or spiritual. If you understand this simple sentence, you hold the key to all expression. The Universal one Soul, is ceaselessly recognizing the one Infinite Spirit, and reflecting her thoughts in Universal Matter, or Ether. Matter, the changeful expression of Soul; Soul, the permanent expression of Goodness; one Goodness, the only reality.

Introduction

by
Joan Cline-McCrary

*And he sent them to preach the kingdom of God, and to heal the sick.
...And they departed, and went through the towns, preaching the gospel,
and healing every where. Lk 9:2,6*
Although many continue *to preach the gospel,* only scattered individuals in 1990 would confess to a belief in present-day "healings" similar to those mentioned by Luke. Yet, only a century ago, throughout the United States, there were several who were *preaching the gospel and healing everywhere.*

But times change, and today's self-proclaimed pundits declare that only today's messages have any validity. Some, declaring anything other than the very narrowest range of traditional Christianity to be "occult" (and not knowing its definition), even label Christian Science as a "cult." They refuse to hear anything but themselves. Others, preferring to hear of global catastrophe and extra terrestrials, by-pass the "old" messages in favor of what they think is NEW.

Too bad! For in some of the messages from 100 years ago are the ANSWERS to today's questions.

One hundred years ago, a Quakeress, named Malinda Elliott Cramer, along with a handful of other pioneers, was bringing a renewed spiritual vision to the world, revealing what had been hidden and espousing what outsiders viewed as a new religion. However, it was not a new religion — it was *preaching the gospel and healing everywhere.*

It was an understanding that enabled healing, whether the individuals were present or not. Great numbers testified to both their own healing and that of others. The pages of *HARMONY* Magazine abound with those who had witnessed healings, healings by Mrs. Cramer — and by her followers. This was "preaching" of a new order.

In fact, the Preface of the enclosed "New Order" announces:

It has been known to the author for some time past that a new order of teachers was becoming manifest on this planet; an order whose teaching and methods would be different from those of the Brethren of Eulis [Eleusis] or any other school of Occultism; whose teachings would surpass those of past orders, and in surpassing, explain them; for the time is at hand when this may be done with wisdom. **Harmony Vol.5:85,86 ***

---

*Ed. note: Henceforth *Harmony* notations will read **5:85** for volume and page number. Notations of other works will be in standard form; brackets [] indicate editorial additions.

The gospel (good news) of the "new order" was not an attempt to replace Christianity but to heighten the understanding of those who called themselves Christians by adding (more correctly restoring) Eastern understanding to that of the West — one might say, by restoring the *heart* of the East to the *mind* of the West.

The gospel of the "new order" was an attempt to reveal the unreality of the sensual world and lead the way for each man and woman's attunement with the spiritual. But despite the new order of teachers, the message found fertile ground only for a time. Two world wars, a depression and a cold war dissipated the message and tied the world even more tightly to its *senses.*

THE ANCIENT WISDOM

In the 19th Century, some called the Ancient Wisdom *occult* (hidden); some called it *New Thought.* Some today call it by the same terms; but a Theosophist, Claude Bragdon, writing in 1910, clarified the terms:

> *What is the Ancient Wisdom, which, antedating recorded history, is yet the New Thought of the present hour? Adequately to answer this question would require an entire literature; yet the answer lies dormant in the mind of everyone: it is the knowledge and the love of what the Chinese call Tao, the Hindus, the Higher Self, the Christians, Christ. The Ancient Wisdom is at once a philosophy, a science, and an art.* [1]

This philosophy, this science, this art — flourished as the 19th Century progressed; and, in the last few decades of that century, it produced remarkable visionaries. Some of these expressed themselves as poets or writers, some as lecturers or ministers, some as teachers and healers. Yet, their genius was nothing new; the understanding had surfaced many times in the history of mankind, just as it is again resurfacing in the last decades of the 20th Century.

However, few recognize that today's enlightenment is simply an extension of what began more than 100 years ago.

THE NEW ORDER

Throughout the United States, Western Europe, and the British Empire various teachers/movements stood out as evidence of the "new order." Not all teachers generated movements; not all movements had heirs; and not all teachers lived well into the 20th Century.

Among the Americans, an impressive group emerged. Malinda

---

[1]"The Ancient Wisdom in the Modern World," *Episodes from an Unwritten History,* (Rochester, 1910), p.89.

Cramer, Emma Curtis Hopkins, Charles and Myrtle Fillmore, and of course Mary Baker Eddy. Their message was neither new nor singularly received (although this was disputed by Eddy).[2]

We are most familiar with the American examples of the *new order;* but judging from the (sometimes obscure) British and European writers found in *Harmony*, this is shortsighted on our part. Certainly Eddy/Christian Science and the Fillmores/Unity are standouts throughout the world for their numbers and longevity. Certainly Blavatsky (et.al)/Theosophy had a lasting effect, although not so visibly to Americans. Certainly Hopkins had her lasting effect.

More difficult to trace is Cramer, the one whose entire operation was burned to the ground, the one who left the scene much earlier than anyone else, the one whose husband and son were apparently so devastated that they never rebuilt. And, yet, it is Cramer who may have been the most prolific writer of the American "new order."[3]

Great portions of the American culture proved themselves open to new ideas, but for the most part organized religion had no part in either maintenance or distribution of the Ancient teachings. While the ancient wisdom had been "retained" by some portions of traditional religion, it was not dispensed to the laity. It was only through this "New Thought" or through secular sources that the common man would hear the wisdom.

Fittingly, with Volume One of *Harmony* Cramer began to "educate" her readers. She established her parameters with her "Meditations" (see

---

[2]A progressive flow of understanding had come upon the Western world in reaction to the Age of Reason. The Western contact with the Far East — particularly Britain's two-century stay in India — had its effect. Swedenborg had revoiced the Ancient Wisdom that was always about; the British Romantic writers had secularized the concepts; and, finally, Emerson and the Transcendentalists had plowed deep the understanding. Only part of the the heritage had been "hidden."

The somewhat cloaked Freemasons and Rosicrucians (and we should add the Kabbalists) had maintained the Western religious climate sufficiently so that by the mid-1800's the Theosophical and Swedenborgian ideas found fertile ground in the Western world, making the Ancient Wisdom of the "New Thought" flower.

As proof, by the 1893 World Parliament of Religions (in conjunction with the Chicago World's Fair), even staid American Victorians anxiously welcomed Vivekananda as a celebrity. Moreover, throughout the entire nation, great numbers gathered to hear various speakers of the "new order," regardless of when or where they spoke.

[3]Although younger than Eddy by 23 years, Cramer preceded her in death by four years (Cramer, 1906/Eddy, 1910); Hopkins died in 1925; and Myrtle Fillmore (1931) was followed by Charles (1948).

Despite the early date of her death, Cramer had finished the pioneer work of eighteen years of healing, teaching, and publishing Harmony Magazine. Through the magazine she not only had unified this "new order" for a time (except for Eddy and Hopkins), she had molded an entire generation, providing a sounder footing for their understanding than it would have had otherwise.

pp. 59-109), and she broadened the understanding of her readers with what she wrote and printed. She printed portions of classical material; she printed portions of Eastern and Middle Eastern wisdom that pertained; she wrote and printed Metaphysical necessities; she presented the wisdom of the Bible in this light; and she tied it all together with what is called *An Occult Novel,* "The New Order" (see pp. 111-151).

It is no wonder that the magazine came under Cramer's sole editorship early in its existence.[4] The magazine is clearly Cramer's vehicle — her TEACHING vehicle. In Volume One's pages, the master teacher gives what basis her students will need to proceed to the understanding of the Ancient Wisdom.

This is the writing of a "master teacher" EDUCATING. Regarding EDUCATION, she writes in the March issue of 1896:

> *EDUCATION is, properly, to draw forth, and implies, not so much the communication of knowledge,* as the calling forth of inherent Truth. *It means* leading out of. *Were we to speak from the standpoint of the babe, we might say the child has no formulated thought to lead out or call forth; but if we speak from the standpoint of Being, we must perceive and know that all thought and possibility IS potential there and can be revealed in the child as well as in the adult. ... The new and true education is from within. It is making known the knowledge of Being, which is manifest in all things; it is making known the truth that has already been revealed in nature.* **8:155**

One could contend that Cramer attempted to educate her readers away from the "intellectual" realms and into the spiritual. It is this *sounder footing* that Cramer spread with her magazine. It could be argued that Cramer was attempting to take her readers from Metaphysics in to an understanding that was MYSTICAL. As author Dorothy Elder points out in her recent book, *From Metaphysical to Mystical,* there is a point where *metaphysical* understanding is transformed into *mystical* understanding; and Cramer had reached that point.[5]

Part of the Metaphysical footing had been in the messages of Theosophy. Cramer begins her magazine as *A Monthly Magazine of Philosophy devoted to TRUTH, Science of Spirit, Theosophy, Metaphysics and the Christ Method of Healing,* but by October, 1891 — after returning home from her extensive

---

[4]F.E.Coote, who is listed as co-editor until June, 1889, resided in Australia (Australasia as Cramer calls it) when publication of the magazine began (nicely for beginning subscriptions in that part of the world), but by 1889 he had returned to San Francisco to set up his own School of Metaphysics; he is not listed as co-editor after June, 1889.

[5]Webster defines *mystical* as 1. *having a spiritual meaning or reality that is neither apparent to the senses nor obvious to the intelligence* and 2a. *of, relating to, or resulting from an individual's direct communion with God or ultimate reality.*

tour — both *Theosophy* and *Metaphysics* are dropped from the logo. It does not seem, from a close study of *Harmony,* that Mrs. Cramer's understanding changed, but that her view of other disciplines changed. Those disciplines which were dropped, Theosophy and Metaphysics, (as well as "mind cure" and "Spiritualism") are tied to the intellect.

However, she recognized, as she says in the enclosed "Review of Theosophy ..." that "this (the intellectual philosophy) the world at present makes great demands for." Nevertheless, Mrs. Cramer and the "New Order" novelette's Mr. Fairchild are mystics, the latter having little respect for those disciplines which remain tied to the intellect.

Cramer never fits snugly into the label of Metaphysician. In the first issue she makes no distinction between Metaphysical and Spiritual *Healing,* saying that her lessons are "instructions ... to attain an illumined or spiritual consciousness." She notes that "There is a certain amount of discipline that all must have before they can heal, or understand why truth does heal."**1:18** As the first volume progresses, however, her position shifts; for the approach of the intellect is, as Cramer says in the enclosed "Meditation" for April 3, 1889, (see p. 82):

> *"...To have our consciousness embedded in things is to be dead; to be concerned ... with the things of earth is to be dead to life ..."*

Most likely, it was the internalization of this understanding that had occurred in 1885 (when Cramer felt she was totally healed from 23 years of illness). Indeed, is this not the healing for all of us, to realize our ONE-NESS with GOD?

SAN FRANCISCO'S SPIRITUAL CLIMATE

Exactly what preceded the 1885 healing is open to question, and the fact that Mrs. Cramer's library and records burned in 1906 leaves the actual history likely untraceable; but we do know that San Francisco in the 1880's enjoyed a cosmopolitan culture. Obviously, given its large Oriental population, proponents of various Eastern religions were resident there. In addition, "occult" organizations could be found in the city. According to Dr. J. Gordon Melton, the Rosicrucians had come to California as early as 1859, and it is likely that Freemasonry was present for many years prior to that. Theosophy, too, was present in the Bay City if we are to believe the enclosed "New Order." In the late summer of 1886, W.J. Colville lectured for several weeks on topics as diverse as Spiritualism, Atlantis, Mind Cure, and Women's Suffrage.

For several years (prior to 1885) the San Francisco *Chronicle* had carried numerous "scientist" and mind-cure advertisements and a large number of "spiritualist" advertisements. Interestingly, these ads were often placed (many of them as churches) on the church page. However, the message varied.

INFLUENCES ON CRAMER

Cramer always tells us that we will be taught OF (a preposition which to her seems to mean both *of* and *by*) the Holy Ghost. This is best expressed in the remarks found in the enclosed "Is Divine Science Theosophy or Christian Science?" (see pp. 164-168), which partially answer the questions posed as to Cramer's spiritual path. She says:

> *This Truth (Divine Science) I did not get from any book, but it was spiritually perceived and intuitively realized, and this before I had read any book upon the Science. (see p. 165)* **10:290**

Charles S. Braden in *Spirits in Rebellion* makes an interesting aside when he says:

> *If, indeed, her system was an original discovery arrived at on the basis of no previous reading or contact with persons holding "metaphysical" concepts of healing, then Malinda Cramer stands out as an unusual figure in the story of the rise of New Thought.[6]*

One of the current misconceptions, one likely furthered by some of Braden's remarks, is that Cramer was a student of Emma Curtis Hopkins. However, in all 6000 pages of *Harmony* Magazine there is no evidence to support such a contention. Furthermore, a simple glance at the dates of the material in the References in this *Hidden Harmony* indicates a vast knowledge and understanding present in Cramer by October, 1888. Such knowledge could certainly not have been acquired in the one year from hearing Hopkins (1887).

In greeting the delegates to the Fifth Congress of the I.D.S.A. (International Divine Science Association — which she founded in an attempt to unite the entire "Scientist" movement), Cramer said:

> *Early in the year 1885, I perceived the true basis of Divine Science, the idea of the Omnipresence of God and Him manifest in Creation. Later, I perceived that the All-in-All is God, His creative activity and creation; this simple law of expression was direct revelation to me. So, I am ready to accord the same (direct revelation) to all people, and I agree that they can know Truth for themselves. When others tell me that they, individually, have received the Truth from God, I am ready to confirm them in it; for, from whom would they receive it if not from the One, Only Source?*
> **12:87**

---

[6] Dallas, 1977, p.270.

Although Cramer would never have used Eddy's term "race-mind" (because she anticipated her students' being above it), she recognized that numerous individuals considered their particular messages to be Truth. The collective consciousness of those living in the Western culture in the latter part of the 19th Century was geared for "receiving" Truth — just as it was geared for "healings."

On the other hand, the thinking (the collective consciousness) of late 20th Century man (Braden was writing in the early 1960's) has become so tied to the intellect that few can conceive of someone having such an understanding as to "receive the Truth from God." Instead, 20th Century scholars place each "teacher" in a linear descent from another.

The understanding of those of "the New Order" of teachers seldom came in a linear process. Quimby was not in direct descent from Swedenborg or Emerson; and even though Eddy had studied under Quimby, she discounted his influence.

Simply reading another or hearing him speak does not establish a teacher/student relationship. Most likely Cramer's training came from her individual studies. She was, obviously, a consumate student of the Bible and apparently an avid reader of the "higher criticism" material then in circulation. Simply her study of the Bible could have been sufficient to produce her understanding. In addition, she had her Quaker heritage, a tradition of hearing — in the silence the "still, small voice."

Cramer recognized the blessing of her heritage. In praising an associate Carrie S. Alden, Cramer said she "was blessed by 'Quaker parentage' and *divinely intellectual.*"

It may be this *divinely intellectual* that the 20th Century no longer recognizes, but have we really fallen so deeply into the materialist's view that we cannot ascribe an individual's understanding to oneness with the Divine Mind, even when the individual is of utmost repute and states such as being true?

Obviously, Cramer does not contend that she had never heard or studied or read spiritual and metaphysical material; and, needless to say, her vast knowledge was not the product of a few short years. It would seem more correct to say that whatever she needed came to her (in one way or another). Most likely, what we are seeing in the more than 6000 pages of *Harmony* was what Cramer received.

Although Cramer calls no one *teacher,* she may have had some earthly influences. As Braden suggests, one such influence may have been Warren Felt Evans.[7]

Mrs. Cramer makes little mention of the Kabbalah, but her comments in Bible interpretations, as well as some of her articles, indicate a familiarity with some of its teachings. Her acquaintance with the understanding may have come through her friend W.J. Colville (who wrote a book entitled *The Kabbalah* in 1916); or it may have come from information that was available to her from other sources. For many years the public had had access to Kabbalistic teachings through numerous writings, and access was made even easier in 1887 through the first edition of *Qabalah Unveiled* translated by S.L. MacGregor Mathers from the Latin *Kabbala Denudata*.[8]

The Victorian knowledge of the occult was probably deeper than is ours, not in a negative sense, but in its willingness to see beyond the intellect. Apparently Cramer considered herself "a student of Occultism." She excuses a review of a year-old book, one of Franz Hartmann's books, as necessary, "as it contains some remarks valuable to students of Occultism."[1:13] But it appears that Cramer remained apart from the established organizations. She was not a follower of Blavatsky or the Theosophical establishment, although she had great respect for what she called *true theosophy* (see pp. 157, 158, 165).

Nor is it likely that Mrs. Cramer was a Rosicrucian (although the novel found in this collection may have been her subtle disclosure of such study). However, she did have close Rosicrucian connections. (Several R.C.'s are listed in the advertisements in the earlier issues of the magazine, and her son Frank's name is followed by R.C. several times.) However, any reference to anything Rosicrucian lessens as the years pass.

There is little mention of Freemasonry in the writing of either Mr. or Mrs. Cramer; yet from Dr. Ruth Townsend's research we know that Charles Lake Cramer's funeral (Dec. 30, 1911) was a Masonic service. Most likely, Mrs. Cramer would have had access to the many writings of Albert Pike, and she may have had access to the esoteric Masonic teachings.

---

[7] In the first volumes, she quotes Evans several times, and upon his death she publishes almost an entire page in tribute (see p. 57). It is unusual for Cramer to dedicate an entire page upon someone's demise. The death of the vice-president of Home College (Mrs. Rose de Groot) warranted only a few lines, and Sir Edwin Arnold's death in 1904 is not even mentioned. The only other lengthy eulogy is for her long-time associate (and a writer for *Harmony*), William Brunton. It is found in the last issue of the magazine, April, 1906, very close to the last page of *Harmony* that was ever printed.[18:213] (The earthquake was April 18, 1906.)

[8] In speaking of her husband's associates in his esoteric school (commencing in 1888), Mathers' wife comments in the Preface to the New Edition (Samuel Weiser, Inc., York Beach, ME, 1970) that "They, with my husband, held high Office in the Societas Rosicruciana in Anglia, and other Masonic bodies." The material in this preface is greatly informative, for Mrs. Mathers is speaking of the activity in Europe at a corresponding time to Cramer's (among others) activity in the United States, indicating that she (Mrs. Mathers), as well as her husband, had been taking part in these studies and organizations.

It appears that our understanding of the availability of esoteric study in the Victorian world is greatly limited. Apparently, a world-wide network truly existed, aided by ever-increasing written communication and by travel between the areas of Europe, America, and the rest of the world. In some ways, Theosophy was the synthesis of the wisdom of this entire network; consequently, Cramer's view of Theosophy touches on many disciplines and is, therefore, hard to pin down. However, her views regarding Swedenborgianism and Rosicrucian tendencies are quite similar.

Part of her feeling about Theosophy is found in the enclosed "A Review of Theosophy..." (see pp. 156-163). She says:

> *The word Theosophy did not, nor does it, mean any of the theories of evolution, or of personal reimbodiment, or of physical causation taught under the name Theosophy. My understanding of the word Theosophy was, and is,* Divine Wisdom, *or wise in the things of God.***10:290**

One sees her partial views of Swedenborgianism in the enclosed piece eulogizing Warren Felt Evans (see p. 57), but a book by Susan Wood Burnham, a Swedenborgian, brings a Cramer indictment:

> *To conclude, we must say that consideration of Health from a psychic basis is as complete a failure as the consideration of evolution from a psychic basis. ... for judgment by the senses is always erroneous, and the psychic plane is just as material as the physical plane, hence judging from the psychic basis is sense judgment and is erroneous.***1:239-240**

Cramer levels a similar indictment at Franz Hartmann, a German (Bavarian) Theosophist, Rosicrucian and spiritualist, in the enclosed "Rosicrucle" (see pp. 153-155), a review of Hartmann's *Adventures among the Rosicrucians*, which, she says, "is not a text book such as is [his] *Black and White Magic* [pub. 1886 as *Magic, Black and White*]."

> *Now both of these books appeal to two opposite classes of readers — one class are the intellectual, who devour the scholastic learning and get led away by the marvelous and remain in the symbol; the other class are the intuitive, who, getting behind the form or symbol, simply understand.* **1:13**

Yet, she has high praise for much of what Hartmann says, and, in fact, quotes him five years later:

> *To die — in the real meaning of the term — is to become unconscious of a lower state, and thereby become conscious of a higher existence.* **5:194**

CRAMER'S LITERARY CHOICES

Who and what influenced Cramer will probably never be known, but she does make a revealing statement in the last paragraph of the enclosed "Review of Theosophy ..." (see p. 158). She lists *The Song Celestial, The Light of Asia,* [both by Sir Edwin Arnold], *Black and White Magic* [by Franz Hartmann], *Light on the Path* [Anonymous], *Esoteric Buddhism* [A.P. Sinnett], and the *Theosophist* (magazine) as among the best works on Theosophy. In addition, she adds, as "**amongst the foremost contributors of recent times to religious progress,**... the works of Max Muller and Mohini Chatterji and the early volumes of the Hibbert Lectures."**1:137** (For Cramer's view of *Esoteric Buddhism* by the turn of the century, see p. 172.) Obviously, Cramer was a voracious reader of both classical and contemporary literature — by those of this "new order." This does not make her any particular person's student. In fact, any argument as to "who was whose student" only points to a failure of the combatants to internalize Cramer's message.

Remember the definition of *mystical*! This "Ancient Wisdom" was NOT something to be intellectually learned! Furthermore, to Cramer, the teaching was being done by the Holy Spirit, not by individuals.

CRAMER'S PART

We come upon Mrs. Cramer as though in the middle of a play (we only have material beginning with the October, 1888, issue of *Harmony*) where the important players (Eddy and Hopkins) are seldom mentioned and the associate parts are played by unknowns. Much of *Harmony* follows the careers of these associate players.[9]

P.P. Quimby and Emerson had already played their parts by 1888, and Warren Felt Evans would die in 1889. Mary Baker Eddy was at her height in Boston having a five-year-old *Christian Science Journal* and a thriving movement (despite the loss of several of her brightest followers) — having twenty-two more years in her productive life. Eddy's former follower, Emma Curtis Hopkins, was just beginning her activity in Chicago, with almost an identical time-table and a similar script to that of Mrs. Cramer — but with a more lengthy appearance on the stage.

Sir Edwin Arnold would die in 1904; Franz Hartmann in 1912; and William Wilberforce Juvenal Colville, not until 1917.

Cramer apparently began teaching formally in 1887; by May, 1888, she had instituted her Home College (at her home address). In the

---

[9]Advertisements and notices in Volume One of *Harmony* indicate the "characters" already on the stage — in their separate roles. Some who may be recognized: W.J. Colville, Josephine R. Wilson, Annie & Harriet Rix, Mrs. Sarah A. Harris, Mrs. Sadie Gorie, George & Mrs. Anna Kimble Chainey, (all related to San Francisco at one time or another); Dr. W.P & Mrs. M.M Phelon and Ida A. Nichols (in Chicago); Miss W.J.Rule, Wm. Oxford, Miss E.J.Taylor (in Australia and New Zealand). Interestingly, many of these "characters" seemed to move from place to place, spreading the word.

Chronicle for June 24, 1888, she advertises under Sunday meetings:

> *Classes in the science of the spirit (or metaphysics) and its application in healing. ... All invited. The normal class for students wishing to graduate opens July 10... This affords opportunity for pupils, **wherever they may have studied,** of becoming duly qualified teachers and healers.*

Over the next 18 years, Home College generated a number of branch colleges. In addition to the College was The Home (actually, the Cramer home address, too), which apparently was a combination of rooms for "healing" and, in some cases, rooms where associates lived.[10]

Nevertheless, the role of Malinda Cramer ten years earlier in October, 1888, at the inception of *Harmony* Magazine, is not that of a singular figure with "healing rooms", a college, and a printing press.

By October, 1888, Cramer already has a substantial following (possibly, more correctly) **network**. She is involved in an international network called Committees of Universal Register, and with the first issue of *HARMONY* (in the enclosed "Meditations"), she suggests to this world-wide network topics for simultaneous meditation. But, it is more than this; Cramer in her divine optimism presents these topics with the following comments:

> *All persons whether belonging to the committees or not are requested to unite in the consideration of the following subjects; all editors of magazines and papers are invited to bring these subjects before their readers, and so promote harmony and union in thought amongst all men. It is not intended that these subjects should be interpreted or considered according to any fixed ideas of any school of thought, but that they should be considered by every individual — laying aside all prejudice — in the highest light that can be brought to bear on them.***1:148**

An editorial aside is appropriate here. Here is the explanation of why Malinda Cramer could heal. She expected healings! She expected coopera-

---

[10] Mrs. Cramer was always quite concerned that there be appropriate housing for young women and, in fact, started the Home Fund which raised money to establish "Homes" for such young women. Annie Rix Millitz' Homes of Truth may have utilized these funds. *Harmony* reports the establishment of each such "Home," as it is set up — throughout California and in a few other places. However, apparently (as was the case with each college and with each "home"), these satellite institutions were totally autonomous.

In the enclosed "Is Divine Science Theosophy or Christian Science" Cramer refers to one lady's regular visits to 'the Home' through which she had become confused (see p. 167). Judging from the comment, she could have been referring to 'the Home' set up by Annie Rix and Sadie Gorie which was relatively close to San Francisco, but which taught ideas not sanctioned by Cramer.

The church which formed around the college, the First Divine Science Church of San Francisco (complete with its Sunday School), was not established until October, 1897. (Its first service was not until January, 1898.)

tion even from the most powerful people in the world. She expected a united world consciousness to bring vast changes!

This is a pattern she repeats several times. First she addresses the world and her network with "teaching" meditations. The Meditations were published between October, 1888, and October, 1889; after this she teaches using much longer lessons. She again addresses the world after 1891 with suggested topics for Silent Unity.[11] In the topics for Silent Unity, she again is suggesting topics for simultaneous world prayer. These continue through the remaining years of the magazine, until 1906. With establishment of I.D.S.A (International Divine Science Association) in 1892, she again establishes topics for unified consideration and meditation. By 1903 she addresses this world-wide network of readers as "Our *Harmony* Class," again urging world-wide prayer. Finally, in the last several issues of the magazine, she even is suggesting world-wide, simultaneous Sunday School lessons.

Harmony was the special teaching vehicle of Malinda Cramer. With it she taught and she united a world-wide network in unified thought. Once having read *Harmony*, one can see why the statements of all of the New Thought leaders — down to the present ones — have a familiar echo to them

The entire reading public of *Harmony* was Mrs. Cramer's classroom. Repeatedly, throughout the eighteen years, she corrects statements made by others — so that her "students" will not be misled. She corrects certain assumptions made by Eddyites; she corrects certain assumptions made by proponents of mind-cure; she corrects Theosophy. She corrects anything that does not speak from a knowledge of the Omnipresence.

One might interpolate that *she taught, not as the scribes and Pharisees, but with authority.*

Often these corrections appear in the reviews of current literature. Probably the finest of such is "A Review of Theosophy and *The Secret Doctrine*." One sees in its pages a Malinda Cramer that is far beyond the common teacher — a Malinda Cramer equal to (if not beyond) her contemporaries. The reader of *Hidden Harmony* can get a better picture of the 1880's as he or she reads the enclosed *The New Order: An Occult Story,* written by "a Rosicrucian." The reader can see the variety of viewpoints which were available to the individual in the 1880's. The novelette, which

---

[11]Cramer's College had always had weekly meditations, but upon returning from personally meeting Charles and Myrtle Fillmore (previous contact had been by mail) on her trip to the Midwest in 1891, she immediately established the San Francisco chapter of Silent Unity, acting as its president for several years and, personally, furthering establishment of such groups in other California locations.

in my opinion was written by Malinda Cramer, nicely parallels Mrs. Cramer's activities. Of some interest are the weekly sessions at "the Home."

Cramer saw her own teaching as *utilizing a systematic approach*;[12] consequently, with establishment of her magazine in October of 1888, Cramer simply expanded this approach to a greater audience. As she said, recognizing that few have access to "Spiritual or Christian Science" colleges or class-teaching in health and healing, "to these dear sisters and brothers our published lessons will be a messenger of peace, giving rest, health and happiness."[1:18]

CRAMER'S EFFECT

Yet, it is difficult to assess Cramer's effect. She taught many thousands, in California and through her several personal, nation-wide tours, as well as through *HARMONY*; and her echo is still heard today in the various New Thought thinkers. But, given the temper of today, one wonders if her effect was lasting.

Mental science has remained mental science; traditional Christianity has remained traditional Christianity. Eddy's Christian Science has continued to view the physical as illusion, and likely, New Thought has been more a product of the Metaphysical League's metaphysics and an intellectual approach to the spiritual than of International Divine Science Association and its approach.

Cramer's thinking transcended all intellectual approaches; she was preaching a gospel that healed.

It doesn't matter if the outside world understood her message; it doesn't matter whose teacher she was or whether she had any teacher. It doesn't matter what her effect was. It is Mrs. Cramer's message that is of importance to today's listeners: MANKIND MUST CHANGE ITS PERCEPTION OF ITSELF; MANKIND IN ITS PROPER EXPRESSION IS GOD'S EXPRESSION.

CRAMER'S TRUTH

Admittedly, Cramer had no question that she had found Truth, and by 1890 she called this Divine Science — and, as she said many times, "when one has found Truth, there is no longer any opinion."

It seems proper to classify Cramer as a mystic. Her information came directly from within, and she eventually saw herself only as God

---

[12]*Divine Science & Healing*, 5th ed., p.21

EXPRESSING. The reader must take careful notice of this line, for herein lies the distinction about Malinda Cramer.

It is with this in mind — THERE IS NO SEPARATION (distinction?) BETWEEN GOD AND MAN; MAN IS GOD *EXPRESSING* — that Cramer must be read. This is particularly true since we are in the material that we are calling **The Hidden *HARMONY*,** for much of the material being presented in the 1990's as "Metaphysics" fails to understand this point. Consequently, it deals with life on the mental plane (as opposed to the physical plane — in Theosophical terms), but it does not go to the spiritual plane.

Through her more than twenty-one years of endless activity and through her eighteen years of *Harmony* Magazine, Malinda Cramer taught her listeners and readers a different view of life. She saw ALL is ONE; she saw ALL is GOD; she saw GOD is ALL. This is not the understanding of many denizens of the latter part of the 20th Century. It is not the understanding of materialism, nor of credal religion, nor of psychology; it is the understanding of mysticism.

Although the "New Thoughters" and traditional Christians of the late 20th Century assume to understand the concepts of the occult (or the concepts of being "born again"), often their understanding has not yet crossed to *mysticism.* Nevertheless, in mysticism both camps are saying the same thing. They have only to cross the bridge from the physical and the mental to the spiritual.

But our 20th Century sophistication makes it more difficult to cross the bridge. We as an audience in 1990 are much more sophisticated than those in 1890. We have bowed to scientists for more than 100 years, we have listened to psychologists for almost 100 years, we have been visited by various gurus for nearly 100 years, and we have been exposed to metaphysicians and clairvoyants and "born again" preachers for the last 100 years.

And in that same more than 100 years, we have moved from Eddy's "race consciousness" to immediate visual notification (and most likely observation) of every global calamity. The mind of the resident of the last decade of the 20th Century likely is even more tied to the physical expression than was the resident of the previous century. Consequently, we may feel cheated that Cramer does not explain everything to our satisfaction. We may feel cheated when Cramer speaks to our spiritual selves rather than to our mental or psychic selves.

THE 'PSYCHIC' OCCULT

The 19th Century was just as enamored with the psychic phenomena and ideas as is the 20th Century. Even as early as 1884 the San Francisco *Chronicle* ran as many as eight advertisements in one day for different psychic-spiritualism speakers. Theosophy and even Swedenborgian disciplines dealt with the psychic, but Mrs. Cramer seldom mentions the spiritualist phenomena — relegating it to the mental realm. Even the topic of reincarnation is taken and turned to her particular bias as the reader can see in the enclosed *God Incarnation -vs- Personal Re-incarnation....*[13]

Only the briefest mention is made of her own experience. It isn't even a full paragraph, but a few sentences in the review of a book, *In the World Celestial,* by T.A.Bland, M.D.. She says:

> *His (the story teller's) experience with a well-known medium in New York is very similar in physical phenomena, to what the editor of* HAR- MONY *experienced thirty-two years ago with the same medium, and witnessed again in San Francisco in her own home.***15:27**
> (Ed. The review is dated October, 1902. This would place the New York encounter as 1870 and fits nicely with her medical journey to New York where the doctor advised her to go to California. In the beginning of the review she had explained that the story teller [a well-known literary man], while in a trance spent time with "those whom the world called dead,... enjoying the society of one who was his lover in early life.")

Mrs. Cramer never answers the question of reincarnation in terms that would satisfy a late 20th Century reader, partially because she always transcends the physical. At one point she says that reincarnation can only be

---

[13]Nor was she alone in her position. This is still true in most New Thought circles. While many of those in New Thought privately admit to a sympathy for the idea of reincarnation, few ministers and fewer movements will publicly admit such leanings. Part of the explanation may lie in the tradition of each of the movements in New Thought.

Ernest Holmes puts it quite clearly in *The Science of Mind* text:

"I do not believe in the return of the soul to another life on this plane. The spiral of life is upward. Evolution carries us forward, not backwards. Eternal and progressive expansion is its law and there are no breaks in its continuity." (pp.386-387)

Rev. Marge Flotron points out the view of Emma Curtis Hopkins as being in *Self Treatment.* While the sheer poetry of Hopkins' writing partially obscures her view, Hopkins writes:

"... We may keep eyes on the flesh, keep fingers on matter through this world, through the next world, through the world beyond that, on into the three heavens of our Bible, the twin heavens of Mohammed, the ten heavens of Dante, we may return again to this planet, or fly to Saturn, Jupiter, Mars, Venus — but the call of Master and king, the inconceivably small One, the every where present One, is still the same! 'Come!'" (p.28)

Of all the major pioneers, only Charles Fillmore of Unity speaks of reincarnation as do most occultists. He writes: "Without doubt the secret of Paul's great illumination ... is that in previous lives he had built up a spiritual consciousness, and on his way to Damascus he **stirred up** the gift that was within him. ..." (*Atom-Smashing Power of Mind,* pp.28-29)

correctly *understood* by one who has attained understanding of Omnipresence — in the Eastern terminology — become illumined. She insists that only the "spiritual plane" must serve as a basis for attention. For Cramer, only total absorbtion in the spiritual plane is true THEOSO-PHY — GOD WISDOM.

This is the Ancient Wisdom, this is the New Jerusalem, this is the speaking in tongues, this is being born again, and this expresses itself in the rapture! This reveals the Hidden Harmony!

In many ways the attention of today's self-proclaimed spokesmen falls short, for it is not always centered on the spiritual; but, then, these spokesmen are not bringing about healings — AND Malinda Cramer was!

The Mystical

EXCERPT from Volume Seven

Ed. note: To Mrs. Cramer, as to the Kabbalists, the number seven is one of the most significant of numbers, for it represents physical completion. Without doubt Cramer considered Volume 7 of *Harmony* Magazine as a milestone. Its first issue came out in October, 1894, and it is almost presented as a declaration of who she is. She lists herself under the title of "Our Workers" (subsequent issues introduce other workers).

Its first page is a photograph of Mrs. Cramer, taken by her husband, Charles. Although Cramer was not overly modest and later on advertised both her photograph for sale as well as that of her husband, this was the only photograph of her ever to appear in *Harmony* Magazine. (The copies available of this particular photograph are too poor to reproduce.)

The photograph introduced Cramer's description of her "healing" and the subsequent revelations that had resulted in what she called *Divine Science*. Prior to this, the magazine had never told her story. The story was later added to the early Lessons to become part of *Divine Science and Healing*.

Two portions of her several-paged article are printed here. While her first statements reveal her familiarity with the teachings of theosophy (the lower and higher self) as well as the understanding of Eddyites (separation of Divine Mind and body), Cramer's combined remarks disclose to the world experiences beyond the physical realm.

"During the hours devoted to silent meditation and affirmation of the good, I realized that the mental change taking place was the mental act of passing from the individual to the universal; and at one time, while making absolute statements of Life, I saw the fallacy of the popular belief that there is a *lower self* and a *higher self*, for Cause and effect must forever be united. With this realization, passed away the belief of the separation of Divine Mind and body. I saw that holiness consisted in oneness—that Spirit and body are at-one in truth. I realized from the beginning, that Infinite Mind and it manifest, was the All in All. When there was no longer two self-hoods, and no body of falsehood to deny, my health sprang forth speedily, and I realized a body free and could say this day: 'A body thou hast fitted me.'

"One day ... I experienced a realization of wholeness beyond all previous conceptions: I realized the passing from, or the blending of, the individual mental conception into the conception of the Universal Mind of Consciousness.

"As soon as I laid my head upon the pillow, I consciously withdrew from the body and looked upon it lying upon the bed, and realized it to be a thought within My Mind. I then said inquiringly: 'Where am I, and what am I?' Simultaneous with this question, I saw another form—white and ethereal in appearance, vapory and cloudlike; this form enveloped the one lying on the bed

and pervaded it through and through. My realization
was that it was (beyond all question) a thought in My
Mind.

"Then I thought with increased earnestness: 'Where
am I, and what am I?' And in answer to my question,
there was before me (within my consciousness) a six-
pointed star, pure and clear as diamond light; its center
calm and clear as pure crystal, and radiating the Light of
Life. I knew unto a certainty that it was a center of consciousness, or conscious action within My Mind. I intuitively understood its connection with the forms I had
previously seen. I knew it to be also a thought in My
Mind.

"Again I said, with even more emphasis: 'Where am I,
and what am I?' And simultaneous with the asking of this
question the third time, was completed the realization of
the full consciousness of Being. 'I' **was** that
Omnipresence which lies back of all form; the **Mind**
which contains within Itself the things that are seen; the
Mind not seen, but which Itself is Consciousness. 'I' was
not only conscious, but was consciousness Itself." 7:9-11

Erroneous Teaching.

No one who supposes that protoplasm is the origin of man, or that he has
evolved from unconscious life, ever gives a treatment for the healing of disease from his assumed source, of protoplasm or unconscious life. This
proves that his theories and teachings are not practical nor demonstrable
even to himself. Every healer who expects healing to follow his treatment, bases his treatment in conscious Mind, pure Intelligence, the unchangeableness of Truth, the inseparableness of Life—the Holy Spirit, the
One All.

To teach that one has evolved from unconscious life is like giving a continuous treatment for poverty ; lack of life, substance, intelligence and
power ; lack of health, ability to succeed and unfold the Truth of Being.
We should give no place to such suppositional theories.   M. E. C.

Ed. note: Although only slight differences exist between the following account (from 1903) and the preceding account (from 1894), the 1903 material has a vitality that Cramer's work had lacked for several years. In fact, Volume 15 (1903) is almost as vital as the first few volumes.

Of particular interest are her comments "... The time came (for plowing) when I experienced a branch within that did not bear fruit of the Spirit." She never states just what this "branch" was, but from mid 1901 a number of Cramer's articles dealt (at least in part) with never accepting dualism; yet, to Cramer even the mention of any difficulty was dualistic. The unfruitful branch may have been the International Divine Science Association (IDSA) upon which much of Cramer's effort was expended between 1891 and 1900 — which somewhat corresponds to the period of lesser works. By 1899 and the fifth IDSA conference, no one else was interested in hosting the gathering — thus forcing its return to San Francisco. The conference in 1899 was the last.

It may have been because she saw the IDSA as unfruitful that it ceased to exist, thus allowing Cramer to concentrate her efforts on her own "Home work," as she said in one place.

What I Have Seen.

WHEN first I commenced to treat myself in 1885, I treated, as I do now, from the plane of Omnipresent Spirit. My affirmations were profuse, and always true of my consciousness of what Holy Spirit was. I was thoroughly imbued with the consciousness of the presence of Spirit within me, and in all, and that the Law of Being worked from within out. My body had been clothed upon, as it were, with beliefs and conditions of Invalidism, not only twenty-five years, as published in "Our New Book," "Divine Science and Healing," but practically so from early childhood, and it was seemingly slow to respond.

I first felt a sense of freedom in the brain, which soon enveloped the entire head with a sense of ease and peace, which was glorious to me, and quite remarkable.

It was sometime before I was able to demonstrate the same sense of relief through the chest and shoulders, but through diligent and earnest work it was accomplished. I continued the treatment promptly at stated times, always recognizing God within, around and as All. That is, I knew I was embraced within the Omnipresence of the All Good, and that I could neither breathe, live, move nor have being apart from it, or in anything different.

Finally freedom, ease and peace were sensed throughout the entire body; then when I concentrated in treatment, either for myself or for others, I sensed the vibrations throughout the entire body; there was a glow of life felt, which was the outcome of my consciousness. My patients enjoyed the same. They would say, "I feel the treatment in every part of my body, either as a soothing glow of warmth, or a gentle, peaceful thrill of electricity." The sensations were even, smooth and harmonious in every part.

This self-treatment was the actual quickening of the Spirit, and renewing, or bringing out afresh the real state of Being. All my teaching and healing has been from the Unity and Presence of the One All. So I have always seen healing follow as the result of both teaching and treatment.

Thomas J. Shelton, in speaking of his spiritual demonstrations in *Christian*, says : " In my own experience there has been much plowing and harrowing before I could see the Truth. You must see everything in the subjective before it can be made manifest in the objective."

This is true with many in the beginning, and they, as he, work faithfully through the plowing season and come to realize the new resurrection body.

In my case, for years there seemed to be no need of plowing. Now you will want to know if the time came when there was need. The time came when I experienced a branch within that did not bear fruit of the Spirit. Just how and where to locate it outwardly I knew not, nor did I care to do so. I moved on in the even tenor of my way, always teaching and healing from the highest, and proving the Principle of Truth with equal power and force for others as before. All the while knowing that what is true of God is true of man, and that deliverance was mine ; that my true consciousness was freedom. I have experienced deliverance, the branch is removed ; the power of the spirit through its own strong affirmations in thought and word that I have voiced worked the works of God. This branch that bore not fruit was not of my own conscious production, and yet was the reflected result of a negative , therefore, a receptive condition to the adverse mental states of some with whom I have been connected. No sooner was this negative mental attitude discovered within myself, than it met with merited destruction at my own hands.

So the principal demonstration that I have seen of late is a most wonderful and marvelous demonstration within myself.

Rejoice with me, I am the way, Christ Jesus made so clear. Gone forever is the seeming branch that bore not fruit.

PARAGRAPHS.

Life is the light of the world; love is the nature of life.

The true light of Life lighteth every man that comes into the world.

To express love in all our ways, is to let light shine.

To be the Life, the nature of which is love, and let light shine in all, is to glorify the spirit of God, on earth.

THE SECOND BIRTH.

Thy Christ has unto thee come
　With remembrance of the truth sublime,
That of all living things thou 'rt the total sum,
　Eternally poised in the *Center* of time.

Time for thee has no beginning, no end,
　For deathless thou standest between
Past and Future, and thus ever blend
　These counter-parts in one *Present* serene.

Being the Center of the whole, thou 'rt the life,
　The heart whose pulsations of consciousness give
To its body the world release from the *strife*
　Of existence, for *to know true Being is to live.*

Thy memory in this *Now* doth contain
　Both what has been and that which shall be,
The fulfillment of all, with naught yet to gain,
　The Seventh Day's rest of eternity.

On thy forehead appearing in living light,
　In letters ready traced by the "Ancient of Days,"
Which through æons have awaited the illumining bright
　That ever is heralded by Heaven's lays,

Is written thy name for Memory to read.
　It contains all that language can ever express—
The create and Creator in One who doth lead
　From circumference to center on the *line of wholeness.*

"I am" is thy name. Thine action is *to recall,*
　When into light and time thou hast thus evolved
From thy dark unmanifest deep the all,
　Thy *One* equals *Seven* and from *works* thou 'rt absolved.

And we know and have believed the love which God hath in us. God is love; and he that abideth in love abideth in God.—*I. John 4: 16.*

Whatsoever ye would that men should do to you, do ye even so to them.—*Matt. 7: 12.*

HARMONY

Is Wisdom's Way of Presenting her Expressions.

Vol. 1.   JULY, 1889.   No. 10.

Mathematics, or Truth.

Mathematics is that science which treats of the exact relations existing between quantities or magnitudes, and of the methods by which quantities sought are deducible from other quantities known or supposed. And the science of spirit is that science which includes all sciences, which treats of the exact relations of souls and of nature to God; in other words, which treats of the true and exact relation of all things that are manifested to their parent source.

A mathematical demonstration is one that accords with unchanging law or principle; so it is axiomatic that there is an unchanging law or principle which underlies mathematical demonstration. A truthful conclusion or harmonious expression, is one that is in exact accord with unchanging law or principle; so it is axiomatic that there is an unchanging law or principle underlying truthful conclusion and harmonious expression.

As the Supreme, Infinite source or Being is one, its method of demonstration is one. As in the study of the science of numbers, all problems solved are in exact accord with the principle, so in the study of the science of Spirit, all truthful conclusions that are formed, must be in exact accord with the Spirit; and the purpose of the study of the science of life or spirit, is that of finding where and what spirit is, that which is "yesterday, to-day and ever the same;" that we may speak the word of reconciliation, and make our manifestation represent or demonstrate it with mathematical precision; also, that we may learn to work in exact accord with the Spirit, in thought, word and deed, by imaging in consciousness its attributes and unchanging truth, by correct and careful thinking.

To have no other God before me, is to acknowledge God in all our ways, which means to have no ways that are unlike His; then He will direct the path which leadeth unto all wisdom, to a perception of all truth, by which the problem of life is solved.

The science of Spirit is the way to truth and life; its teaching instructs how to express, according to principle or the law of Being in thought, word and deed; and when thought is according to law, we demonstrate with mathematical accuracy in the body, and in word and deed. "Mathematics has not even a foot to stand upon, which is not purely metaphysical. All parts of knowledge have their origin in metaphysics, and finally perhaps, resolve into it."—*De Quincy.*

Metaphysics is the science of first principle, law or cause, that which precedes the physical, as the principle is prior to the problem. There cannot be an example without the principle; an example is an idea symboled, so that the senses may cognize it.

There cannot be an expression without an expressor; there cannot be a visible appearance without the presence of the invisible cause; there cannot be a form of matter, a form of thought or speech, nor course of action, without the presence of the formless or maker of forms. A form of any kind, is a symbol of an idea, i. e., an idea spoken that the senses may cognize it—principle imaged.

Principle means highest, first, that from which anything proceeds. Wisdom is the principle source from which knowledge is gained. As in the science of 'mathematics, the principle is the highest or first, and is that from which the problems proceed; so the Spirit of God or Goodness, is highest and first, and is that from which creation proceeds. As the principle of mathematics is prior to the example, so the Spirit of God or Goodness is prior to creation.

Physical forms hold the same relation to God, that examples do to the principle. The examples are symbols of the ideas in principle, in mathematics; and created forms are symbols of principle or Spirit; neither are life, substance, or power. We must find ourselves as one with that which is prior to creation, and place it first and foremost in our thought before we can demonstrate harmoniously and mathematically, or interpret ourselves truthfully. "As the harmony of a sentence is promoted by adapting the sound to the sense or idea to be expressed," so the harmony of expression is promoted by adapting our thought to that which is to be expressed, and that which is to be expressed is the spirit of God or Truth.

Harmony in created things is to be promoted by perceiving their true relationship to their source, and then adapting thought, word and deed to harmonize with things as perceived. Harmonious expression and truthful interpretation is one, so the truth of God, which is wholeness, health and happiness, is as simple as the multiplication table, and as easily understood. Science is truth ascertained, which is exact knowledge; we cannot ascertain truth, or gain exact knowledge, but of that which is exact and unchanging. So true knowledge consists in knowing first cause, law or absolute power, considered apart or as pure from application. The application of science or truth, is the application of cause, law and power. So the application of the science of Spirit, brings forth manifestations from Spirit according to the law of Spirit, which is love.

Through sense seeing, personal will and desire, the consciousness is veiled from a perception of truth and perfect understanding. The perception of truth is light unto the soul, is rejoicing in wisdom.

Expressions of life are in the power of thought. That which is called death is a denial of power. That which is loved, is held in thought and bears its fruit.

The ear that heareth the silent voice is understanding. To maintain a deaf ear to the senses, is to open it to the silence. We are taught from life eternal, the Spirit of Truth.

"The man which wandereth out of the way of understanding, shall remain in the congregation of the dead." Prov. xxi, 16.

Image God in thy thought, and thus wilt thou prove thy faith, peace and truth to thyself. Compare thy deed with the goodness of God, and thus wilt thou know the master thou servest. The faithful servant doeth the will of the master, and thus is the edenic order maintained.

He that heareth the reproof of truth and rejecteth it not, but abideth in its decision, is in the way that leadeth to a realization of eternal freedom.

To account for our existence is to solve the problem of life.

The awakened are those who have become conscious that it is not they personally or individually that live, but the Father in them.

━━━━━ **The Basics** ━━━━━

HARMONY

IS WISDOM'S WAY OF PRESENTING HER EXPRESSIONS.

Vol. 1.   NOVEMBER, 1888.   No. 2.

IN all the Earth—we speak again, dear friends, of what to most in mortal flesh appears most real—there is not one of all the many Souls of all the many forms but what perceives, each within herself, that which is like herself. In her unconsciousness she surely sees in Absence her unconsciousness; and in her consciousness is One with omnipresent Consciousness. This is the Presence that lights the soul to Oneness, her predestined goal.

Perceiving the Presence, that eternally resides, still amidst motion, amidst change abides; wrapt in attention to the Silent Chord—that Nature in her loudest rending, or a planet's burst, quells not, though every atom of the boundless deeps vibrate, and echo upon echo like a rolling wave reach on and further on in time and space; wrapt in attention to the Still Small Voice, of which the ceaseless Melody of Harmony divine is as a spoken word—we pass to The Inner World of Soul—the Lord. And here perceive the Heavens, that first—first as to state, in time the now; while yet the Outer or the World of Sense was as a prophecy of fulfilment void—in perfect Thought, in perfect Likeness rest; of God the Image—God manifest.

Perceiving the Presence, that within abides—within in state, but as to space unbounded; in excellency supreme; created not; pervading all of Soul—of Thought—created first in Mind of Substance permanent, whereof in imitation is the seeming Light, the Matrix or Akasa, within which all Bodies, Worlds and Suns in fitting likeness find a place. Perceiving thus in Principle the Presence—Nameless, Placeless, Senseless, All—we three in one to the Innermost attain; to Oneness with all Life; to the Absolute; the Essence of all Souls; Substance of Individuality; Thinker of each Thought; of every Word, the Speaker; of Act, the Actor; of Time, Eternity; of Space and Place the Here. The Sabbath of the six days' Labour; of seeming Far the Near.

*   *   *   *   *   *   *   *   *

The beginning and the end are in the present. Now is the accepted time. The Day of Creation, the Day of Judgment and the Day of Atonement are now.

There is a Prayer, which is the seeking of an earnest heart for Truth; and there is a Prayer, which is the recognition of the Truth sought. The former is the Prayer of Hope; the latter is the Prayer of Faith, and is both the Substance and evidence of The Truth sought.

The Awakened perceive not evil, but perceive the good. To be undivided in Consciousness of good is to be pure in heart.

Upon what do you pass judgment? Is it upon what you perceive through the senses? Then, as like perceives like, you who judge have within you that which you sit in judgment upon. Therefore, judge not that ye be not judged.

"God! be my life and blessing"—is the prayer of many a Soul. "I am thy life and blessing," is the Father's ever-present reply. It is a matter of recognition, dear friends.

The Soul's education consists in experience in expressing Ideas, which are forms of thought, and speaking them into external forms, and in expanding the consciousness to perceive that which is permanent, and in harmonizing her will, loves and desires to the Father.

Statements of Truth are never cutting to those who are in Truth.

The object of Buddha's investigation was to find the cause of misery, and the remedy for it. Gautama Buddha found the cause to be ignorance; Jesus Christ demonstrated the remedy to be understanding.

As long as the individual believes that he has two natures, one good and the other evil, sometimes one belief will rule and sometimes the other; and just so long will there be doubt, uncertainty, no knowledge of the Permanent.

Christian Healing is healing by the power of Spirit. Spiritual Healing is healing as Christ did; therefore the two are one.

The individual should make the experiences of others his own; only in so far as he does so does he learn from them.

Shrink not from identifying yourself with God " in which you live," for this is the truth that frees you from limitations and suffering.

The word of God is spiritual truth, and can only be understood spiritually. The attempt to understand the Bibles or spiritual truth by the intellect or sense perception, is like trying to measure the Infinite by personality.

The Way of Approval.

If it be difficult for us to love our neighbours and acquaintances because of something they may have said or done, of which we did not see fit to approve, then to love them is the thing we most need to do; we should never allow the error of a Sister or Brother to prevent us from expressing the all-saving power of love toward them; we cannot expect to be strong in good and be healed ourselves until we arise and do difficult things. "To him that overcometh will I give to wear the crown of life."

Sensation.

All sensation is mortal.
Time is sensation, Eternity is Truth.
Sound is sensation, Silence is Truth.
Sight is sensation, Understanding is Truth.
Place is sensation, The Formless is Truth.
Motion is sensation, Stillness is Truth.

Sympathy and Emotion are Sensations, and are mortal; for they are personal participations in what pertains only to personality.

To judge of our true condition by examination of the physical body is morally wrong. To judge of our capabilities by our present degree of consciousness and understanding is mental darkness. It is setting up our present degree of knowledge against the government of Spirit. Error is without the reality of truth, therefore it is without reality. As we awaken to the reality of Spirit we lose consciousness of Matter; and the less we think about our bodies the more harmony do we express.

Mind.

There is but one Infinite, therefore there is but One Mind, which is absolute and perfect. To the extent that we are unconscious of the Attributes of Divine Mind we are unconscious of our own life, and have not control over our thoughts, which precede external expression. This unconsciousness is sometimes erroneously called 'mortal mind.' It is but a lack of recognition of what mind is. When we turn from principle we turn from Love, Wisdom, Truth and Justice, and we are not capable of thinking truthfully. There is not a truth spoken that is not in the image and likeness of Spirit, and is a harmonious expression.

" The Spirit itself beareth witness with our Spirit that we are the children of God." This is the recognition by the individual of the Infinite Spirit within all; and is the Christ method of healing.

ONENESS.

ONENESS is the Creator of One; One is the idea of Number. All numbers are varieties of the number One, which proceeds from Unity, which is Oneness manifest. Thus we complete the circle from Oneness to Oneness.

There is one Spirit, one Soul, one [1]Body. Within Spirit is Soul; within Soul is Body. Within the Universal Soul are all Souls that take to themselves bodies, Within the Universal Body are to be found all bodies that exist.

There is One Mind, one [2]Idea, one Word. Within the Mind is Idea; within Idea is Word. Within Idea are all thoughts. Within Words are to be found all letters.

There is one Creator, one [3]Man, one [4]Woman. Within Creator is Man; within Man is Woman. Within Man is the type of every creature. Within Woman is to be found the nature of every type.

There is one Principle, one Solution, one Book. Principle, Father; Solution, Son; Book, Matter. Principle contains Solution; Solution contains Book. Principle perceives and solves; Solution is its work. Solution perceives and solves; Book is its work. To Solutions there are no beginnings, to Books there are no endings. Solution is end without beginning, Book is beginning without end.

Whoso understands Oneness the flaming swords touch not, but he passes again within the Garden of Eden to eat of the Tree of Life.

＊　　＊　　＊　　＊　　＊　　＊　　＊　　＊　　＊　　＊

In truth we live; and if we do not think the truth, we are untrue to truth. Every unpleasant feeling is a sign that we have not been true to the truth.

----

[1] Matt. xxvi, 26.
[2] i. e., The Word in St. John I, 1.
[3] Gen. I, 26.
[4] Gen. II, 22; 1 Cor. xi.

An effect is the appearance of what has past. **Then if we live in any** effect—i.e., in that which is dead—we have no consciousness of life; for life belongs to the present, but death to the past.

For those who are of the world, Imitation is by no means justification. For those who are not of the world, Imitation becomes Being and is in every way Justice.

Affirm for yourself everything that pertains to Eternal life. Deny from yourself everything that pertains to the Body. For you are not the Body, but you are Eternal life.

Thirdly—I have brains. Secondly—I have thoughts. Firstly—I am the thinker. Then firstly, what relation are you to your thoughts ; and secondly, what relation are you to your brains, or body ?

In what is your faith based ? God's works are the evidence of His Faith. Each individual's works or manifestations are the evidences of his Faith. What does your evidence prove ?

Thought being an effect can only affect effects. Furthermore, the only effects that thought can affect are the appearances, that are eternally without reality. No one can be affected by anything, but anything by its constant changes is a constant evidence of continuous effect. He who states that he can be affected by any thought, or anything, identifies himself with an effect— such as a post ; and this is death, for every effect is dead.

A consciousness of Truth is Eternal Life. Truthful thoughts or declarations are the buds which bloom and produce the fruits of Spirit.

The aura, or thought emanations of the awakened, electrify the atmosphere with the healing balm of truth for all who come within their mental sphere ; as the flowers extend their fragrance to all who come within their sphere.

CORRESPONDENCE.

The New Doctrine.

"WHAT thing is this? What new doctrine is this? for with authority commandeth He even the unclean spirits, and they do obey Him."
—St. Mark, i: 27.

The same wonder as of old still asks of truth an explanation, and the same answer of deed and word is given. The sick are healed by mind, and the power of Christ heals them. Modern religion does not teach this as possible, but the life of Jesus as recorded in Scripture places an emphasis upon this fact, too important to be overlooked or lightly treated, as both are proof of His divinity, and that by which He gained authority to command obedience from the unclean. Modern religion leaves out these proofs, and demands only ritualistic ceremony, forms, and external observances, which hinders the Spirit of Christ from becoming a conscious help to man, giving him the authority of health to body, or making practical the highest truth of Christ.

No one can dispute the work of healing performed by Jesus as being divine. He did not call upon matter, but spirit, which he claimed all men reflect. Such a doctrine was new to that age, and it is new to this. Truth is always new and marvellous 'till its light is understood. Man has scarcely learned the Alpha of his spiritual being; he knows next to nothing of the simplest laws of body, and less of the laws of mind in relation to it. Hear the cry, "What new doctrine is this?" that even the sick are healed, and by the power of Good.

The action of one thought upon another thought is not realized, nor is their vibration upon external manifestation clearly seen, scientifically explained or comprehended. Spirit alone heals the sick. Body is always responsive to mind, and the world will acquiesce if man admit, "to some extent," as if the cause of any result or condition could be at one time matter and at another time mind. As if heat could one time come from light, and another time from darkness. Christ is truth, and if Christ heals, truth must do the same wherever it is found, and in accord with the spiritual unfolding. Christ also is love, and the more love we have the more of Christ is ours, and thus more of the good work is done. Could this be seen and appropriated what a struggle for good the world would make.

Man in ignorance and sin, or contented with the pleasures of sense, does not see the necessity of the good, hence he leaves his soul to the pulpit, and to the drug store his body for restoration to health, as if the power of Christ was on draft, or at the bidding of human command. "Work out your own salvation ; occupy till I (Spirit) come," is a lesson all must learn to gain spiritual light. This must begin in the moral life of man, and when that is righted, the body will be healed without delay. This work is not all expressed in healing the body. A good man's life is a constant rebuke to the evil doer, and though often unconsciously so, is a powerful antidote to sin. The prayers of Christian parents for their children are not lost, nor is the love of the pure for an unworthy object of no value. "To pray for them that despitefully use you" is a power when manifested, that refines better than the most eloquent theory, and is the soul sunshine that chases away the darkness of discord, and the fear that creates disease.

The whole life of Jesus bears the testimony of love by healing the sick, as well as reforming the sinful. His disciples followed His divine teachings, and never forgot this. We find Peter healing the blind man at the gate, restoring the paralyzed Eneas, and raising the dead Dorcas, and if Scripture is true, each disciple did what love ever commands, viz., destroyed physical suffering as well as sin. This is taught in Science and Health also, and its author made it equally important with all other christian work. But above all else, our own convictions should guide us, and who does not concede that sickness should be handled, and by spirit ; that body should be governed by mind, and that man should be "Christ-like in triumphing over sickness, sin and death, to open the prison doors to the captive; that is, to break the fetters of personal sense and give to being full scope and recompense."

How limited our knowledge has been of this truth, but how glorious that its eternal light is dawning upon human thought, and the darkness of sense, tradition, is fading from our land, from body, and from man, and the new doctrine of love, life, and truth is recognized as a science and can be practically applied to the ills of body, for the promulgation of moral strength, the uniting of mankind in brotherly harmony, and the omnipotence of the Fatherhood of God.

"THE Primitive Trinity represented neither three originant principles nor three transient phases, but three eternal inherences in one Divine Mind."— *R. Williams.*

"FOR by what anyone has been overcome, to this also he has been enslaved. Truth never enslaves."

HARMONY

Is Wisdom's Way of Presenting her Expressions.

Vol. 2.   OCTOBER, 1889.   No. 1.

THE HOLY TEMPLE AND THE INNER SANCTUARY.

THE temple of the Spirit of truth and goodness is the divine soul or the divine man, wherein the human knowingly or unknowingly lives ; where the thought and consciousness knowingly or unknowingly resides.

The altar of this temple, from which the Spirit of truth and goodness instructs the human in ways divine, is the absolute consciousness of the union of Spirit and soul, or of God and man.   In this temple and from this altar, or in the soul and from this consciousness, has the Redeemer, from time immemorial, taught the truth, the unity and oneness of life.   From this altar the truth is ever saying, let there be light.   Let my unity, the way of understanding, be known.   There can be no division in the One—Being.   And this Redeemer will ever continue to proclaim this truth, irrespective of the Scribes and Pharisees—or intellect with its pride of attainment, with its boasted knowledge based upon deductions drawn from illusive appearances.

Mortal temples, with their unillumined altars, will decay and pass away ; but this eternal temple, altar and teacher, are One, it passeth not away ; neither is it supported by the mortal, but its unity remaineth permanent from eternity to eternity.   It is the God-head, and is omnipresent.   The mental constitution should willingly and knowingly become a pupil therein, and thus from the altar of truth image forth its teacher in the visible universe.   The teaching received in this holy temple admits of no doubt or mortality, it is of the Spirit, and bears the golden fruit of the Spirit.   That which is evolved and comes forth from this altar, or absolute consciousness of unity with God, is the tree of life whose leaves are for the healing of the nations.   This teaching needs no intellectual aids to make more clear its light ; it is self evident to all who enter therein, for they who enter this temple have eyes to see and ears to hear the voice of the Supreme, for the veil of delusion or materiality must be laid aside before the thought can understandingly enter into this holy of holies, this temple of God.   And when the mask or veil of illusive appearances is rent in twain, the student, or thought, images the Teacher, the Christ, or Truth, and sees face to face. The foundation of the holy temple, or the principle upon which all is based, is the love, truth and wisdom of an omnipresent One ; and where the temple, altar and teacher rest upon one foundation, and that foundation is the trinity—love, truth and wisdom—there is no argument, no distinction, for in that which never differs, beliefs of differentiation find no place.

Therefore all who are taught from this temple obtain the same knowledge, for there is but one truth of which to obtain a knowledge. The incentive which prompts the student of truth, in this holy temple to be good, is goodness. The incentive to be loving and charitable, is Love and Charity. The incentive to be truthful and harmonious, is truth and harmony, and they who enter therein and reason divinely from the plane of Spirit, are illumined by divine wisdom.

The reward or penalty for every student of truth, or thought and consciousness, who obeys or disobeys the teachings of the Holy One in this temple of God, is the fulfilling of the eternal law, that with what measure ye mete it shall be meted to you again. And this truth is written in letters of living light on the walls of every temple of God ; that is, it is included within the divine idea of God, which is man.

Therefore, the first lesson that understanding reveals to the heart of the student, is a silent realization, that to measure forth wholeness and perfection in our thought, is to experience wholeness and perfection. That to measure forth universal love and truth in our thought, and give that thought expression in all our ways, is to experience universal love and truth in creation, which is God manifest in the flesh. Therefore to consciously enter this temple of wisdom, and measure forth its life and truth, it is essential that we love the absolute goodness of the All-pervading One. In this temple, the first of all commandments is, hear, O son of man ; The Lord thy God is one : and thou shalt love the Lord thy God with all thy heart, and with all thy soul, and with all thy mind, and with all thy strength ; and with what measure ye mete the same do you experience and know !

If you measure *wholeness* in your thought, you experience wholeness. If you measure *love* in your thought, you manifest love. If you measure *truth* in your thought, truth is expressed in you.

Upon this law depends knowledge or ignorance. It is necessary therefore, for them that would enter this temple and consciously perceive the workings of Infinite Mind in creation, that they worship in spirit and in truth.

That is, that they perceive the true worth of Spirit, by thought proceeding in a divine and orderly manner, thereby discerning the true relation of things to their source. Then do they truly partake of the bread of Heaven and drink from the fountain of life, and are filled with wisdom, and manifest the way of understanding.

WANT, LOVE AND WORKS.

B E not conformed to this World; but be ye transformed by the renewal of your mind; that ye may prove what is that good and acceptable and perfect will of God." Rom. xii, 2.

There is an essential requirement, threefold in its nature, to be fulfilled by every student of Divine Science if they wish to attain to a high spiritual consciousness and deep realization of the Esoteric truths underlying the expression or creations of Divine Spirit, and of how to work with the law of expression. Understanding comes of experience. We only know the attributes of Divine Mind by perceiving them within our own thoughts, feelings and consciousness. Think divinely, and we are at once conscious in feeling of what we think; think loving thoughts and we feel loving.

To gain a permanent consciousness of the Divine presence of good, is to be unwavering in Divine thinking. To be able to hold steadily to truth, with undivided faith in good, is to be renewed in the Spirit of the mind, which transforms every external expression, word, deed and feeling into harmony. Truth is harmony, and when held in consciousness it is a messenger of peace, bringing glad tidings from the unmanifest Spirit into form of word or outer expression. Truth is life, and when spoken it is health and ease—not dis-ease.

"He knoweth the way that I take." Job xxiii, 10. The first requirement on the way to a consciousness of eternal life—the permanent good—is to *want.* The Student must want the truth because it is truth; want it sufficiently to put away preconceived ideas and beliefs, and work to attain it; want the truth sufficiently to be energetic in refusing errors' claims, and in casting out intellectual rubbish that does not harmonize with the great central and "all-saving truth" or basic principle of Divine Science.

Another requirement is *Love*—Love for all truth, because it is truth —Love and regard for the Omnipresent, silent and invisible God, the only source of life and power. "Except ye become as little children ye can in no wise enter the kingdom of heaven." This means that unless we consult "the Father," the one principle of good underlying all expression, and are governed by Him in our thought, we can in no wise express perfect harmony, which is true happiness and heaven ; for heaven is a condition and is within each one of us, and to think spiritual truth is to realize the presence of the eternal within.

The third requirement is that of *Works.* Not until the student wants the truth, and loves it because it is truth, will he perceive it with reference to himself, and of his relation to the Infinite One. He will see with the eye of understanding when he dares to draw the line between the Creator and the created—the manifestor and the manifestation—himself as immortal and the mortal body, his beliefs which stand in opposition to himself—and when he dares to think of self as invisible, immortal and divine now and here ; that he in being is in the "eternal now" what he ever will be, and that his manifestations and mortal body are alone visible to him on the sense plane. He can only be spiritually perceived and understood ; and until he reverses his decisions of himself he will not perceive himself and understand his relations to Divine Being. The student must dare to rise up and throw off all beliefs of limitation and inharmony, instead of waiting for them to desert him : he must banish from consciousness the accustomed mode of thought concerning self, and all beliefs that are opposed to the spiritual and clear realization of himself as immortal. Then identify himself and feel his union with the one self-existing Spirit in which he lives, and with all life that is manifested. Yes, dare to think that by doing the Will of Spirit, and speaking its Word, he can conquer selfish personality.

The way to strengthen the Will is to sacrifice the individual will to the permanent good, by acting under all circumstances in obedience to the law of good, and by daring to realize Self as Immortal—a divine reality now ; and by facing and conquering life's seeming difficulties as they come. Our expressions are ever changing, and therefore are mortal, and are passing away. Hold fast to the invisible and to the immutable—the Soul, and the Life behind this veil of shows ! If the Student of Divine Science wants to know the truth, because it is truth , and if he love the truth for the same reason and live it as rapidly as he becomes conscious of it, he is taught of the Spirit or Christ within and attains a high spiritual unfoldment.

THE LAW.

A LL religious or divine systems of teaching should point the way by which individuals can perceive the truth for themselves. Unless we see and gain the knowledge for ourselves, we can have no conviction ; and without conviction we cannot have perfect faith ; and without perfect faith our expressions are weak and inharmonious. Even the teachings of the world's great masters—unimpeachable as they are—and the sacred and unalterable truths of a Christ or Buddha can only instruct. We must take the steps upon the ladder of progress for ourselves.

Teachers can point the way to Truth and Life in spoken word and silent thought. Sometimes it is better for the student to have the silent instruction of the treatment in connection with the oral lesson ; especially if it seem difficult to understand the science of spirit, and to hold the truth in consciousness.

All must see and know the truth, and depend upon its practice if they would have permanent health and harmony. To state this in another way we may say, that we must become conscious that we are Divine and Permanent, and speak the unalterable truth for ourselves. We must look beyond the temporal kingdom if we would find the Staff of Life that never fails us ; we must seek the permanent kingdom if we would be conscious of eternal life. " Seek, and ye shall find." Hold the first bit of unalterable truth that you perceive by practising it, and it will act as a magnet to relate your consciousness to more and more of truth. Then, with energetic effort in Truth's practice, and with aspirations attuned by the truth to harmony, the Spirit will lead to all truth. The Consciousness will expand to perceive more and more of that which is permanent.

If the individual be obedient to " the Law"—Love—then, perversity is overcome ; and the student will hold with a divine steadfastness to truth, and rapid will be his growth into a spiritual consciousness. He will be surprised how quickly he will surmount life's seeming difficulties and pass the border line of elemental thought and consciousness, from the mortal to the immortal, from belief to knowledge, from error and dis-ease to truth and ease ; from a belief in death to that of life, and from all illusion resulting from not knowing into the light of understanding.

That which is called the evolution or progression of the human soul is the soul's experience and process of awakening to the God within ; or the process of individual effort in expanding the consciousness to a realization of that which is, and is permanent. And resulting therefrom in an unwavering and perfected faith, based upon a knowledge of self, and of our union with the Father ; and that we are in and of the kingdom, the power and the glory. For when our thoughts and expressions are reconciled or adjusted to the good, we are at one with the Universal Harmony.

Vol. 1.   AUGUST, 1889.   No. 11.

BIBLE LESSON.

" AND WITH WHAT MEASURE YE METE, IT SHALL BE METED TO YOU AGAIN."

WHAT man thinketh in his heart is his belief. Our fixed beliefs are imaged in consciousness and made manifest by our thought. And resultant from our beliefs and general line of thought, are words, deeds, and feelings. Therefore with what measure we mete, the same is meted to us again, or manifest by us, for our measure is an assertion or affirmation of the dimensions of our present state of thought and consciousness. If our thoughts measure the idea of wholeness and perfection for others and for self—they measure the idea from the spirit, and wholeness and perfection is measured to us, for the same is our measure. But if our belief and thought measure limitation and imperfection for others and for self, then limitation and imperfection is measured to us, for the same is our measure. So, it is axiomatic that in proportion as we recognize Truth, to that same degree do we manifest it and know ourselves, the invisible I am.

2. For not until our ideas measure wholeness, have we cast out the beam from our own eye, or rendered the eye single to Truth—which is life; nor do we clearly see to pluck the mote from our brother's eye. As we must ever see through our own eyes, that is, according to our beliefs or our degree of understanding, therefore as long as the beam of error or belief in imperfection remains, we see with the eye of error or belief in imperfection, as through a glass darkly. The belief in imperfection cannot perceive or realize perfection. " Blessed are the pure in heart, for they shall see God." Purity perceives and acknowledges its own. It being omnipresent, recognizes the truth that it is omnipresent, and sees Itself in all, with the eye of purity or perfect understanding. The beam of doubt, which is hesitation, leads not to understanding, it is not a cause for, neither is it a guide to a perfect perception of the entity

and wholeness of Being. Therefore it must be erased from, or cast out of our mental vision, before the consciousness can receive a true image, or perfect idea of its origin. The beam of judging according to the senses, which is made apparent through thoughts of uncharitableness, criticism, and fault finding, must be cast out of our own mental sphere before we can see face to face the absolute truth of the omnipotence of the ever present Goodness. For as long as we have a belief in imperfection, we have a belief that is the opposite of God, for God is *Infinite perfection*, and through such belief we see imperfectly, for our judgment is not of Truth, nor is our measure of wholeness; it is through such believing that error and imperfection is seen in others. By allowing our thoughts to pass judgment, or by yielding them servants to obey appearances, they, through criticism, confirm our consciousness in error.

3. The acknowledgment of the whole truth that God or Goodness is infinite, i. e., All in All, and that there can be but one Infinite or one All, is the one step that leads from Earth to Heaven. To many the thought may occur, a road too short, a truth too simple to be true. When this acknowledgment is made or step taken, and we find the kingdom, and the truth is realized that we are in God or Goodness, and that God or Goodness is in us, and that the two are one in Being, the greatest truth has come, and "when that which is perfect is come, that which is in part shall be done away." When the truth is perceived we must lay off the garb of sensuous judgments, with all carnal thoughts, and make the eye single to the all inclusive truth of the Unity of Being, that is, reconcile and conform our expressions to it, if we would gain a full realization of the wealth and power of the kingdom in which we live, and clothe ourselves in the garb of immortality, and wear the pearl of greatest price, which is perfect illumination. Not until a perfect understanding reveals the Unity of Being, will the expression in earth, the body, be perfect and harmonious.

4. They who would hasten toward Goodness or God, must cease false interpretation and perceive the true worth and position of Spirit; that is, worship in *Spirit* and in *Truth*, or in *single, fervid faith, by holding all in Spirit, and by thinking and speaking truthfully of Spirit, as the truth was spoken by Jesus.* And if the consciousness be illumined by truthful thought, the expressions are light and life manifest or made apparent. If the consciousness be not darkened by false belief and erroneous thought, the ever present truth will illumine the understanding and take away the branches which bear not fruit of the Spirit. When we rise above delusion, to us there is no delusion, and we are able to remove false belief from others; that is, we are able to see clearly to pull out the mote from our brother's eye.

CHRISTMAS.

THINKING back now over nearly nineteen hundred years of the world's history, we reach that particular period during which happened the event whose anniversary is to-day. From the days of Noah to the time of which we are now speaking, the world was passing through the experiences which were heralded by its baptism by water—the flood—a symbol of the Lord, or the Soul. The chief characteristic of this reign of the Soul or Lord was individuality; or, perhaps we will be better understood if we say, the experience of the world at this time was one that pertained to the individual. Hence we find it a period of what may be termed, Individual Law; of law setting forth carefully and in detail all the observances necessary for each man, for each woman, and for each child, both in moral and material affairs, for public or private observance; of law setting forth the different sacrifices and sacraments, fastings and feastings, each in its proper season; of law setting forth the natures of the planets and the stars, and their relation to individual life; of law whence came records of the past and prophecies of the future. Thus we find, that the Old Testament and bibles of pre-christian times, are in general histories of individuality. As to the New Testament and contemporary bibles, we find on the other hand, and for reasons hereafter made clear, that they are witnesses or records of universality and unity.

A truthful interpretation of St. Paul's Epistle to the Hebrews, Chap. ix, will throw much light on the two dispensations; the dispensation of law and the dispensation of love, which is the fulfilment of the law, to which the Old Testament and the New Testament respectively bear witness. The first tabernacle wherein the priest went always accomplishing the service of God, is the symbol of the body; the second tabernacle, wherein the priest went once a year, is the symbol of the Soul. But into the holiest of all, which symbols the Spirit, went no man; for under the old dispensation the way into the inmost sanctuary had not been revealed; nor could it be, because the old dispensation was of the Soul, of which the second tabernacle is the symbol, the world had not yet reached beyond the worship of a personal God, the Lord or Soul. It was known by a few enlightened souls, that in pursuance of Divine law and order, the world would sometimes reach a further consciousness, a consciousness of the Spirit or impersonal God—the symbol of which was the inmost sanctuary—and which consciousness could not be revealed by one who manifested a personal consciousness (so to speak), but would be revealed by one who manifested an impersonal consciousness ; by one who was high priest of a tabernacle not made with hands; by the Messias, who was expected. This expectation was fulfilled in the coming of the Christ—or the consciousness of universality and unity manifested in Jesus of Nazareth. Hitherto the world had not known the Father, but had known His child— the Soul—the Lord; and until the Christ consciousness is reached no one can know the Father ; thus through Christ all come to Him. Hitherto the law had been the observance of Individual Will ; now came the law to observe the Father's Will.

The birth of Jesus of Nazareth marked the transition from personality to impersonality, from distinct individuality to inseparable unity, from Lord to God. The teachings and works of John the Baptist are the link that binds the old with the new, the expanse out of which the present emerged from the past. John baptized with water—the symbol of the old dispensation, at the same time declaring the baptism with fire, or the Holy Ghost, of which the Star of Bethlehem is the sign, the symbol of the new dispensation.

The above remarks apply in principle to the world as a whole ; whether under Buddhistic, Confucian, Zoroastrian, Brahmanic or Mosaic teaching.

Let us look still further back, and see the condition of the world before the days of Noah and the Flood. We will find it thoroughly materialistic ; we will find that the people on the earth in those days expressed a degree of sensuality and ignorance, that was the very ultimate of sensuousness and idolatry. These were truly the dark ages of the planet. It will be noticed we are dealing with the planet as a whole, whose history is that of the nations and people inhabiting it And it is in order that a clear idea may be formed of the earth's evolution, that we refer to antediluvian times.

During the materialistic period then, prior to the days of Noah, the consciousness of the whole earth was thoroughly immersed in the darkness of sensual desires, to such an extent as can scarcely be conceived of in these days. And the manifestation of that consciousness, or the appearance of the world (and its people) in those times. would correspond exactly, that is, the latter would be the appearance of the former. Thus we understand, that the dark ages were the product of dark thought ; and in it the Nations lived until they saw the folly of darkness and longed for light. The whole world longed for better times—it was tired of materialism, found nothing substantial in sensation, nothing of peace or rest, but only perpetual war and discord.

Thereupon the World's thought changed; a universal demand set in for a holier and healthier state of affairs; and the first appearance of this thought upon earth was the flood; the cleansing waters of the Lord were an answer to the general demand for a consciousness of something higher than material things. Then we have seen that the period extending from this time to the days of Jesus, was marked by a consciousness of a Soul of things; that the worship of the Lord was the worship of the Universal Soul, of which the Sun is a symbol. This period was one of phenomenal appearance and phenomenal worship; (e. g. sun worship); but in time, the people of the earth began to aspire to something beyond this, still the numbers of the gods that were worshipped, increased and uncertainties arose as to the true God; and uncertainties drove men, that they began to seek something higher than phenomenal worship, something nearer than a far off God. In answer to this came the prophets, who foretold of better things, of a Messias who would come and lead the children of God into the way of truth and eternal life, into a certain knowledge of The One God. Hereupon, great expectations set in; and the whole World looked for the coming of a God, who would deliver them from uncertainty and its results, who would deliver his people (all people,) from their enemies, (their own unconsciousness), and who would abide with them forever. The dispensation of which the Old Testament bears record, marks the true Middle Ages in the Planet's history. These, however, passed away with the coming of a new consciousness, in which the whole Earth is folded to-day.

In order to understand fully the import of the mission and message of Jesus to the World, we should understand the state of the World prior to his birth; and what led up to it. We have only laid a foundation for such an understanding in the foregoing remarks, but sufficient perhaps to enable our readers to realize, that the appearance of Christ upon Earth was an answer to preceding universal thought and search, or demand. What led up to that demand has been in few words generally set forth.

With the coming of Christ, the World entered upon its last days. Hence the event was one of two-fold importance; first, as marking an era in the history of the World's progress; and, second, as being the second coming of God Himself to the Earth. His first coming was on the Day of Creation; His second coming was in the Day of Christ; His last coming will be in the Day of Awakening. Just now we have to deal with the Day of Christ—let us see how it was the second coming of God. That the first coming of God to the World was in the Day of Creation, needs no explanation—for God is the

Creator of all things. That no similar manifestation of God was expressed between the Day of Creation and the Day of Christ, will be clear if the Order in the evolution of the Planet be comprehended, and if the evolution in expression be understood as the corresponding consequent of activity in thought; and this may be gathered in principle in the preceding pages. Then, it only remains to show, that Jesus was Christ or God manifest, which will appear in the following remarks.

From the Day of Creation to the Day of Christ, the Planet passed through all its stages of unconsciousness. By which we mean, that although God was just as much present to the World during all these stages, as now or at any other time, still the World had no knowledge of that. In its evolution—or involution, if the latter term be preferred, as we are treating of the Soul or consciousness—it had to pass through all the experiences that were necessary for the unfoldment of the Christ consciousness, which is knowledge of the Omnipresent God and at one-ment with the Father. This knowledge is the consuming fire before which ignorance or unconsciousness disappears as grass in the furnace. That Jesus had this knowledge, was and is manifest, i. e. proven; hence Jesus was Christ or God manifest.

Now, then, we can plainly see, that as soon as the Soul becomes conscious of the Omnipresent God, God has come to Her; and forthwith she manifests that consciousness—upon the plane of manifestation. Let us apply this to the Earth; the consciousness of the World is its Soul; when the Soul becomes conscious of God, she knows herself to be one with Him. The Soul of this Planet Earth reached that consciousness at about the time of the appearance of the Star of Bethlehem in the East. Then having reached that knowledge she proceeded to manifest it—yet, no longer SHE, as in the last dispensation, but HE, the Father, through her; for she was at one with Him —and thus came Jesus, the Christ, God manifest on Earth.

CHRISTMAS, 1888. Where do we stand in consciousness to-day? If you had been asked this question nineteen hundred years ago, you might have answered—well certainly the World at present does not afford conditions for the appearance of the Messias it expects; one nation is intent upon its Hippodromes, and another upon its material aggrandizement, and others are in barbarism, and so forth; certainly the Messias cannot appear now. In thus passing judgment you would have lost sight of the fact, that the Messias would appear when the World was ready in Soul and Thought. Appearances are not the cause of thought, but the result of thought; thought is the forerunner of every appearance; therefore appearances are no index of the present. Then, remembering this, where does the World stand in consciousness to-day? Far indeed from where appearances would indicate; on the threshold of a great awakening; in the dawning of a Light that has already come. OLD THINGS HAVE PASSED AWAY, BEHOLD ALL THINGS AS NEW!

FOR THE NEW YEAR.

Be Life *Eternal*, good and true,
 Be just and loving, heed the deep
Silent voice of faith; thus the "New
 And living way," will ever keep
  Thy thought in light of perfect day.

In loving words and loving deeds,
 Is actualized whatever could
Be found of *Truth*, in all the creeds,
 Hold to the Truth that all is good,
  And of it give, and thus receive.

Give and receive; and you will bless,
 And know no empty hand nor heart.
Than this true work of faithfulness,
 There is no higher, better part
  To bring "Eternal Life to light."

AFFIRMATION FOR HEALING.

The Almighty Good has blessed me,
 With *Its* own heavenly store,
And the fullness of its presence
 Will be with me evermore.

HARMONY

Is Wisdom's Way of Presenting her Expressions.

Vol. 2.   MARCH, 1890.   No. 6

The Glory of God is the End of Personality.

THE hour is come, that the son of man should be glorified. "Verily, verily, I say unto you, except a corn of wheat fall into the ground and die, it abideth alone; but if it die, it bringeth forth much fruit." John xii: 23, 24. As every thing in nature is symbolic of truth eternal, truth which nature symbolizes is the essential substance to be understood. And when the method of nature is looked upon with understanding by the Spirit of Truth, the perfect and eternal law of correspondence is apparent; for it is ever true that nothing is hidden from the perception of truth, the only mask or veil that mystifies is error. So we find that the above text is symbolic of what each individual must witness and experience as taking place within his or her self, if beliefs of separateness and selfishness cease, and if the unity of Infinite Spirit be established and enthroned in existence.

Let us, then, ask you to consider the spiritual meaning of this scriptural text written everywhere in nature by the hand of Divinity. When the corn of wheat falls into the ground, its death consists in yielding the seeming separativeness of form to unity, and by so doing it blends with the whole earth as dust unto dust, and because of this impersonal act it is glorified in bringing forth much fruit. As long as it stands alone it yields no fruit, for the reason that belief of separateness is limitation, which pronounces itself to be one among many; but when that which seemingly stands alone—and in belief is isolated—gives up all thought of separateness, and when word and deed express divine love, the unity of Spirit is manifest, and the result thereof is fields of wheat; or resultant therefrom is spiritual food to the nation.

"The hour is come that the son of man should be glorified." Every one who perceives and realizes the truth of Being, and the unity and oneness of expression, knows that the whole earth is the Lord's, and that truth and life is the Being and the Cause thereof. To such the hour is come to be glorified with the consciousness of Infinite Good, for as the corn of wheat relinquishes form and blends with the whole earth, so they have relinquished form and belief in separate personality, and have blended thought and memory into the consciousness and understanding of the Universal Spirit of God, and no longer do they abide alone. To the Christ consciousness, or to the truth, personal existence is but seeming, for by that consciousness form is seen and known as by the eye and understanding of spirit.

The above text is representative of the method which all will pursue when they lay aside belief of limitation, thought of distinction and of separateness from God and from humanity, as a whole or in part. As long as the individual stands alone with personal opinion that he or she is both separate and different from God and from the rest of humanity, selfness, distinction and limitation will be the measure which they mete to themselves. Therefore each one must in time perform the act that will bury or sink, as it were, the belief of personal limitation into the thought and consciousness of the infinite and impersonal God; and by this means find his or her life and true self. This is the death that all must die to find eternal life; that which is found in any other way will be lost, because it is mortal effect and is therefore subject to change, and abideth not to the end. As the Omnipresent One which pervades all things, at all times, is impersonal love, not until the individual as perfectly symbolizes the one living God in thought and action as does the corn of wheat, can he be glorified as it is glorified, with an abundant harvest, nor can he consciously bear the golden fruit of the spirit of truth. But when the individual knows himself to be impersonal being. he knows that he brings forth in every grain of wheat, and in many, many forms of expression. He that loves to sustain thoughts of personal existence and separateness from God and from nature, shall lose that which he loves and tries to sustain, because what he loves is but seeming—appearance only. Existence is a perpetual circle, a never-ending change of generation, dissolution and regeneration; or of birth, decay and re-birth; "such is the work from summer to winter, from seed-time to harvest." The law manifest everywhere in nature, is the law of the moral world, which is the way of truth and light. All may observe how this law of inmost principle when brought into human action disciplines the character and blends it with the divine. It is universally realized and understood that good comes, or is manifest for others and for self, in exact proportion as we extirpate beliefs of selfishness and desire, and practice love in the Spirit of Unity. The belief is general that except a man loves something, and lives for something beside himself, he does indeed "abide alone," and his life is barren; the wealth and blessedness of his Being is not brought forth and imparted to others. But when man comes to know that he is love, and that love possesses all that it loves or includes, he will find himself loving because he is love. Then will he know that he stands not alone, but is one with God everywhere present in humanity.

When faith is based in the person, which is an effect, instead of in the impersonal Cause, which produces that personal effect, beliefs of limitation unavoidably arise, and desire is engendered thereby, and this it is to abide alone. Therefore, to be alone, one need not go into a desert or a solitary chamber. The most gloomy, and impenetrable loneliness there is, is the isolation of the belief of personal ability, will, strength and desire. Since life, substance and power is impersonal, if the foregoing beliefs are entertained one may live surrounded by a multitude of people without realizing a thought of sympathy, or a feeling of love; to such an one how lonely is a great crowd or city. No one can believe themselves to be alone who through truth is consciously free from self-made limitation and desire; but through sense and desire personality always seems to stand alone. Therefore, if narrow thoughts and small beliefs of self-regard fall away, truth and universality will take their place. When we start from the basis of Being with truthful self-appreciation, we are armed with righteousness and wholeness to go forth and do the will of the universal, which has sent us into the world to give light unto the world. In proportion as our acts are loving they are just, and that which is just is for all time identified with the all good. So it is true that expressions which symbolize the unity of Being live in memory, and are as boundless as light, and free as air.

The thought and word of truth builds an immortal structure, and humanity recognizes itself expressed therein. " Verily, I say unto you, except a corn of wheat fall into the ground and die, it abideth alone; but if it die it bringeth forth much fruit." How sacred the law and sublime the process which this text proclaims! what vast possibilities does it unfold; how full of faith does it fill our thoughts for the world and for the individual ! with how much calmness and certainty all may take up this truth; and obey the divine law as the corn of wheat obeys; and be glorified as the son of man is glorified in bringing forth much fruit in the thought and heart of humanity.

———

He who walks by the light of experience gained, walks by the light of things created; but he who walks by that which gives experience, walks by the Creator, and is himself the light that guides existence aright.

PERCEPTION, OR CONSCIOUSNESS.

" WHEN Jesus came into the coasts of Cæsarea Philippi, he asked his disciples, saying, Whom do men say that I, the Son of man, am? And they said, Some say that thou art John the Baptist; some, Elias; and others, Jeremias, or one of the prophets.

" He said unto them, But whom say ye that I am? And Simon Peter answered and said, Thou art The Christ, the Son of the living God.

" And Jesus answered and said unto him, Blessed art thou Simon Barjona, for flesh and blood hath not revealed it unto thee, but my Father which is in heaven. And I say unto thee, That thou art Peter, and upon this rock I will build my church; and the gates of hell shall not prevail against it· And I will give unto thee the keys of the kingdom of heaven, and whatsoever thou shalt bind on earth shall be bound in heaven, and whatsoever thou shalt loose on earth shall be loosed in heaven."—*Matt. xvi*, 13–20.

If we consider the subject of perception, we shall readily see that belonging to perception is the perceiver and the object perceived. Now objects perceived are in two distinct classes; those that are perceived with the senses belong to the Material Class, and those that cannot be perceived with the senses belong to the Immaterial Class. To the Material Class belong all words, worlds, and sensations; to the Immaterial Class belong attributes and principle. The Mind perceives Immaterial objects (that is, principle); the senses perceive Material objects.

Perception is the consciousness in the perceiver of the objects perceived, which, in the case of immaterial objects, is true consciousness, and everlasting; but, in the case of material objects, it is a false or reflected consciousness, and dies with the memory of its concepts.

Like perceives like; the senses perceive sensible things, but the Spirit perceives spiritual things. Nor is it ever otherwise; as, that the Spirit perceives sensible things. Mind never perceives Matter; nor do the senses perceive Essence or spiritual things. To the pure all things are pure; to the good there is no evil.

Now, if Christ belongs to the Material Class, if he were a person, or visible being, flesh and blood (the senses) would reveal him—but they do not and did not. Then, not being a sensible thing, he or it cannot be perceived by the senses or in a sensible way. But if Christ be the Truth, or principle, then the Mind of man, which is the Mind of God, will reveal it; " flesh and blood hath not revealed it unto thee, but my Father which is in heaven."

Perception it is, or consciousness, that reveals to us the way, the truth and the life. This consciousness is the rock upon which I will build my church, and the avenues of delusion can never prevail against it; because the avenues of delusion are the senses, but consciousness of spiritual things belongs to Spirit. And I will give to thee—*i. e.* Spiritual Consciousness—the perception of Love and Wisdom, which is the keys of heaven.

You will notice that in this interpretation of the wonderful passage before us we have got rid of Peter's personality altogether; and in its place we have the true Peter, which is Peter's Consciousness or perception; or, to speak more correctly, we have the invisible Peter, his perception and the truth he perceived—three in one. This is the rock upon which the Church of The Christ is built; built not by hands, attained not by ceremonious effort nor prolonged works; but now, and by the simple recognition that "I and the Father are one."

If we reflect for a moment upon the Material consciousness—or carnal or mortal mind—we shall determine that it is sensation; for we call the consciousness of sensation—sensation itself, just as we call the consciousness of truth—truth itself. Then, if the soul's consciousness be sensation, she herself is no different from sensation. Now sensation, or the concepts of the senses, belongs to Matter, or the Earth, only. Therefore the Soul that is sensation is bound by her consciousness to Earth; but if her consciousness be not sensation, then is she loosed from Earth. Moreover, heaven is a state, and is right here—nevertheless the Soul that is bound to the Earth perceives not heaven, neither in this life nor in the life to come. What more shall we now say of Consciousness? Whatsoever thou (Consciousness) shalt bind on earth shall be bound in heaven; and whatsoever thou shalt loose on earth shall be loosed in heaven. When the individual has overcome the world, the desires of the flesh and the delusions of the senses, she is freed from all earthly ties and enters into rest, heaven or nirvana.

We are all seeking to attain to this conscious at-one-ment with the Father, which Jesus here speaks of as the rock upon which the true Church is built, and we shall all express it when we have become impersonal—when we have sacrificed personality. Some, who have realized the truth that life is eternal and one, and that it is one and the same life that manifests and has manifested all forms at all times, also realize that they must have lived in the past; and immediately the question is apt to arise, Who—what personality—was I? Possibly they may identify themselves with some great person; possibly such identification in thought may lead them into absurd expression. So in these

last days—in these last states—about which we are speaking, many shall come
in my name, saying, I am Christ. And again, many shall affirm, saying,
Thou art John the Baptist, or Jeremias, or one of the prophets or apostles.
But, friends, all such questioning, all such affirmation, belongs to sense
perception; weary not yourselves with any such thoughts; for *now* is always
the time of day, let us live what we are now. Fear not, if you be conscious
of Peter's perception, that your Father in heaven will not recognize you. But
seek not recognition amongst men, for this is personality and belongs to the
sensation of this changeful world.

We have said that spiritual perception is the rock upon which the Church
of The Christ is built. Let us conclude with a few words upon the Church.
The word Church means the Lord, that is, the expression of Truth. The
Soul is the true Church of God—the Soul, in which the consciousness of her
at-one-ment is awakened, is a Temple of the Living God—it is the expression
of Truth. Yet, if we speak of a still more external expression of the same
Truth, namely, the perfect body, we may say, too, that it is a Temple or true
Church. And further still, we may call the buildings, in which we worship,
Churches—for they are symbols of the one eternal true Church, in which God,
the Father, and Christ, the Son, meet in conscious at-one-ment. Consider
that meeting, that moment, that state; and no matter the name or form of the
Church, remember that the Father and the Son are there.

BIBLES OF THE AGES.

THE COMFORTER.

John 14, 15—26—If ye love me, keep my commandments, and I will pray
" 15, 26,   —the Father, and He shall give you another Comforter,
that He may abide with you forever ; even the Spirit
of Truth ; whom the world cannot receive, because it
seeeth Him not, neither knoweth Him ; but ye know
Him ; for He dwelleth with you, and shall be in you.
I will not leave you comfortless ; I will come to you.
The Comforter, which is the Holy Ghost, whom the
Father will send in my name, He shall teach you all
things, and bring all things to your remembrance,
whatsoever I have said unto you.

" 16, 7,   —   It is expedient for you that I go away ; for if I
" 16, 13,   go not away, the Comforter will not come unto you ;
                         but if I depart I will send Him unto you.

FAITH.

Just as the New Testament of the English Bible is the expression of the
Truth, so the Bagavad-Gita of the Hindoo Bible is the expression of Truth,
i. e., of the same Truth.   This Indian new testament has been translated out
of the Sanskrit into many languages ; in the English language it may be read
both in prose and poetry.   In its poetical form it is " The Song Celestial,"
by Edwin Arnold; and perhaps this work is the sublimest of all we know anything of, if indeed we allow that truth in the garb of poetry is more sublime
than in prose.

At the present day the poet's name is most generally associated with "The
Light of Asia," but by the future generations, Sir Edwin Arnold will be
known as " The Poet of The Song Celestial."

We would put this beautiful poem into the hands of every true student,
that from it they might gather clear interpretations of the loftiest truth of the
Bibles.

The following poem, " Religion by Faith," is but one song out of eighteen,
that compose "The Song Celestial."   It is in the form of a dialogue:—

Arjuna, Prince of India, seeking for the Truth with the sincerity of a
princely soul, asks :

    " Lord, of the men who serve Thee, true in heart
    As God revealed ; and of the men who serve,
    Worshipping Thee Unrevealed, Unbodied, Far,
    Which take the better way of faith and life?"

To this question, God makes the following answer to the soul :

    " Whoever serve Me—as I show Myself—
    Constantly true, in full devotion fixed,
    Those hold I very holy.   But who serve—
    Worshipping Me The One, The Invisible,
    The Unrevealed, Unnamed, Unthinkable,
    Uttermost, All-pervading, Highest, Sure—
    Who thus adore Me, mastering their sense,
    Of one set mind to all, glad in all good,
    These blessed souls come unto Me.
                        Yet, hard

The travail is for such as bend their minds
To reach th' Unmanifest. That viewless path
Shall scarce be trod by man bearing the flesh !
But whereso any doeth all his deeds
Renouncing self for Me, full of Me, fixed
To serve only the Highest, night and day
Musing on Me—him will I swiftly lift
Forth from life's ocean of distress and death,
Whose soul clings fast to Me. Cling thou to Me !
Clasp Me with heart and mind ! so shalt thou dwell
Surely with Me on high. But if thy thought
Droop from such height ; if thou be'st weak to set
Body and soul upon Me constantly,
Despair not ! give Me lower service ! seek
To reach Me, worshipping with steadfast will ;
And, if thou cans't not worship steadfastly,
Work for Me, toil in works pleasing to Me !
For he that laboureth right for love of Me
Shall finally attain ! But, if in this
Thy faint heart fail, bring Me thy failure ! find
Refuge in Me ! let fruits of labour go,
Renouncing hope for Me, with lowliest heart,
So shalt thou come ; for, though to know is more
Than diligence, yet worship better is
Than knowing, and renouncing better still.
Near to renunciation—very near—
Dwelleth eternal peace !

        Who hateth nought
Of all which lives, living himself benign,
Compassionate, from arrogance exempt,
Exempt from love of self, unchangeable,
By good or ill ; patient, contented, firm
In faith, mastering himself, true to his word,
Seeking Me, heart and soul ; vowed unto Me—
That man I love ! Who troubleth not his kind,
And is not troubled by them ; clear of wrath,
Living too high for gladness, grief, or fear,
That man I love ! Who, dwelling quiet-eyed,

Stainless, serene, well-balanced, unperplexed,
Working with Me, yet from all works detached,
That man I love ! Who fixed in faith on Me,
Dotes upon none, scorns none ; rejoices not
And grieves not, letting good or evil hap
Light when it will, and when it will depart,
That man I love ! Who unto friend and foe
Keeping an equal heart, with equal mind
Bears shame and glory ; with an equal peace
Takes heat and cold, pleasure and pain ; abides
Quit of desires, hears praise or calumny
In passionless restraint ; unmoved by each ;
Linked by no ties to earth, steadfast in Me,
That man I love ! But most of all I love
Those happy ones to whom 'tis life to live
In single fervid faith and love unseeing,
Drinking the blessed *Amrit of My Being!

*Nectar of immortality.

NOTES.

Our beloved brother, Dr. W. F. Evans, has passed from this plane of existence, has laid aside the worn-out garment, the earth mask. In his disappearance, there is withdrawn from visible manifestation a life in which the spirit of love and truth shone with unwonted brightness. We shall miss him as a co-laborer in the field of Truth. But he has garnered many golden sheaves for which we are thankful, as his "Esoteric Christianity," "Primitive Mind Cure," " Soul and Body," etc. These remain a valuable monument of his diligent search for Truth, and of his scholarly investigations along her paths. Dr. Evans was a Swedenborgian minister, and was not only conversant with the voluminous and subtile productions of that celebrated theologian, but was profoundly versed in all modern metaphysical teachings. He received his first ideas of the practical application of metaphysics in mental healing from Dr. Quinby ; he, having been himself healed by Dr. Quinby, concluded that he might use the same means to the same end. He thus became one of the earliest and most earnest of modern investigators into the effect of mind over matter, and its application to mental healing, and has done much to turn the current of modern thought into the line of truth. He has labored diligently in Truth's vineyard, and has borne much fruit to her during a long and beautiful life of loving devotion to her cause, and from his pages there gleams the sweet spirit of a practical life which charms the reader. The truth through him has expressed and recognized its own.

METAPHYSICAL OR SPIRITUAL HEALING.

To be healed means to be in a spiritual or normal condition. It means ease for dis–ease, love for fear, charity for unkindness, faith for doubt, truth for error, knowledge for belief, happiness for sorrow, harmony for discord, spiritual understanding for mental darkness. To be healed means unity and wholeness.

We have prepared these lessons so that you may heal yourselves, and teach and heal others. They will be in lecture form, so that when you have studied them, you will enjoy reading them to your friends ; and will profit by your efforts in explaining them to their understanding. In so doing you begin to teach and heal, and expand in spiritual consciousness. There is a certain amount of discipline that all must have before they can heal, or understand why truth does heal.

58

Cramer's Poetry

Ed. note: Throughout the eighteen years of *Harmony* Magazine, Malinda Cramer included a great deal of poetry. She included much of both Sir Edwin Arnold's *Light of Asia* and *The Song Celestial* throughout the years. She included a great number of poems by William Brunton as well as by numerous others.

In addition she published her own poems from time to time. The following is one of her better efforts. As with most of her work, it is unsigned (the magazine masthead announcing that all unsigned work is by the editor). In the last few volumes of the magazine many more Cramer poems appear. Apparently, poetry was one of her passions that she neglected during the years of her greatest activity, and it was only as she was beginning to relax again that she returned to it.

The Blessed Christmas Bells.

Ring, gladsome bells, love's message clear and true,
That God in man eternal friendship finds;
That to himself he every creature binds;
And is in us as light in gems of dew:
He is for all and not a favored few,
The inspiration of aspiring minds,
That blows delight as soft as summer winds;
In him we live as stars in yonder blue!
O, tell the world in your vibrations sweet,
It need not weary, toil, and mourn and fret;
It need not suffer from sharp cold and heat,
But may in God a pure protection get;
Christ is our truth, hope's child in every soul,
Now born in us creation to control!

Meditation

The circulars issued by the Committees of the Universal Register furnish suitable subjects for Meditation on every Wednesday evening at eight o'clock. In each number of HARMONY we will give short explanations of the subjects for the month, and suggestions as to how they may be thought about.

What is Meditation? The derivation of the word itself may be traced to the Sanskrit ' man,' which means to think. To be active in thought on a particular subject is the true signification of the term Meditation. It will be noted that this definition excludes a discursive and argumentative method of thinking ; it excludes, too, a negative, passive attitude of "mind" (*i. e.*, consciousness). To comply with the above definition a close attention and concentration to the subject under consideration is necessary ; that we be active in thought is likewise necessary. In our next number we will give directions how to attain concentration, or an undivided attention to whatever one is occupied about.

Wherever a few gather together in the spirit of truth, there truth will be with them. Whatever the subject of thought may be—no matter who are the thinkers—the object of study with all is to get understanding ; *i. e.*, Truth ; to obtain understanding one thing is necessary, namely—that we approach it in a spirit to receive it. This is simple, and reasonable. Let us think of it.

If in our investigations we set out to arrive at a particular goal, some particular standard of knowledge, we set out with a certain amount of prejudice as a guide to keep us in the road we have in idea, or in the groove that we anticipate will bring our desired object—Truth ; then, if in our investigations we come across a train of thought—perchance the very truth we are seeking—that agrees ill with our preconceived idea, the chances are very much in favour of our ignoring the gems by the way ; with the possible result that after praiseworthy perseverance, we pass through the goal we set out to reach, and receive the gratifying plaudits of our friends. And what we have thus done was to strengthen the prejudice that guided us to our destination. But do you honestly expect, that from prejudice truth will come? No, you do not. Yet if one be so unreasonable as to expect it, he will continue on his course to the bitter end—for prejuidce has its beginning and therefore its end—and written large thereat is disappointment. The trouble was we did not enter the path in the Spirit of what we sought to attain. No man can attain to understanding by the Spirit of prejudice, but by the spirit of understanding.

Neither will one get truth by following in the footsteps of any other— no matter what perfection that other may have reached—but if he follow the Spirit of Truth he will walk in the footsteps of those who have walked similarly, and know that those who preceded him shined with no borrowed light. Yet if he follow a leader, and be not in the truth himself, by what shall he know his leader? Truly the light of such a follower will become darkness as the sun sinks behind the first hill top.

Please to consider this further, friends, in your own thoughts ; and it will seem, that nothing but the little prejudices—that arise perhaps from motives of excelling and sensations of competing—prevent us from entering the true way in the spirit of the true wayfarer. Then nothing but the spirit of truth can lead us into the way of true knowledge or understanding. And what is this Spirit of Truth ? Consider the little child whom the gentle Master of Nazareth placed in the midst of his disciples ! Even as the little ones whom we see receive from a visible source, so the little ones whom we see not receive from the invisible Source. But every one who is willing to receive truth, is one of those little ones whom we see not. Therefore let us be willing to receive from the invisible source, for this willingness is the Spirit of Truth that leadeth into all knowledge.

Then in our Meditations, having put away prejudice, we shall surely sit in the very presence of what we seek ; and being willing to receive we shall receive. And this is true acting—true prayer. Then, whether alone or together with others, we may sit in silence, attentive to our subject, for a quarter or half an hour : after which we shall *express* the thoughts we have had either by writing them down, or by speaking them to our companions. Our Correspondence department will from time to time be open to those who will forward us the result of Meditations that will be helpful to others.

OCTOBER 3RD.

The subject for this evening's thought is " All is One ; and One is All:" —Now it may be that some friends will not agree that "All is One, and One is All," but the subject is stated as one to be thought about. There may be differences of opinion about it : let each give it his or her honest, simple consideration and whatever the result may be, it will be well. Let us take two examples of Oneness,—first, to the senses any individual appears as One, but there are many individuals, therefore to the senses All is not one, but many : neither is one all, for there appear many besides the one ; now, second, putting the judgment of the senses out of the question altogether, and using the understanding only—truth is one, and it is not many ; e. g., 2 added to 2 make four: if this be true it cannot also be true that they make 3 or 5 : and whenever you add 2 to 2 they will make the same number to all eternity. It is similarly true that 3 and 3 are 6 ; there are myriads of true things, but each is permanently true ; and thus all Truth is permanently unchangeable ; that is it is one. In a similar manner we may consider every attribute of God, any one in its infinity is the same as any other considered in its Infinity, and is no different from the One God. Thus to the understanding All is One and One is All ; but to the senses, All is many, and nobody knows how many is All.

OCTOBER 10TH.

Subject:—"Thy Kingdom Come."

The Kingdom of Heaven is a State. The Kingdom of Heaven is Permanent. If it were a place it would not be permanent. The Kingdom of Heaven is the Kingdom of God and is therefore an unlimited domain ; and being unlimited it is everywhere and ever present. Thus the Kingdom of Heaven is within. If then the Kingdom be already come—and how can it be otherwise? the prayer of the Earnest Soul to her Father is, "May thy heavenly state become a conscious reality to me !"

OCTOBER 17TH.

Subject :—" Thy Will be Done."

From what has already been said on the simple willingness to receive, much may be gathered on this subject.

What is Divine Will ? God being complete in Himself, His Will cannot be a wish ; for what would he wish. He who has All and is All ! And if he have All, and is All, then he is conscious of All—He is consciousness itself. Now the supreme God having created Souls—it is His Will that Individuals should through experience come to know Him ; and thus does God become manifest. With Him to Will and to do are identical. But Will, in the individual, does not become Divine until personal or individual exertion or effort has been supplanted by the recognition of the Father working in all and through all to will and do of His own good pleasure.

As there is but One God, there is but One Will—the Will of the Father, and the Will of His Child—BE ME expresses it all—BE ME.

OCTOBER 24TH.

Subject :—" Faith ; the substance of things hoped for."

The substance here is the reality of the thing hoped for ; and at the time that the individual has a hope, he has faith in the reality of what he hopes for, and expects that when his hope is fulfilled he will receive something real and substantial ; otherwise he would have no hope. Whether the thing hoped for is real and substantial will be ascertained by experience ; and it matters not what is hoped for, faith will be the substance of it. Faith is the substance of wealth hoped for ; and when the wealth is obtained, the individual will experience whether or no there is any substance or permanent reality in it ; if it have no reality the same individual will not again

hope for it with faith. in its reality. The faith is all right, the thing hoped
for may be visionary. Then should we not see to it that we place not our
heart upon treasures that are corruptible ? This is wisdom.

OCTOBER 31st.

Subject :—" Faith ; the spoken word or result of Knowledge.

Having once found the experiences spoken of in our last subject, the individual has gained something permanent—namely *Knowledge ?* In the
future he will act upon that Knowledge, and this is faith as the result of
Knowledge. By faith worlds were made—*i. e.*, by the application of Knowledge. Applying theory—experimenting—experiencing—are an application
of faith that will bring Knowledge ; and again the application of Knowledge is
Faith. There is but One Faith.

WE have said that a close attention and concentration to the subject under
consideration is necessary to true Meditation; that inactivity in thought
is not by any means a desirable accomplishment.

This becomes a plain truth if we do but consider, that the object of
manifestation is that the individual may know the principle or creator of all
individuals; just as the object of doing a sum upon the slate is that the pupil
may understand the principle underlying the sum—the proof that he does
understand the principle is the correct working of the sum. Matter—the
Earth—is the slate upon which individuals are learning to demonstrate the
principle of life—of God. And the senses may reveal many mistakes indicating that the Soul has not yet solved her problem—that is all. Because the
pupil has failed to work his sum correctly, he is not therefore a sinful, evil or
diseased pupil; we may call the sum—the appearance—incorrect, but the
pupil is not his sum; the principle is all right, though the pupil has not yet
understood it. And so it is with the Soul; her body is the sum upon the
slate; and all the imperfections, sorrows and sins that the senses reveal are
mistakes in the sum, indicating that the Soul or individual does not understand herself, *which* is the principle of life she is endeavouring to demonstrate.

Then the purpose of manifestation is that we may know God. Consider
the pupil at his slate once more, and you will see that he puts down what he
thinks; if he were inactive in thought he could not work his sum, if he were
inattentive he would at best work carelessly. Just so it is with the Soul;
thought must precede manifestation; inattention will produce imperfect work.
Hence it behoves us to be active in thought, and attentive to our subject.

Many methods have been given to the world by which to arrive at concentration, and with which our readers will probably be familiar. Different societies, both secret and proclaimed, of Occult Students, have their different methods—but there is nothing hidden that shall not be revealed; first find the kingdom of heaven, and all knowledge is yours. Now the reason why we write thus is that every one may break any spell of fascination that holds them to the mysterious or secret. There is not anything mysterious or secret; all knowledge is ever present and as free as the air; you are the very knowledge you seek; mystery only comes in by believing otherwise. Imagine the pupil taking himself to be his sum—all incorrect, all wrong, liable to be rubbed out—what confusion! what a mystery he would be to himself! Friends, friends, you are nothing that is wrong or liable to be rubbed out; will you not hear us, when we tell you—you are the truth and the life. The way is within you all. Therefore let us make nothing mysterious nor secret; remembering always that Knowledge is Wisdom. He that wisely gives of the tree of knowledge is the heavenly physician.

Now thoughts of concealing seem to belong to a consciousness that is desirous of effect, that is forgetful of the truth that behind all effect is the object of true admiration and wonder, namely, the cause. Are we quite sure, when we sit quiet-eyed, gazing on some spot, with muscles and passions under control, seeking illumination and power, that we are seeking power in the spirit of truth; or are we seeking it with the motive of effect? Do we thus seek the kingdom of heaven (cause), or the kingdom of phenomena (effect)? Are we not by thus doing seeking to build up an individual will, a personal power, a house upon the shifting sands? But if we seek the Will of the Father, the power of the Invisible, a mansion not made with hands but permanent in heaven, we shall find it by seeking in the Spirit of what we seek. Do we seek Power? then Knowledge is the Spirit of Power; do we seek Knowledge? then Truth is the Spirit of Knowledge. No amount of sitting and external concentration; no amount of travelling and careful selection of mountain heights will bring us Power or Illumination; but the quiet recognition—at the counting-house, or in the kitchen, or wherever we are and whatever engaged in—that all the Power of God is omnipresent, is true illumination, and to know that that power and illumination is you is true concentration (this conclusion we shall hereafter show more fully).

In the performance of our daily duties we are putting into practice rules for the attainment of perfect concentration; whether at school or occupied at home or in business, we are more or less continually engaged in unfolding the necessary qualifications for Adeptship.

Directions how to gain that concentration or undivided attention which will bring the success and the contentment and the consciousness into this World of the World to come:—WHATEVER THY HANDS FIND TO DO, DO IT WITH ALL THY HEART. WHATEVER THY HEART FINDS TO DO, DO IT WITH ALL THY LOVE.

NOVEMBER 7TH.

Subject for this evening's thought is "The purpose of Creation." In the foregoing remarks much has been already said on this subject that will be found to contain substance for to-night's reflection.

NOVEMBER 14TH.

Subject: "I AM the life of everything." In the consideration of this subject, let us endeavour to forget time, by realizing that eternity, like God, is ever present. Time belongs to the senses, to limitations; it can only be conceived of as relative to changeable and impermanent things. Things appear and disappear in time; but God is forever the same; past and future are always present to Him. Therefore He is always "I Am"; and nothing (*i. e.* no power) but God can say "I Am." Should we not then always bear this in mind? We who are continually saying "I am," should we not cease to live in time? But the body is a thing of time. Eternal life then is the life of everything; the Father and His children are One.

NOVEMBER 21ST.

Subject: "Ye are Gods." God is the invisible, omnipresent, first and only cause, omnipotent and omniscient, the Father. Then, are not those wise souls who are at one with the Father, Gods? And have we not seen that in the affairs of God there is no past or future? Then if ye are Gods, ye—without distinction—are Gods now.

NOVEMBER 28TH.

Subject: "The One Mind." Mind is the present and all-pervading Consciousness of God. (See further our remarks in October number headed "Rosicruciæ.) Did you ever consider what chaos would reign if there were more than one Mind? If in imagination we divided the earth into sections, each of which was pervaded by a distinct and different consciousness, no one section could possibly understand another, for there would be nothing in common by which one could recognize another. But throughout all space, in all times, we perceive similar objects similarly; and the Providence and Order of One Mind is thoroughly manifest.

When we speak the word of Spirit, we speak to all, for all.
When we commune with Spirit, we commune with all. for all.
Such speaking, and communing are impersonal.

When our speaking is personal, we commune with like states of consciousness, which is in part, but " when that which is perfect is come, that which is in part shall be done away."

. . . .

MEDITATION.

OUR remarks under this heading this month follow closely upon those of the same subject in the last number of HARMONY. Our readers will remember that we are considering the subject of concentration, and how the same may be obtained. And we said that the recognition, that the Power of God is omnipresent, is true illumination ; and that to know that that power and illumination is you (the reader), is true concentration. First, let us proceed to understand how you are what we have just claimed for you ; and second, to understand that this knowledge is that perfect concentration which is necessary to perfect meditation.

You are the Power of God ; this will be clear if we can prove that there is nothing else for you to be. As God is forever unchangeable, He must be truth (not creation, for all creation is changeable) and hence power. And He is infinite, therefore you are within Him. Therefore you are truth or power. Of course persons may believe themselves to be something changeable, but beliefs do not alter truth ; and this is truth, that there is nothing real but the unchangeable. Now if you recognize this truth, you recognize that you are truth ; and truth is the light of understanding or illumination. To thus recognize yourself is justice, and in no other way can you be just to God.

Now, secondly ; we must refer again to the meaning of the word meditation, which will be found in the October number, " to be active in thought on a particular subject (not object) is its true signification." Any attribute of mind—e. g., truth, is a subject ; but any form or appearance is an object—e. g. the Astral form. Then consider truth ; that is—from what we have already said—think of yourself. Now your attention is upon that which is universal, unconfined to place or time, upon that which is real ; and the more fully you realize truth, the more are you conscious of it, and are it. From which it follows that true concentration is BEING. Therefore, wisdom's rule for attaining perfect concentration is, CONTEMPLATE THAT WHICH TRULY IS ; AND BE IT.

December 5th.

Subject—" I and my Father are one."

Perhaps we can best understand who is meant by " I," if we first understand who " My Father " is ; therefore let us direct our attention to the Creator of all things. The Creator must be the cause of all ; now we know that all expression is created, therefore no expression can be the Creator. Everything formed is created, therefore the Father must be formless. And he is the same yesterday, to-day and forever ; therefore he is *invisible*, for everything visible has form and changes ; therefore He is the *Silence*, for sound is a production or a creation ; therefore He is *stillness*, for motion pertains to appearances only ; but if He moved, whither would He move—He who is the fullness to infinity ? Then, He must be life, truth, love and wisdom ; hence he who said " I and my Father are one," also said " I am the truth and the life." Now, the Father is infinite ; therefore we, who meditate, are life and truth, we must be or God would not be infinite. To realize that we are the invisible, the silence, the stillness, it is necessary that we shake off the psychology of the senses under which we have allowed ourselves to fall. We are not the body which we see, is a plain fact, if we but give it a little attention ; then we are the life ; for what else is there ? We and the Father are one.

December 12th.

Subject—The Holy Ghost, the Comforter.

We as individuals, by what faculty do we perceive a truth ? Is it not by perception, or the eye of understanding ? And this is the spirit of truth, who is with us at this present time leading us into all truth. We see the necessity in meditating on divine subjects, of getting out of consciousness of matter into consciousness of essence. Out of identification with body, into identification with being. If on the other hand, we were meditating on material affairs, dealing with a material trinity, we should say that it was the light that enables a father to perceive his son. But the Father in the Holy Trinity is invisible, the Son is the truth, and the Holy Ghost is His perception of Himself. Therefore the Spirit of Truth, the Comforter, is given us by the Father, that we may perceive Him.

December 19th.

Subject—Christ Manifest and Unmanifest.

Christ is the anointed one, the soul that has become one in consciousness with the Father. Then Christ unmanifest is no different from the Father ; what the Father is Christ is. But that the world might know God, this soul, that had become conscious of its oneness with God, took upon itself a material form, Jesus, and manifested, by thought and deed the attributes of the Father hitherto unmanifest but nevertheless present. How apt mankind has been in mistaking the instrument by means of which the principle or divine attribute manifests itself, for the attribute itself, e. g.—the love of dear friends; when the appearance by means of which they demonstrated their love for us has disappeared, we are very apt to think that their love has gone with them ; whereas the love, which is our friend's reality, is ever present with us, but the body which is not our friend at all, is absent.

December 26th.

Subject—" Time and Eternity."

In approaching the end of one year and the beginning of another, it is customary for us to indulge in looking backward and looking forward. In so doing we linger in thought on the past, on the trials and pleasures that we have long since buried ; we seek a little pleasure in these burying grounds of past experience, but with a sigh pass on to what the future may bring. One thing is noteworthy, that whether we have been looking backward or looking forward we have been dwelling on effect. We know that the effects we have been looking back upon belong to the past, and are dead and buried; but do we know that the effects we look forward to, also belong to the past and are dead ? Is this a very strange thought, dear friends ? Then what are effects ? Are they not results of a cause ; are they not products of mind ; are they not things done ; appearances of past thoughts ; the shadows of by-gone ideas ? Effects are always things DONE—done with and past ; and whether we think of them as belonging to yesterday, to-day or to-morrow, they are equally dead, equally and forever past. Let the dead remain buried, and beside the past with gentle thought let us bury the memories that belong to them. What a delusion, then, is time ! All yesterdays are always yesterdays, and to-morrows are a mirage that no traveller ever comes up with. But to-day is always NOW, is eternally present ; and only that which belongs to the present is eternal. Years come and years go ; bringing with them all the wealth, friendships and happiness that in the world can be supplied, again taking them with them and supplying poverty, enmity and sorrows, that alone in the world can be supplied ; in this world nothing is stable and certain, but all things change in time. In the coming year, then, shall we not live in the present? If we turn over a new leaf shall it not be one that will carry a permanent record, and on which is written Truth? This we may do as follows:—LIVE IN THOUGHT OF WHAT IS, AND NOT IN THOUGHT OF WHAT APPEARS. IF OUR THOUGHTS BE ALL RIGHT, EXPRESSIONS (e. g., BODIES) WILL BE ALL RIGHT.

Thus all our years will be happy new years ; and our lives which may hitherto have been measured by time, will become measureless in eternity.

GOD BE WITH YOU.

REFLECTION.

Flower in the crannied wall,
I pluck you out of the crannies ;—
Hold you here, root and all, in my hand,
Little flower—But, if I could understand
What you are, root and all, and all in all,
I should know what God and man is.

Tennyson.

THE PEARL OF PRICE.

A rich return is ours in life,
    When recognizing good in all.
The richest gems doth come of strife
    Into lives both great and small.

Then let us work with truthful thought
    Prepared for life as it may come;
For then it is that we have wrought
    The richest gem, the diamond won.

The judgment of this world is its own opinions. To it the day is light because of the Sun; but the night is dark because it sees no light. But, when the world does perceive the light in the darkness, then is the prince of this world cast out.

Love is our being; and this we seek to manifest by our thoughts. Thus we may base our love either in the spiritual or in the material. That is, we thus think we are Spirit or Matter. In the one case we decide we are Goodness; in the other case we decide we are its forms. We cannot serve *both* God and Mammon.

By our works and not by our claims shall we be known. If any one would be an Apostle of Christ, let him do the works of The Father, but let him refrain from outward profession of Apostleship.

On Earth we gain knowledge by experience; therefore let us work now, while we can, that at night we may rest.

Truth is the food of which, if ye eat, ye shall not hunger.

Whosoever trusts to the light of another will stumble at night by reason of his darkness; but whosoever walks by his own light shall not fall, for truth fails not.

God. The Infinite Spirit is everywhere the same (The Unchangeable).
Therefore He is One (The Perfect).
Therefore He is indivisible (The Atom).
Therefore He is invisible (The Unmanifest).
Therefore He is silence (The Still Voice).
Therefore He is stillness (The Motionless).

MEDITATION.

THE questions are frequently asked—What is the best time to meditate? Is it best for all throughout the world to meditate at one time?
TIME.—What is time? Will you re-read the few words of suggestion

for December 26th on this subject ?

Time is the period of changes.

Time is the necessity of appearances.

Time is the record of thought.

Time is limitation; is false.

Time is not, but appears to be.

Time is for the changeable, eternity for the unchangeable.

Time is the appearance of eternity, as light is the appearance of truth.

Time is effect, created.   Eternity is cause, creator.

Time, in short, is the absence of all real, which by virtue of the continuous changes of things and their endless variety, assumes the appearance of eternity.   To time belongs every unreality: but all, that really is, is eternal.

We would not convey the meaning that because times, bodies and sensations are unreal, therefore they are to be utterly ignored.   On the contrary, we would affirm the utility of all things, times, bodies and sensations.   But this is *the* point—let the real be understood as the real, and the unreal as the unreal; and *not* mistake the real for the unreal, nor the unreal for the real.

What is the best time to meditate?   Simply the most convenient to yourselves.   But if you go further than this, attaching any more than a mere temporary importance to the question, you fall into a train of external thought, that is out of all harmony with true meditation; because you attach to time an importance that is completely foreign to it.   The time of meeting in different places is not of the least consequence; but the motive for which we meet is important.   And the question—What should our motive be? will be considered in our introductory remarks under this heading next month.

January 2d.

Subject for Meditation—"The Incorruptible Body."

Read I Cor. 35–58.

In the portion of Scripture above referred to St. Paul speaks of a corruptible or natural body, and an incorruptible or Spiritual body—two bodies. Let us see what we shall understand by "body."   And we know that the body profiteth nothing; that of itself it has no life or power; that of itself it can proclaim neither yea nor nay; that of itself it is nothing but a form led about by the mind of man, and acted upon by his thoughts.   And when the mind ceases to lead and the thought to act upon it, the body returns whence it came—dust to dust—corruptible to corruptible.   Looking thus upon the body, we see that of itself it is nothing, NOTHING.   Let us have no thought that it is in any respect real—The Infinite is the only real—for without this understanding we cannot understand the subject before us. Then if "body" be nothing real, what shall we say of it? It is an appearance of the mind in the mind; it is an image of the thoughts in the thoughts. Your body is an image or expression of your thoughts. The fact that we have a corruptible image signifies that we have erroneous or imperfect thoughts; but the image of knowledge or perfect thought is an incorruptible one. When—but not before—we cease thinking imperfect thoughts and think perfect thoughts, we shall put off the corruptible body of the old man and shall put on the incorruptible body of the new man, which is Christ. Have you not heard that a tree is known by its fruits? Then you know that the thought (the tree) must precede the body (the fruit). Your corruptible body is an image of your thoughts; your incorruptible body is an image of yourself.

January 9th.

Subject—Blessed are the poor in spirit, for theirs is the Kingdom of heaven.

The Kingdom of heaven has been thought of as a place; but few now think of it as such because place or the things in place must be changeable; because the invisible, the all, can alone be unchangeable. The Kingdom of heaven is unchangeable, because it is the completeness of perfection; it is therefore the state of eternal life, which is God.

To whom then does this kingdom of heaven belong—who can enter into the state or knowledge of eternal life?

They who are conscious of love; who love to give life, and who live to give love.

They who are mothers, and fathers, ministering to the orphans in consciousness—orphans bereft not of earthly parents, but of the knowledge of their heavenly Father.

They who have overcome pride and personality by gentleness and universality.

They who have overcome the desires, which are the spirit of this world; they who have become poor in the spirit of this world.

Blessed—happy—are you if you have become poor in temporal desires; for to you belong the riches of happiness that are eternal.

January 16th.

Subject—Thou Shalt not Kill.

What is it—to kill? Is it to deprive of life? But life is infinite and ever-present, and cannot be increased or diminished. Nobody can be deprived of life; the physical and mental savage does not know this. But life may be deprived of body. The immortal soul cannot be deprived of life, but the immortal soul may be deprived of body. God—the life—and the Soul can never be affected, they are forever unchangeable. Whatever is, is forever. But the body which appears may disappear.

To kill means to deprive the soul of its manifestations or bodies.

Every creature has soul and body.

The object of creation is that God may be made manifest.

Whenever you see any creature, dear friends, say to yourselves—there is a soul trying to manifest God. You cannot through your own physical eyes see the soul, but only its body. Do not allow the senses which can only see visible things, to conclude for you any questions concerning the invisible. To the senses the soul is invisible, but to the mind it is visible. There is not a creature upon earth but is a living soul manifesting the highest form it is conscious of. We all gain our knowledge by experience; our bodies, sensations and deeds are our experience. Let us help one another; help those whose forms belong to the vegetable kingdom; those whose forms belong to the animal kingdom—even from the least of all, to man.

Thou shalt not kill any creature.

Thou shalt not deprive *any* soul of its body.

This is the command, which will never be broken except by those who know no better.

January 23rd.

Subject—Blessed are the peacemakers, for they shall be called the children of God.

God is Peace.

They who make peace manifest shall be *called* the children of Peace. All are at all times the children of God or Peace, but every expression is not one of peace; when, however, we see persons peaceful, unmoved by what the world calls insults and wrongs; refraining from litigation and dispute, we shall know that they are—that is, they shall be called—the children of God. The sensations of wars and discords, and of wrangling for superiority, belong to superiority. But in heaven upon earth, or in heaven above earth, there is no superiority, but all are peacemakers and children of peace.

January 30th.

Subject—" Ye are the Salt of the Earth."
See Matt. **v**, 13.

Salt has a peculiar meaning amongst Alchemists, the significance of which may be expressed by saying that it is the synonym for Matter, or the "gist" of bodies appearing in Matter. Except for its flavour it would be no different from the earth; that is, its savour, called saltness, distinguishes it from the earth. So the salt is not the earth, but its invisible quality is the true salt. Savour, Salt and Earth, correspond to Spirit, Soul and Body. You as individuals are the salt of the earth; but you must not stop there, for without the savour the soul would not be salt, therefore ye—not as mere individuals, but as one flavour—are the savour of the salt of the earth. Similarly—you as individuals are the Soul of the Body; but you must not stop at that, for without the life the Soul would not exist; therefore, ye—not separately, but as one with the Father—are the life of the Soul of the Body.

. . . .

MEDITATION.

FROM our last remarks under this heading it will be gathered, that time is a sensation belonging to the World; but eternity is Heaven; and in order that God may be known upon Earth, we will heaven to come to Earth. "Thy will be done on Earth as it is in heaven." We do not will or pray for Earth to come to Heaven, for that would not be possible. Now, this is tantamount to saying we *will* to do away upon Earth with that sensation called time, in order that eternity or the kingdom of heaven may be our consciousness here. Then, if we sometimes pray, "Our Father which art in heaven, Thy kingdom come, Thy will be done on earth as it is done in heaven;" and sometimes will (or pray) to make time any importance, we are like a house that is divided against itself, and which will ultimately fall, if the division continue. Whenever we meditate divinely, or in truth, we (i. e. our consciousness) are *then* in heaven. Or, if not, then some truth or divine meditation is dependent upon some time; which we know is not the case. Where we meditate, dear friends, all are one; and neither time nor place is a consideration. Though, whether we get there (i. e. into the spirit of truth) in consciousness, or not, depends entirely upon our thoughts. For our consciousness follows our thoughts. And our thoughts depend upon our motive, or will, or faith. And if you should ask what your individual motive or faith amounts to, we should answer, that your thoughts are the measure of it; and remember, that your motive, will or faith (these three terms have the same meaning) is the cause, of which your thoughts are the result. Now, if our faith be in times, places, sensations, results or material things, our thoughts will be of times, sensations etc. The study of motive is very important, for —

Motive is the substance of thought.
Motive is the basis of all words and speech.
Motive is the foundation of all actions and behaviour.
Motive determines the character of appearances.
Motive is the reason of existence.

And just here we see the necessity of getting understanding; for, if we do not understand what goodness is, we may think our motive to be good, but it may not be (and if it be not good it will be nothing). Now to apply this more exactly to the present consideration; if we understand what it is to meditate or think truth, our thoughts will express truth. Our motive being truth or knowledge determines our thoughts, that they are true and wise; and determines our actions and speech that they are truthful and wise. On the other hand, if our motive be not goodness and knowledge—even though we may think it is—our thoughts will be occupied by such things as exact times and particular places; and our actions, writing and speech will manifest a corresponding want of wisdom, knowledge or understanding. These remarks, be it remembered, refer to motive, faith, or will in the individual. Let our motive be all goodness with understanding; then let us *be* our motive, for that is just what we are.

February 5th.

Subject:—God.

"God is one spirit." John iv, 24.

In many editions of the New Testament this verse commences—"God is a Spirit," and in some it reads—"God is one Spirit." The latter is without doubt the correct translation. Moreover it is the correct interpretation; for God is ONE and ALL. The English word God is probably derived from an old Sanskrit word meaning 'to conceal.' In any case, if we consider Nature, Words, and Expressions as the revealed, we shall consider that which is the cause of Nature, Words and Expressions as the concealed; and cause is God. That which perceives Nature—every external expression, from the blade of grass to the body of a man or of a planet—is the senses; but from the senses God is concealed for ever, the senses can but perceive His manifestations. On Earth God is concealed but revealed or manifest; in Heaven God is unveiled, unconcealed, unmanifest. To be unmanifest is to be unexpressed, unformed, uncreate, impersonal; and the unchangeable unmanifest God is not any expression, or form, or creation, or person. Hence, He (or It) is Infinite; but otherwise he would not be. Goodness and truth are essence or attributes that are eternally unchangeable; they are God. Again, goodness and truth are Mind, or The Thinker, or cause forever, without varying or shadow of turning, but which produces all variety and all shadow. Goodness and truth ARE; they are God; everything else seems to be.

God is one goodness, or one truth, or one spirit.

God is all goodness, or all truth, or all spirit.

February 13th.

Subject:—Love one another.

Why? Because you are love; and because you are one another.

God is love. Your love is not only God's love, but it is God.

While concluding thus, let us be aware that mere affection is not love, mere attraction is not love, mere like is not love, because they are respecters of persons, place, things, and sensations. But love is no respecter, has no dislikes, feels no repulsions or antagonisms, thinks no thoughts of aversion, preference or distinction. Will any ask—Is it possible for me to be all that love is? We answer—You are it already, always will be. Did not you know it, friend? Still there is nothing else for you to be; for there is but one being. Will any one ask—Then, is it possible to manifest what I am? Yes, you will continually manifest yourself; and in order that you may do so now—love one another.

February 20th.

Subject :—Blessed are they that mourn, for they shall be comforted.

Mourning is an expression of sorrow. What for? In the world we would say for a friend, or some advantage or material loss. But Jesus did not mean this; for he taught—set not your affections upon anything changeable. Then, what did he mean? Now, no one mourns but for a loss; and the loss over which one is blessed, if he mourn, is the loss of consciousness; and this loss the Master came to supply. The Christ or Truth is the supply, which makes good any loss; it is the presence now recognised where once an absence was thought to be. Then, the text may read—Happy are ye, if ye seek the Christ or consciousness of the Father, for ye shall find it; and finding it ye shall be comforted. This is the only blessing, the only happiness, the only Comforter: and all who seek shall find.

February 27th.

Subject:—Blessed are the merciful, for they shall obtain mercy.

Mercy brings mercy.

Each individual attracts to herself from others that which she metes out to others. This law of individual compensation is regulated by individual thought, and in such a manner that absolute justice is the portion of each—no matter what may seem to be to the contrary. /Each attracts to each that which each has made arrangements or conditions to receive/ This is destiny; and it is under the control of each. There is no chance, although people, forgetful or ignorant of the law of compensation, speak of chance or accident as possibilities.

Your thoughts mark out your destiny; and neither Sun, moon, stars nor any material thing ever has or can affect or in any way whatever shape the destiny of any individual or the events of any one's 'life-time;/but you alone regulate them according to the knowledge you exercise in *thought./* This is the law—If you be merciful you shall obtain mercy.

And this is to be merciful—To do unto others (without exception) as you would be done by. Deal with all men, and with all animals, exactly as you would wish to be dealt with. If you would be universally trusted, trust all; for this is the law. If you would be loved by all, cast out all prejudice and aversion from you own thoughts, and you will be loved. Deal gently with all creatures, and all creatures will deal gently with you; but not otherwise—*not otherwise.* Verily you have your own rewards.

The Father devotes Eternity to the Works of The Father.
The Son devotes Time to the Works of the Father.
The Children devote Time to their own Works.

The life of Jesus may be written in these few words "He went about doing good."
BE, then DO.

If we think we live by our daily food we are deceived. But if our consciousness be truth we shall know that the truth sustains us.

Not until we claim the truth of Infinite Being as the truth of all being shall be known for ourselves, that God is in us; or have we perceived righteous judgment.

The harvest of Truth is always ripe; postpone not gathering in your harvest, thinking that in weeks or months it will be ripe. To-morrow never comes, to-day is the harvesting time.

MEDITATION.

LET us state shortly the substance of our preliminary remarks under this heading during the last few months. When we have been advised to "look within" during our meditations; to concentrate by looking "within"; to seek the kingdom of heaven " within "; we have very likely directed our

attention within the physical body to a region near the heart where impressions may be felt; or we have, perhaps, concentrated by focussing our attention to a centre within the brain, where pictures may be perceived. But
neither of these methods is true concentration; within the material body is
not the mystical "within." Consider any living thing—say a man; one
thing we know about him is that without life the body is useless; in other
words, that the life is the reality of the man, that the body is an instrument
by means of which the life manifests itself; the body is visible, the life is
invisible; the body is in particular places, at particular times, but the life is
everywhere at all times; the body is, as it were, something focussed or bound,
but the life is free—pervading all space; body is external, or the "without,"
life is internal, or the "within." This is the true "within", in which, if we
be concentrated, our attention will not be focussed, and our brains contracted; but our attention will be simply *on the subject*, and the brains relaxed.
True concentration is not to a place, but to a state—namely, the "within," or
life, heaven, Truth, etc. True concentration cannot be attained by object
gazing, but fixity of gaze and all external things will be added to whomsoever attains the "within". Thus, instead of feeling focussed, let us feel
expanded, not in place but in state, even to life itself, which is omnipresence.
And the best way of attaining to this highest blessedness is—to pay attention
to whatever we have on hand, and attend to it with Love. If we follow out
this rule we shall quickly realize that heaven or life is now—eternally; consequently questions of time dwindle into insignificance, and as a mere secondary consideration we arrange to meet together at some particular hour of a
day; the hour thus fixed is not because of any particular benefit that is to be
gained by members sitting in different parts of the world at the same time,
for there is no particular benefit to be gained by so doing; but it is because
where a few meet together in the spirit of truth they may help one another in
the search for it. Truth is the importance, not time; our motives should be
based not in temporal things but in the eternal. How we base our motive or
faith in the one or in the other may be easily understood. For consider how we
become conscious either of temporal things or eternal; is it not by our
thought ? We are not conscious of anything except we think about it; even
the most familiar object might be prominently before our eyes, but it would
remain unrecognized by us until we thought about it. By our thoughts we
place our faith where we will, either in the material or in the spiritual. But
we now no longer seek the kingdom of heaven in sensational enjoyments, for
these pass away; for we know that our Home is permanent and passes not

away, we therefore seek the permanent by recognizing it in our thoughts and thus base our faith or motive aright.

March 6th.

Subject for meditation:—**Man.**

" The first man Adam was made a living soul; the last Adam was made a quickening spirit." I Cor. **xv, 45.**

The knowledge of ' man ' is, perhaps, as much veiled from most men as is the knowledge of Genesis itself. We are accustomed to think that man is the male portion of the human family, and there we generally let the matter rest. It must be remembered however, that man is a living Soul in the image of God. Now what is an image of anything? Is it not a *complete* representation of that thing ? And an image or likeness of any principle or truth must be its complete representation. Hence the image or likeness of God, which is all principle, every truth, must be the complete represesentation of Him or Life; it must contain all forms in one form, all images in one image, all likeness in one likeness. And this is the Universal Soul, God the Son or Man in the image of the Creator. Oh Man! awaken from thy sleep and know thyself.

"And Adam begat a son in his own likeness, after his image ", etc. **Gen. v, 3.** That is, and Man commenced to create forms in his own image. These forms that are in the image of man are all the forms in the whole material universe; in other words, the whole material universe is the demonstration or image of Man. Let us then think of ourselves as we are, and not as separate from any form of life; let us not think of the human race as merely containing man and woman; all life is man ; " Woman" of the bible is not the helpmate of man as most understand it [See opening lines on Oneness]. Whoever knows man, as he is, is the last Adam—a quickening spirit. We are all Adam, but not all have eaten of the tree of the knowledge of good and evil to the attainment of wisdom; yet whoever has attained Wisdom, as a god, is a quickening spirit.

And finally, just as a representation could not exist without the thing represented, just as a demonstration could not appear without the principle; so, neither could Man exist, nor his demonstrations appear, without the Spirit of God which is eternal life, truth, wisdom and justice; with which we are one; to whom alone be all glory for ever!

March 13th.

Subject:—**Swear not at all.**

" But let your communication be, Yea, yea; Nay, nay; for whatsoever is more than these cometh of evil."   Matt. v, 37.

An oath is a symbol by which one places himself under bondage to do or say, or refrain from doing, saying or accomplishing some particular thing. Now to be under bondage is not to be free, and no good can come of it; if we be not able to restrain ourselves from thieving and wantonness, then are we under bondage to these adverse propensities; and if for a time we end these propensities by reason of some pledge or other bondage, then are we in double bondage, firstly to our dissipations, and secondly to our pledges; but if we break the bonds of disobedience by preferring knowledge to ignorance, we shall stand free from corruption by reason that we are free indeed.   Therefore, let us not place ourselves under any promises, pledges, or other bondage—or require it of others, whether in law courts or out of law courts; nor emphasize our remarks beyond the straightforwardness and simplicity of a simple affirmation or denial, as the case may require.   To do more than this is to place oneself under suspicion; for oaths are only for the bond, the free are beyond suspicion.

March 20th.

Subject:—**Resist not evil.**

The word " evil " is intended to designate an absence of goodness, *not a presence of the opposite of goodness;* but sheer absence, or ignorance, or unconsciousness.   Suppose that some one offer us, what is commonly called, an insult; now we know that it is nothing, or prompted by a not knowing any better; then if we resent the insult we seem to make something of it.   We allow it to become a reality in our thoughts, and this strengthens the one who offers the insult in his opinion that the insult is something.   We admit a reality of whatever we struggle against or resist; it does not make evil absolutely real, because we think it real; but if we allow ourselves to live under the belief of falsehood, we are in darkness or falsehood ourselves.   If any one would injure you, stand unmoved, denying the possibility of injury, and you have deprived injury of its sting and made a friend of an enemy.   If any one would deprive you of worldly goods, resist not; but show him your unconcern and that you value not earthly things; then you place upon earthly things their proper value, and make a convert of your prosecutor. If any one act meanly towards you, do not you so to them in return, making them your example; but be generous and liberal towards them that they may see your good works and glorify the principle that prompted you. Therefore let us not make another's injustice our injustice; or another's wrong-doing our wrong-doing, by resistance. But let us walk in all respects according to our own light, and not according to another's darkness; with personality under subjection, and desires outgrown; so shall we in this life attain to life eternal—and not ourselves only, but those also who would have had us resist their evil. Let this be our example to our neighbours, that we resist them not; and this is the judgment that is come upon the world through Christ, that the absence called evil no more appears where the presence of truth is recognized.

March 27th.

Subject:—Ask, and it shall be given you.

When the subject of "thought" is understood, it will be found, that we neither attract to us nor are conscious of any thing or any principle that we do not attract or recognize by our thoughts. To ask is to recognize and attract to us what we ask for; whatever we receive, we receive in this way, and in no other way. Each is responsible for their own gifts; but only when the impersonal Goodness or Spirit of God is sought and recognized, will we receive on Earth that Ease which is the true image, representation, or manifestation of health, life, or the Kingdom of Heaven. "Thy will be done on earth as it is done in heaven!"

We are *servants* of what we obey.
We are *doers* of what we condemn.
We are *masters* of what we overcome.

*   *   *   *

*   *   *

Round things belong to Roundness. We have found Truth to be roundness itself and Universal. And the Earth we find is round, and all upon it in
their nature are inharmony. And we conclude that the Earth and all upon it
belong to Truth.

Truth is the bread of life, for it is the remedy for all misconceptions or
seeming *inharmony.* Know the truth and live it, and it will free you from
all limitations.

Just as much of Truth as we recognize, just so much—and neither more
nor less—do we manifest. To each one is given according to the measure of
the gift of Christ. To the degree that we think truth, to that degree do we
manifest Christ.

MEDITATION.

April 3rd.

Subject:—What is it to live?

Surely to be conscious of life.

Suppose we ask ourselves, what are we conscious of? We should answer
just what we think about. And one thinks about his business, past failures and
future prospects; another about her home duties and the detail of providing
food and amusement; others about grievances, sicknesses, expenditures,
socialties and so forth. Now take any one of these occupations, or any of the
others that occupy the thoughts of ninety-nine people out of one hundred,
and we shall see that they are *things;* in other words, that the attention of most
people is chiefly confined to what the senses perceive, to things that pertain to
existence, and are frequently called "necessities of life;" and of all the
things that are to be found on earth, of all the sensations, whether of joy or
sorrow, we get out of them. Is there any *one* of them that can be called life?
The food we eat is dead; the houses, churches, etc., are dead; gold and silver

are dead; our bodies and the earth to which they return are dead. No, there is not one thing that is perceptible to the senses, that is life; and yet the majority of people are worshipping these things of sense—a dead god, not a living God. To have our consciousness embedded in things is to be dead; to be concerned or taken up with the things of earth is to be dead to life, and to such ones it matters not whether they have a physical body or cease to exist here, they are equally dead in either case. Death is not a question of losing a body, it is a question of losing a consciousness. The Soul, whose consciousness is in things, is dead now; the Soul, whose consciousness is in Being, is alive now. "And this is life eternal, that they might know thee, the only true God, and Jesus Christ, whom thou hast sent." (John xvii, 3.) Then the Soul whose thoughts are of, whose attention is upon, the world and things of the world, is—*so far as she knows*—dead. What then is it to live? He that knows eternal life lives; and as the soul has become dead by basing her consciousness in the letter, so, shall she become alive by basing her consciousness in the Spirit. Death is not a species of annihilation, nor life a species of becoming; death is not a deprivation of life, nor life a something that becomes dead. There is Being which is forever life, and there appear its manifestations, which are forever dead; we are life forever, but to identify ourselves with the dead is to believe we are subject to death. The body is always dead, the life is always life; we are always life and will always have a body; we may identify ourselves with either, by placing our thoughts or consciousness in one or the other. "Choose ye this day, whom ye will serve."

April 10th.

Subject:—Perseverance.

"We are made partakers of Christ, if we hold the beginning of our confidence steadfast unto the end." Heb. iii, 14. "Prove all things, hold fast that which is good." I Thes. v, 21.

The subject for this evening's meditation is one of great importance to every one; for it is only through perseverance, or holding to what we want to attain, that we attain what we want. In considering it many thoughts will suggest themselves; we must learn *what* to hold to, then we must learn to hold to that steadfastly; next we must learn *what* to let go of, then to let go of that steadfastly. All that we wish to hold to is the real, all that we wish to let go of is the false. But to know what is real and what false, each must learn from experience; each must partake from the tree of good and evil, in order to become wise. We will persevere in what we think it important to attain to, and the strength of our perseverance will be regulated according to the importance we place upon what we are striving for. But the listless and indifferent, those in doubt and nervously shifting from one issue to another, positive in nothing, remain unanchored and unstable, until the weariness of their situation forces them to take some decided stand. Such as these should guard against flying off into the other extreme, and placing an extravagant value on some supposed pearl; for the reaction of this is the old listlessness. Steadfastness is the secret of Wisdom; and whoever seeks steadfastly with discernment shall find that Pearl of great price, which is the Peace of God passing mortal understanding. If from experience we have learned not to place our confidence in Earthly riches, if we have learned to place our trust in Christ, or the heavenly riches, let us hold the beginning of our confidence with perseverance unto the end; and what is that end? It is reconciliation to the Father, knowledge of the unknown, happiness of happiness, and joy with full consciousness forever. Then let go of prejudice and prove all things patiently and perseveringly, until we find good in all things; hold fast to the good, let go of the things.

April 17th.

Subject:—" It is finished."

" I have glorified Thee on the earth; I have finished the work which Thou gavest me to do."—John xvii, 4.

Even as in the school-room and workshop, we commence and end the education fitting us for a particular occupation; so in the world or in nature we commence and end our experiences necessary to a consciousness of eternal life. The testaments from " In the beginning" of Genesis to " Amen" of Revelations, are but records of the Soul's work from Monday to Sunday. Just as any one on Earth works six days of the week without intermission, so any Soul in the Universe works six days—any one of which is as a thousand years—without intermission. The sleeps at nights, or the sleeps at deaths, are but rests during the one continuous period of labour—the six days' labour of the Soul. And to what end does the individual with ceaseless activity labour? To the end that he may receive eternal life. And this is eternal life, that each may *know* God. Eternal life is for each one of us, and that life is absolute knowledge of God. Therefore, dear friends, cease to think yourselves as unworthy to receive so great a gift; but make yourselves worthy by facing your perplexities, by taking up your cross and walking according to principle, and not as a blind follower of Example. "Take My yoke upon you;" for just as your yoke makes the carriage of material burdens easy, so " my yoke"—which is the consciousness of the all-powerful—makes the carriage of all burdens, mental or other, easy. Thus will the last day's journey be along the banks of still waters; and ere the sun has set, our work will be finished. " Enter thou into the joy of thy lord."

April 24th.

Subject:—Sensation.

All feelings are sensations, and are the result of thought. It is our thought then, that we feel. We perceive objects intellectually, that is, through the senses—and the feelings that follow such perceptions are sensation Harmonious sensations follow true thoughts, inharmonious sensations follow untrue thoughts. It is in thought that we work out the Problem of Life, but if we were not sensible of our workings we should not gain any knowledge from our work; thus the lesson of creation would be lost. The difference between Being and Sensation is this; the former is consciousness of the principle or Spirit, the latter is consciousness of the Solution or letter. Sensation is not to be despised, but to be understood; it is not to be loved, but the love of Sensation is to be overcome. Sensation or the perception of objects cannot be killed out, but the loving and living in feelings is to be outgrown. And just as the problem on the blackboard is the Student's method of learning, but is not his Master, so sensation or experience, is our method of learning, but is not our Master. Therefore, although we may seem to learn from Sensation, it is in nowise our master; and we have to learn not to be guided by any feeling or impression, but in all our ways to be guided by principle, and our paths will be paths of peace.

Perfect and complete from eternity is God, and we through unfolding truthful thought and perception, express more and more of his perfection and completeness; perfect and complete from eternity is the *I am* of every one, and through the cycles of eternity, we shall realize more and more of the *I am*, and of self.

MEDITATION.

May 1st.

Subject:—Ye must be born again.

"Except a man be born from above—of water and of the Spirit; he cannot enter into the Kingdom of God. That which is born of the flesh is flesh; and that which is born of the Spirit is Spirit. Marvel not that I said unto thee, Ye must be born again."

The term "ye" means "each one individually." And if each one must be born *again*, it must be allowed that each one has been already born. The true meaning of "to be born" is "to become or to be derived from some source," and that which is derived is expression. Thus we say thought is born or derived from the thinker; or that the Soul is born or derived from God.

Now there is a consciousness or soul pertaining to and appropriate to every creation; and as a natural sequence to this self-consciousness, which makes the individual a living soul, the soul or consciousness identifies itself with its image or appropriate symbol; and this descent into matter is the birth that precedes the rebirth spoken of in the sentence "ye must be born again." That consciousness, which we have seen corresponds to any expression, is the Soul of that expression, and is that life mentioned in Matt. x, 39, which after a man findeth he shall lose, and losing this he shall find that life or consciousness which animates all forms.

A man must be born from above of water and of the Spirit. The term water here means the individual consciousness or life which a man shall lose; and the term spirit means the universal consciousness or life which a man shall find on losing the individual consciousness. Before the individual's realization of his own immortal soul his consciousness is so based in the material things his attention is occupied with, that his soul is said to be dead; that is, it is unconscious of the consciousness or life that animates his form or body. And if the soul's attention or thought were continually to remain taken up with its phenomena (which are of course dead,) such soul would be continually dead—that is, without knowledge, and thus the purpose of manifestation would be defeated. Therefore "marvel not that I said, Ye must be born again." As every experience brings added knowledge to the individual consciousness, it is inevitable that a time must come when such individual will realize life, and this is the regeneration at which we should not marvel.

May 8th.

Subject:—Blessed are the meek for they shall inherit the earth. Matt. v, 5.

The meek are the gentle, unassuming, and not acquisitive. One way to get at the meaning of the above text is to answer the question, Who are the meek? And by inference these opposite shall not inherit the earth. Then the opposite to the meek are the pretentious and acquisitive of material wealth and earthly power, and who do *seem* to rule and possess the earth. But such ruling is in seeming only, and the potentate who says—"I rule," speaks ignorantly, not knowing that all things are ruled and governed in order and harmony by the invisible and universal Mind. Likewise such possessing is the merest pretence and seeming, and instead of considering that such a man possesses the wealth, it would be much nearer the mark to say that the wealth possesses such a man.

But they who have passed through the ordeal of experience necessary to a knowledge of life, know better than to again bow down before idols. These make no pretence or ignorant assumptions, but being borne out of a consciousness of dead things into a consciousness of eternal life overcome the world, and are no more overcome or possessed by it, but are the true possessors of it. Thus only the meek shall inherit or possess the earth, and enter into the kingdom of heaven or life eternal. "Fear not, little flock; for it is your Father's good pleasure to give you the Kingdom." Luke xii, 32.

May 15th.

Subject:—Ye are the light of the world.

"Let your light so shine before men in such a manner that they may see your good work and glorify your Father which is in heaven." Matt. v, 16.

We can meditate upon this subject from more than one point of view. For instance we could take the word light as a symbol of truth; and considering the beneficent part light plays in the world we could point out how this example, which appears to the intellection (or senses), corresponds to the province of truth, which appeals to the intuition (or perception.) And as valuable practice we hope that our readers will carry out this suggestion. But instead of taking the idea light and following it out, let us now take the idea suggested by the word "world," and follow it out. Now this word as here used signifies a state of darkness, a dependence on some outside source for light. We have said in a preceding paragraph that all symbols are expressions of a corresponding consciousness; and if we take this earth—in appearance opaque, dependent upon the Sun for light—as a symbol with a corresponding consciousness, we should say its consciousness was chiefly material, which is in fact the condition of the world as a whole at the present day; though that condition is fast being changed, and humanity is beginning to seek the light within instead of being dependent on some light without. In comparison with such a consciousness, then, as is wrapt up in the darkness of matter or illusion, what is the light? Surely that consciousness that is wrapt up in the light of Spirit or reality. "The light shineth in the darkness, but the darkness comprehended it not." John i, 5. Ye (that is, all who are manifesting truth), are the light of knowledge that shines in the darkness of the world of ignorance.

Then, dear readers, suppose you are conscious of that true light which is the light of the world, how are you going to use it? Certainly you cannot hide it; any more than you could a city which is built upon a hill. Besides, even if you could, it is not meant for hiding, any more than a lighted candle is meant to be covered up in some little cupboard. Then how are you going to use your light? Do you intend that it shall make you a famous philosopher, an illustrious teacher, a marvellous healer? Beware, beware, friends; a wolf is here hidden in sheep's clothing! For it is good to be a philosopher, a teacher, a healer—to bring the lost sheep into the Father's fold; what greater mission could there be! But beware. Press not forward to the work anxiously, or lest some one should be before you; but come into it naturally and orderly, and the time will be directly, when YOU WILL NO LONGER SEEK TO BE KNOWN but you will use your light to the glory of God, that your Father in heaven may be known, and that his children in darkness who see your light may follow it to the Manger of Truth and not to some shrine of your personality.

Let us determine well, firstly to use our talent, and secondly to use it wisely; for great responsibility attaches to those who are a light in the world.

May 15th.

Subject.—Take no thought for the morrow.

"Take no thought, saying, what shall we eat? or what shall we drink? or wherewithal shall we be clothed? For your heavenly Father knoweth that ye have need of all these things. But seek ye first the kingdom of God and his righteousness, and all these things shall be added unto you." Matt. vi, 31, 32, 33.

To-morrow never comes. When the time we did call to-morrow arrives, it is no longer to-morrow, it is to-day. So to-morrow is always in the future. All things unaccomplished, unfulfilled, unadjusted, lie in the chaos of the unapproachable future, and so long as our thoughts are for the future, the sensations that will follow these thoughts will be of dissatisfaction, of chaos, of a craving after we know not what. Oh, the longings for something in the future, the regrets about something in the past! What sorrows they bring, what wounds they reopen. For they who indulge in looking backward and looking forward have not yet outgrown the belief in sorrows and wounds.

You may ask the question, Is it not desirable and even scientific for me to hold in thought the results I wish to externalize? No, friend, it is neither desirable nor scientific; for your consciousness is thus taken up with material things—you are living in results. But live only in the consciousness of God and his righteousness, and all proper, happy and needful results, conditions and circumstances will naturally come to pass for you. By living in the present, as one with CAUSE, we control effect; by living in EFFECT our consciousness is controlled by the changeable and illusory. And of course it is no more desirable to hold in thought unsuccessful results than successful results. But the advice is often given to those who are looking upon business or any other thing with eyes of despondency or despair, to look upon the same business or other things with eyes sanguine of success; whereas that which is really needed is the eye to look upon that which produces the success or favour.

Have we accepted, and are we living this teaching of Jesus given to the world nearly two thousand years ago? Or do we continue to provide for the future? If we do, then we have not yet awakened to the Christ teachings, we have not learned the lesson of undivided faith in the Father from whom all provisions come. The saying, God helps those who help themselves, is a very true one; but it must be remembered that they only truly help themselves who walk after the law of truth, and not after the desires of the heart. Consider the sparrows, how they are provided for; certainly He whose law is of universal application will also provide for you.

Is there then nothing to be done by you? Yes, live contentedly a life of affirmation of goodness; never identifying yourself either through sympathy or antipathy with your own or another's sensations; but identifying yourself with that principle or God in which there is neither any want nor shadow of change. And so living you shall come to realize the fullness of eternal life.

May 29th.

Subject:—"All things are delivered unto me of my Father."

"And when all things shall be subdued unto him, then shall the Son also himself be subject unto him that put all things under him, that God may be all in all." I Cor. xv, 28.

Here Jesus speaks of himself as the Soul that has overcome the world, and through experience in the world has revealed the consciousness of eternal life and oneness with the Father. He that is one with the All-power has power over all things; and therefore all things are delivered unto such an one. But this consciousness could not be imparted to any Soul except by the Infinite; therefore Jesus says plainly that he has received the consciousness enabling him to master all expression from the Father.

And what lessons are we to learn from this for ourselves? That He that imparted a knowledge of himself to one Soul will impart the same knowledge to all. That all will come into this same consciousness on earth through experience. Now we are all in our different ways striving to reach the same goal of happiness—and it is within the reach of all. But the world must be overcome by each before this happiness is attained. Let us then hold to the perception that God is in all things; and let us not judge from the perception of the things, but from the perception of that which pervades them. Thus, resisting not evil, we outgrow it and overcome the world.

THINKING.

THINKING is being.
Thought is the evidence of the thinker.
To be, is to be a thinker.
To think, is to create.
To create is to make an image of the thinker.

Walk in the Light.

Attachment for mortal things; ambition for worldly fame; desire for what is called worldly comfort; blinds to the true interest and inward happiness. They are the clouds which darken the way, that lead to a realization of life eternal and union with all Good.

Feed not upon husks, for the forms of the world are but symbols of the real, which is substance and truth. There is therefore, now, no condemnation to them which are in Christ, who walk not after the flesh but after the Spirit.

All goodness that is recognized, is enjoyed; that which is, and is unrecognized, is unenjoyed. Postpone not the time for re-cog-nizing the Kingdom of Heaven, which is always at hand. They who recognize and enter there, rest in faith and certainty.

MEDITATION.

June 5th.

Subject:—What is justice?

The Uncreate, Unmanifest Being, is Justice. Prior to manifestation, Justice is, and is the attribute of being just, right and impartial. It weighs our inmost thought and the expression of thought, in the balance, and if found wanting of the Spirit of Goodness, or, if not in the image and likeness of the attributes of Infinite Spirit, they are cast into the fire (spirit) and consumed. The imperfect is of short duration, appearance only.

Justice renders to every one his or her due, and to every expression according to the perception and thought producing it. The method of Infinite Spirit in creation, is exact justice. The science of expression of Infinite Being, is exact justice. The science of mathematics, is exact justice. Divine Truth, is exact justice. Just and right is The One—The All.

Conformity to truth in thought, word and deed, is Justice manifest. Thoughts of love are just and righteous, they are the fulfilling of the law. "To refuse Justice and bestow love, is an affectation of mercy and a reality of insult." A manifestation under the name of love without justice, is pretence—

false.   Love, the Royal law of Being, is administered with exact justice. It recognizes neither friend nor foe, all are one to it.   In manifestation Justice has no attachments; it is passionless, unaffected by emotion or sensation.   It is that which finally brings all to re-cognize first and final truth, which is, harmony.   It acts not for affection, hate nor gain.   The just act free from self desire, humble, yet steadfast and unwavering in truth and right.   Content to be just, without seeming, content to do right and practice truth without fame, for the love of right or truth.   The practice of Divine and unchanging truth, is justice to God and man.

June 12th.

Subject:—**Harmony.**

Harmony is the divine and orderly method of the Infinite in creation, which is unity   See article, "Divine love and Unity," No. 6.   The variety of created things in the Universe, is harmonious expression of the Infinite ONE. Knowledge is harmony.   Ignorance is seeming inharmony.   Truth is harmony; it never varies nor changes.   The truth is always truth, its foundation is knowledge and wisdom.   Error or falsehood is seeming inharmony, it is ever changing, its foundation is ignorance and folly.   The perception of the true relation of nature to God, is the perception of harmony.   In truth there is no inharmony.   The Creator perceives perfect harmony in creations; which is within himself.   The Perfect knows not imperfection.

"Good citizens live in harmony."   They who are conscious of the presence of Goodness, are unconscious of seeming inharmony.   Good is in harmony with all goodness.   A goodly act or deed, is in harmony with good or truthful thought; good or truthful thought, is in harmony with the goodness of the thinker or being.   If thought be in the image and likeness of the thinker, the act will be in harmony with the thought and the thinker.   This is the method of proving the harmony of Being in creation.   Harmony is wisdom's way of expressing truth.   It is the perfect adaptation of the part to the whole, or of expression to the expressor.   It is infinite order, and there is no other·

June 19th.

Subject:—**There is none good but ONE.**

One is the number of Unity; Unity is as permanent as THE ONE.   There is but One all; hence all good is that One.   Infinite Being means that which is, was and ever will be.   It is interior and anterior to the finite, which is the expression of the Infinite.   Being and good are one; therefore to be, is to be good, that which is, and is uncreate and unmanifest. A knowledge of what being is, furnishes a basis, which prepares us for just and harmonious thought and action. Without this knowledge we are at a loss to know how to control thought and action, hence they are like a wave tossed to and fro by every wind of doctrine. Not until we become stable and unwavering in our thought, is it possible to understand and work with the orderly and harmonious method with which the law of Being works. When thought is controlled and is representative of Being, the *Edenic Order* is maintained in consciousness; then all expression is dressed and kept in order, for if thought be adjusted to God, the effect therefrom is harmonious and pleasant—this is reconciliation—regeneration—or atonement; thus the individual will becomes a manifestation of universal faith, and love expands to include all. God or Goodness made everything that was made, and pronounced it good. It is race belief—a self notion—a false and perverse method of interpretation, which presumes to claim and clothe self with the corruptible, the opposite of God or Good. When false interpretation ceases, we shall see as spirit sees, that all is good. All of anything is one, and there can be but one All, which is all goodness.

June 26th.

Subject:—"Thy faith hasth saved thee."

If by faith one was saved and made whole, by faith all are saved and made whole. All are alike under one law, all error is subject to the law, all truth is that law. If all are saved by faith, from what are they saved? Not from truth, for truth is the law and is salvation. Is it not clear that we are to be saved from error, which is false interpretation, erroneous thought and action, or from taking things for what they are not? And that spirit perception, truthful interpretation and right action can alone erase, save and set free?

How is spirit perception gained? They who would witness the perception of Spirit within themselves, should lay aside blinding prejudice, and accept truth when and wherever perceived. Acceptation of truth is faith based aright, and is life, substance and Harmony. By accepting the present truth perceived, and demonstrating it, in word and deed, we make it our own, or we accept in thought that which we are, and thus the way is opened to all truth. They who would climb the ladder of progress, which leads from earth to Heaven, or which guides the consciousness from matter to Spirit, from error to truth, must climb it step by step; thus it is necessary that they accept truth perceived, and stand firm therein and adjust the thought and act to it, before they can ascend to the next round or take an advance step. Through spirit perception, and thought made perfect, all is adjusted to the source of Divine Being. This is faith which saves. They who fulfil the law are in love with truth ; and when all are loved, all *is* forgiven; but to whom little is forgiven, *the same* loveth little.

To hold all in love and truth, is to be just and do right, so the recompense at the resurrection of the just is justice. "With what measure ye mete, it shall be meted to you again."

MEDITATION.

July 3rd.

Subject:—Freedom.

Freedom is the state of being free. It is that which is exempt from control, and which is unlimited and unenvironed. That which is free, is not under the law of being, but is the law. Can it be said that the visible Universe or any visible thing therein contained, is exempt from control ? or, is not subject to its source ? That which is made is subject to its maker.

Manifestitation and appearance of every kind, be it the physical form, or that of health or disease, joy or sorrow, truth or falsehood, love or hate, knowledge or ignorance, is subject to the manifestor, that which is not apparent. That which is uncreate and which creates, is unlimited freedom. All Being is uncreate, hence to be, is to be free, not to be subject to the created. "Whoso looketh into the perfect law of liberty and continueth therein, he being not a forgetful hearer, but a doer of the work, this man shall be blessed in his deed." They who *forget not* what Being is, will come to realize the freedom of Being. The forgetting or losing consciousness of the immortal self, is the cause of all belief in limitations. To know ourselves is to know that we are freedom, one with the unlimited and boundless. Dear friends, they who try to realize these truths, seek in the right direction for true freedom.

July 10th.

Subject:—"Blessed are they which do hunger and thirst after righteousness."

It is written that they which do hunger and thirst after righteousness are blessed, for they shall be filled.

Righteousnes is a state of thought and consciousness, which is in unity with, or conformity to Divine love, which is the law of God—Omnipresent Goodness. To hunger and thirst after righteousness, is to desire to work with the law, and to realize oneness with the whole Spirit of Goodness. They who have that desire are receptive, and are seeking to know and to fulfill the whole law of God or Goodness. When seeking that which is, which is the Infinite, we enter the straight way that leadeth to exact knowledge—perfect faith or power. To be receptive to Omnipresent Goodness, is to quench the thirst at the fountain of Life. So to hunger and thirst after righteousness, is the blessed condition which precedes its attainment.

It is blessed to seek and blissful to find. We cannot expect to find unless we hunger for, and seek to work with the Spirit of Goodness. So "to do truth is to practice God's command." His truth adjusts all to himself; His word is Goodness manifest, or made apparent.

July 17th.

Subject:—Hope.

Hope is where the affections are. What we desire we hope to attain, and hope causes the effort necessary to the attaiment; in other words, if we have a desire or aspiration and make an effort to attain it, it is hope that prompts us to make that effort. If it were not for hope, effort or seeking would cease. Faith is the silent power or substance of hope, effort, or seeking. St. Paul said, "we are saved by hope: but hope that is seen is not hope: for what a man seeth: why doth he yet hope for; but if we hope for that we see not, then do we with patience wait for it." So when we work diligently and patiently, as if already possessing what we hope for, faith is manifest which brings the condition desired. If our hope be in God or Goodness, we hope for that which is, and is for us. If it be not in God or Goodness, it is based in negation or denial of Him; verily both bring their reward.

July 24th.

Subject:—Faith or Divine Will. .

Faith or Divine Will is the substance or power of Infinite Spirit or Mind, and is prior to thought, and is that which prompts mind to act or think, and which causes us to express our thought in word and deed, so it is the substance of thought, word, and deed, and of things hoped for.

Through faith worlds are framed, and forms are created; without it, is not anything made that is made. As there is but one parent source or uncreate cause, there can be but one method of creation or manifestation. The method of the parent source is manifest in the son or child; they who understand this, consciously work with the Father, and do His will; then the Father's will is manifest in perfect faith. Faith is the power which enables us to successfu ly perform our every day duties; by it we think, speak, and act, and move our bodies from place to place; by faith we accomplish all that is accomplished. It is faith in our ability to succeed that causes success in all our undertakings of life. All our works are done in faith, beside it there is no power. Consider the lilies how they grow, they toil not neither do they spin, etc. Faith is fullness of power and substance, and is manifest in all things; it knows not fear or anxiety; the more we use of the fullness of power, the more powerful we are in manifestation. They who have watched a little child making its first effort to walk, have witnessed the increase of power, as it expressed faith with each successive step, with the result that in a few days it was walking about the house with perfect faith in its ability to do so. And this simple, child-like faith which wavers not, is the power which removes mountains, and enables us to rise to the pinnacle of the temple in consciousness and understanding, above temptation and limit ation of the senses, into eternal freedom and power. Without this high perception and faith, it is impossible to realize the parent source and do what we see the Father doing. Use faith every day, hour, and moment, its source is inexhaustible.

July 31st.

Subject:—How should desire be overcome.

To desire, is to long for the enjoyment or possession of something, to feel the want of, to mourn the loss of. So desire is the result of a limited consciousness, and a lack of recognition of our divine inheritance ; it is the result of a consciousness limited to manifestation; hence, an unconsciousness of the oneness of the parent source, and the result of believing self to be the manifested. They who do not know themselves desire much.

In the universe there is the unmanifest, and the manifest. The unmanifest is one and inseparable, perfect and complete, from eternity to eternity, and in the manifest there seems to be many, hence limitation. So when the consciousness is based in manifestation, it is limited and environed, and the delusion which arises from sense-seeing and belief in separateness prevents us from realizing that the whole parent source is the life of all. Desire is caused by not having true knowledge, and can only be overcome by gaining it. True knowledge consists in perceiving one inseparable, omnipresent spirit, manifest in all that lives, and in the manifestation, one manifestor. Desire should be overcome by making what we find to do, accord with the Spirit of Truth and by unremitting effort to realize that we are the unmanifest, one with the all, which has all things. When we realize what we are, desire is overcome ; we do not hunger and thirst after righteousness when we are filled. With this consciousness, deeds are not performed with the hope of reward, nor with anxiety as to results. Truth is the food which feeds the hungry Soul. Partake of it freely, and desire and anxiety will be done away, and all things made new.

—As pillars support whole houses, so also do the divine powers support the whole world.

—Justice, above all things, conduces to the safety, both of mankind, and of the parts of the world, earth, and heaven.

—The most perfect, and greatest of all good things, are usually the result of laborious exercise and energetic, vigorous labor. It is absurd for a man, who is in pursuit of honors, to flee from labors by which honors are acquired.

—The extremity of happiness is to rest unchangeably and unmovably on God alone.

—The virtuous man is a lover of his race, merciful and inclined to pardon, and never bears ill will toward any man whatever, but thinks it right to surpass in doing good rather than in injuring.

—Let us not fear the diseases which come upon us from without, but those offences on which account diseases come, diseases of the mental, rather than of the body.

MEDITATION.

August 7th.

Subject:—" Come unto me."

The purpose of silent meditation should be to realize what Being is and what its possibilities are.

If the attributes be expressed in thought, the will of Spirit is done and the motive is based aright, resultant therefrom are expressions of Being—the " I Am"—which is Harmony manifested; this is *the way* to get illumination or understanding.

That is, meditation on any subject should be for the purpose of realizing the principle underlying the subject, of which words can only be symbolic or representative. Not until we arrive at an understanding of the meaning of Being can we know that creation or expression is symbolic and representative, for we cannot be certain of what things are, until we find the cause which produces them. Therefore, not until we find Being, and perceive from the plane of Being, is it possible for us to distinguish between Being and existence, i. e., between ourselves and our expressions; therefore all endeavor should be for the purpose of getting understanding of the reality underlying the subject on which we meditate or think.

" Come unto Me," is an invitation by the speaker to move hitherward, to draw near unto that which is first; i. e., to approach Being, which is prior to thought and word. Me, means Myself, the invisible Speaker, or the " I Am." Therefore the meaning of this subject is, that all are asked to come unto Spirit and learn of It, and find rest from labor, or from the burdens which arise from a denial or negation of the Me.

Though spirit be omnipresent, the only way to accept the invitation, and to " come unto Me," Spirit, is to think truthfully, with undivided faith, and right motive, and they who come in this way will find rest, for realization of our oneness with the omnipresent One is eternal peace and rest.

Jesus spoke not of himself as the body, nor did He act as if His expressions were Himself, and in this He has revealed *the way* to us, and they who think and act truthfully, will think and act as did He, and with the same intent; not because the personal Jesus thus spake and acted, but because He, the Spirit, revealed the true way of life, by which every one may manifest the same truth and come unto Me. The invitation to " Come unto Me" would be meaningless, if it meant no more than that one material form should appear in the presence of another material form.

We may as justly and truthfully expect, that because the furniture of a room is associated together while in that room, or that because a row of houses are resting on a certain block of land, that they can give life and power to each other, as to expect that physical contact, or that the association of physical forms can give life, peace, or rest. They who labor, and are heavy laden, do so because they do not come unto " Me," Spirit, and recognize and claim to be life, peace and rest; such are seeking in effects, expecting to realize life, peace and rest therefrom; such expectation is negation, and never is it otherwise. We cannot manifest the gifts of Spirit, unless we go to the Spirit for them. We do not find them in expression, for the reason that expression has them not to give. Spirit is "*the way, the truth, and the life;*" then to find the Me, the Invisible Speaker, is to find God, and in Him eternal truth, life, and rest.

The yoke of Truth is easy, and the burden of spirit is light. The spirit of truth, which is wholeness, gives all, yet it labours not, neither is it heavy laden. So to "Come unto Me," is to get understanding and awaken to truth; and *every one* who comes, finds. And they who live in a full consciousness of Being, can give to others rest, by imparting to them the truth that brings them into the same consciousness; therefore the awakened can point the way, because they know that they are the way of wisdom, and all who follow in that way, no longer labour, or are heavy laden. But they who continue in the error of believing their manifestations to be themselves, or that that which is made is real, and that visible things are a cause for happiness, are trying to make visible things serve as the cause for what the invisible spirit alone can give. And not until they cease to partake of this forbidden fruit and place the true worth on spirit, and see existence by the light of truth, can such know self, or "Come unto Me." Not until we cease believing the manifest and unreal to be ourselves, and believe ourselves to be the Unmanifest and real, can we know and reveal the wealth and power of Being. Neither have we "worshipped in spirit and in truth" until we have placed the true worth and value on spirit by acknowledging the Me—which is prior to expression—before all that is made in all our ways.

August 14th.

Subject:—What is Mesmerism?

It is said that "mesmerism is a supposed influence or emanation by means of which one person can act upon another, producing wonderful effects upon the body and controlling his action and thought." "Or the art of inducing an extraordinary, or abnormal state of the nervous system, in which the actor claims to control the action, and communes directly with the mind of the recipient."

If we would know by what means one individual seems to control the action of another, we must first learn the cause of action, and the means by which we control our own.

The science of expression teaches that thought precedes all visible action, and that Being precedes all invisible action, that of thought; hence it is true that the mental constitution, which is born of Being, is maker of this visible plane, and is the action thereof; for thought, will, and motive is our action, the controller of the body, hence it is the thought, will, and motive that seems to control the action of the mesmeric subject.

The subject enters what is called the mesmeric state, by yielding the thought and will to that of the operator, and the control is due to the fact, that the subject changes his own thought and will to harmonize with the operator's.

Individual thought and will cannot be used to control the thought and will of one whose consciousness is universal, nor can such an one become a mesmeric subject. To think and act as the operator dictates, is to yield the thoughts to obey or work in unison with his. It is therefore the subject's own thought and will, acting in concert with, or according to the operator's, that produces that which is called the mesmeric state or condition ; both conditions are temporary and mortal.

They who live in a full consciousness of Being, or truth, are exempt from the influence and control of individual thought and will, for when the absolute is come to the individual consciousness, it has come for the reason that the thought and will have become that of the universal, or of Being.

And when that which is absolute is perceived, that which is in part rules not.

August 21st.

Subject:—" Jesus wept."

As it is a truth, that men to whom the word of God came, clothed the truth in language descriptive of things natural, so the words of our text are purely symbolic.

" He groaned in his spirit and was troubled." " Jesus wept." St. John xi, 33, 35.

To groan means to strive after earnestly, as with groans. Thus to groan in spirit is symbolic of effort made to concentrate in thought, and express the power of spirit. And " He troubled himself," symbolizes the fact, that he exerted himself to raise Lazarus, and thus do his Father's work. Christ raising Lazarus from the dead, symbolizes the purpose for which he came into the world, i. e., to raise the dead consciousness of the race into a living consciousness of Truth and Life Eternal.

The Spirit of God, which is eternal, is fullness, stillness, and goodness; and is brought forth or manifested by the power of faith, and the interior action of thought. Therefore groaning in spirit, or weeping (in Scriptural language), is symbolic of effort made for the bringing forth into manifestation the power of spirit, is symbolic of preparation for the birth of great power, which precedes the joy that comes to all that are raised from the dead, that is, from unconsciousness to consciousness; also of the joy that is for those who are privileged to be witnesses to the raising up, or they who see truth face to face in the expression of the power of spirit. In no way could Jesus have wept, according to the unillumined definition generally given to the word, and to the text of the disciple. The fourteenth and fifteenth verses of the same chapter, read as follows, "Then said Jesus unto them plainly, Lazarus is dead."

"And I am glad for your sakes that I was not there, to the intent ye may believe; nevertheless, let us go unto him."

Again Jesus saith unto Martha, "Thy brother shall rise again." He also said, "I am the resurrection and the life," which means, I am that which rises again, and am the life which causes to rise. "He that believeth in me, though he were dead, yet shall he live." "I am the Truth and the Life." They who believe in Christ, believe that Truth and Life is the maker of everything that is made. They who thus believe, though they were dead in consciousness and understanding, shall rise up and live, or return to truth and live in understanding.

For that which we believe in, we are conscious of, and to believe in the power of truth and life, is to awaken, and be conscious of Truth and Life, and the awakened know that they have eternal life with God.

August 28th.

Subject:—"Seek and ye shall find."

To seek is to go in search or quest of, to endeavour to find.

As useless as it would be to go in search of something that we believed did not exist, or that we knew was not for us; so would it be to seek of God without believing that what we seek is, and is for us.

So, if our seeking be in faith, we will believe that what we seek for is, and is for us, and we have a definite idea of where and what it is we wish to attain and manifest.

And as God, the giver of all, is omnipresent, if we seek in truth we must recognize that what we want to manifest is at hand, and in this state of consciousness we realize that we possess what we seek.

"Seek and ye shall find," is a promise fulfilled in every one that truly seeks. To find is to gain a knowledge and to have a realization of spirit. And this knowledge or realization, is only to be gained by true seeking, that is, through the acknowledgement of the presence of the ever present Wisdom Spirit working in us, and by adjusting and conforming our will and way to It.

For if we would act from the Spirit, we must not be unconscious of its presence and of what it is, but must be able to acknowledge It unmanifest, and recognize It manifest in all our ways. "Canst thou by seeking find out God?" True seeking will bring to us a full consciousness of God, for we are ever conscious of what we recognize, believe in, and conform our thoughts and words to.

Therefore, acknowledgement is the way of conformity to the Spirit, and is reconciliation, regeneration, and atonement.

. . . .

MEDITATION.

Sept. 4th.

Subject :—Understanding and its realization.

Understanding is knowledge or discernment of truth. The word comes from the latin verb, " sto" to stand, and " under," meaning under, below, after. Understanding is therefore an attribute of the reality or spirit which underlies and supports all existences ; a perception or consciousness of the Supreme Deity, it is absolute and unchangeable. So, to realize that we have understanding, is to know that we are one with the Eternal.

The word realization is derived from the root, real, and the suffix, ize, to become, and ion, the act of. Hence the act of becoming conscious that we are the real, is the process of turning from error to truth, from nature to spirit, or

from the example to the principle ; and thus realization is gained that we are
the real, that understands the absolute truth, and that we cannot understand
that which we are not ; therefore we are truth.

Realization is the understanding of Spirit, or reality, manifested ; so to
know that we are the spirit of truth, which we realize by manifesting it, is
divine understanding.   Nothing but spirit can understand the truths of spirit,
which are its own ; and truth manifest is the only begotten of God.

The creature cannot understand the creator, but the creator which pervades
the creature, understands itself and the creature.   The creature is a symbol or
example of an idea in the creator.   Power is not given to the example in mathematics to understand and demonstrate the principle, but the power is in the principle to understand and demonstrate itself. /The question will arise, if the finite
be that which is manifest by the Infinite, and it cannot understand the Infinite
or the absolute truth, how are we, as separate individuals, to understand the
Infinite or the absolute truth, for God is truth. / As it is not given to the
belief of separateness, to understand unity and wholeness, so is it impossible
for one to realize and know the spirit, until they cease to look through the false
belief of separateness that would say, I am separate from God, and from any
thing that is made.   Not until we acknowledge in thought the same relationship
with God, as did Christ, that " I and my Father are one," and hold steadfastly
to this truth, sustaining this relationship by truthful word and deed, is the eye
and ear of understanding opened, or are our manifestations universal.   In other
words—not until the individual is merged into the Universal Spirit, is the
consciousness entirely freed from the belief that we are the creature or example.
And to be free from this belief, is to know that we do understand the universal
spirit, and that we are that which we understand, and that that which is manifest, is the manifestation of Spirit, or the I Am.

We may have faith to know, that if we practice the truth of God, we will
come to realize that we have the understanding that Christ had.   Be the law
of love, and manifest it, and you will know God, for God is love ; be one with
Infinite truth and manifest it, and you will realize that you understand God,
for God is truth.   If we acknowledge that God is Infinite Being, Spirit, or
Mind, and that there is no finite being, spirit or mind, then we know that
there is but one mind to perceive the truth; and as that mind is Infinite and is
perfect, it admits of no error or imperfection, then we are that Being or Mind,
or else we are an existing creature without Spirit, Being, or Mind.   Hence
without truth, reality, or immortality.   Therefore it is an eternal truth, that

no one knoweth the things of God but the Spirit of God ; or naught but the Spirit of Goodness can realize or manifest the Spirit of Goodness.

Like comprehends like; to realize the above statements, is the understanding of Spirit or Mind realized ; and upon this rock we may build a structure of truth against which the gates of negation or false belief cannot prevail. Understanding and its realization means the Infinite or divine idea manifest. The absolute understanding of the Infinite, is realized in the expression of every truth.

Sept. 11*th.*

Subject :—Great religious teachers.

The great teachers of religion, are the men and women who in their daily lives have demonstrated divine love and truth according to the Spirit of Truth, thus proving their faith by their works. Religion is defined to mean, to collect anew, to bind back ; properly interpreted it means bound back, relationship or unity with God or Goodness. This carries with it the meaning that that which is bound back must have been bound before. As all individual consciousness has its origin in God, to be bound back is to bind the consciousness again to God. It is the individual thought that wanders out into the wilderness of material effects, recognizing no master save effects, which is an effort to put the example where principle should be. It is therefore deceived by the senses, not knowing the unreality of effects ; this is unconsciousness of truth. Therefore it is the individual thought that returns to God and binds the consciousness anew to the universal. This is to be accomplished by a divine and orderly method of thinking, by adjusting all conclusions to God, as all problems in mathematics are adjusted to the principle ; and thus it consciously returns to God, knowing that every decision is based in goodness. And so we come to realize that we, the I am, were never lost ; that from eternity we were in the bosom of the universal, the Father. And though the thought and consciousness be veiled by sense, yet we are never veiled from the presence of the eternal Father. Religion is subjective, and designates our unity with Good in word, feeling, and deed. It also designates the oneness of will, thought, love and motive, with God or Goodness. A great religious teacher is one that teaches humanity that they can be as perfect as their Father in Heaven is perfect, who teaches the way by which they can recognize the same mind within themselves that was in Christ Jesus. For it is written, " Let this mind be in you which was also in Christ Jesus ; who being in the form of God thought it not robbery to be equal with God." A great teacher of religion is one who reveals the unity of the way of Truth and Life ; he is one who teaches that God is Infinite Spirit, and reveals the way by which we can worship in Spirit and in Truth, and how to be like Him in all our ways, prefacing all our ways with truthful thought. The greatest of all in the kingdom of heaven, or in divine realization, is one who without omission thinketh Truth, and speaketh it in word and deed. One who without omission manifests the love of God for neighbor as for self, and whose worship consists in the practice of Truth.

Sept. 18th.

Subject :—" Take my yoke upon you."

A yoke is a bond of connection ; a chain or link which connects or unites. The yoke or bond of union of which Christ spake, was his consciousness of the truth of his union with God, or absolute Goodness. Hence he said, take *this* yoke upon you, and you will realize what I realize, and find rest unto your souls. The consciousness that understands the truth of the unity of Being, and which perceived the idea of being perfect as Spirit or Goodness is perfect, was one which realized that it understood the idea of Spirit or Goodness.

As personality and false belief cannot comprehend the impersonal truth and life, so, form cannot understand the impersonal. None but the meek and lowly who are willing to love all alike, who have turned from pride, ambition and worldly desire, can come to realize the full meaning of the divine and impersonal idea of Spirit. The consciousness that "I and my Father are one," is the yoke that connects our expressions to all goodness, to all truth, to all life. Therefore, if we take the yoke of our great exampler upon us, it will make all seeming burdens easy and light ; it will give peace and rest to the weary. We, as he, should not deem it robbery to be equal to the Spirit of Goodness, we should not deem it robbery to put on the whole armor of righteousness, the whole armor of truth, the whole armor of perfection. None but the meek and lowly in personality can take this yoke upon them and learn of Spirit, or consciously realize their unity with Infinite Spirit. But they, who through meekness rise above personality or beliefs of selfishness, distinction or separateness, will be able to take this yoke or realization of truth upon them, which is freedom from limitation and rest from fear. Unity, and not division, is the pathway of truth and life. Be not divided in consciousness by sense-seeing, and you will cease to labor with the shadows or symbols of life ; give up the testimony of the senses and all the things of sense for truth and life, and dominion will be gained over the world of sense, and you will know as did Christ, that you are the truth and life. The same consciousness and truth that bound Christ to God or Goodness, is the yoke that will connect all, to God or Goodness. Therefore take this yoke upon you and you will have nothing between you and God, and this is rest.

Sept. 25th.

Subject :—Eternal punishment.

To solve this question, which has troubled the thoughts of so many persons, and which has caused so much fear, doubt and anxiety, that bear not fruit of the Spirit because they are the opposite of love, faith and rest, it is necessary that we learn what the word eternal means, and what that is, that is eternal. All are agreed that life, love, truth, that power, wisdom, goodness are eternal ; or that mind, idea, or Spirit is eternal ; the word represents that which is without beginning or end—without end of being or duration—the state of being the same at all times. Then naught but the unchangeable is eternal ; and naught but the eternal is unchangeable. No existing thing or form is without change. The action of thought is a continuous or never ending change. Therefore it is unthinkable that that which is eternal and which is unchangeable love and goodness can create or manifest, or cause to be manifest that which is not in the image and likeness of itself. Universal love, which has no respect to person, cannot inflict eternal punishment on anything that it makes, for all that it makes is good, and is like unto itself, which is goodness. Punishment is supposed to be inflicted upon immortal souls for the violation of divine law, and as God's law is infinite love, if He were to inflict eternal punishment upon any of His creations for not fulfilling the law of love, He would violate His own law thereby. It would be like the blind leading the blind, both would fall into the pit. Then, dear friends, consider the meaning of the word eternal, and you will clearly perceive and know that that which is real cannot punish or be punished, cannot afflict or be afflicted, for that which is in the image and likeness of Spirit is in perfect harmony with Spirit, as the mental problem is in perfect harmony with the principle. It is an eternal truth however, that the testimony of the senses, when unillumined by the spiritual perception, testifieth against the Spirit, or all that is eternal ; and this has ever been and will ever be the same. As the consciousness is ever based in the premises from which we draw our conclusions, so if the testimony of the senses be taken as authority, the consciousness is based in effect, not in Spirit ; and thus we calculate from our incorrect work, and not from principle. It is truth that we ever feel our own thought, and it is the source of our pleasure or pain. From a false premise, one that is ever changing, we cannot draw truthful conclusions, and feeling or sensation will ever suffer or be punished, as it were at the hand of sense judgment; and this is eternally true, or ever the same. It is fear, doubt, anxiety, falsehood or all negation of God, that will weep and wail when they are cast into the fiery furnace of eternal truth, and are consumed; and not the reality or immortal soul. Again, it is an eternal truth, that sensible conclusions, or false beliefs, which are neither reasonable nor truthful, are the punishments inflicted, and this is ever the source of all suffering. But as thought is continually changing, so every one that is instructed unto the Kingdom of Heaven, bringeth forth divine love in their thought, and by fulfilling the law—love—are in Heaven, a realization of the presence of God or Goodness, for God is love.

──────────────── *Oct. 2nd.* ────────────────

Subject :—*The Sabbath Day.*

The Sabbath day is a day of rest; a day or time when the individual consciousness is borne back into the absolute and limitless, when Divine Unity is understood and realized. The time when the intellect is illumined by intuition and is taught by the wisdom Spirit. When the understanding of the holy Spirit is made apparent in us. Is it not indeed a day of rest, when we realize or experience our union with God, with all of Goodness? The Sabbath day is that time when the individual has finished his work in materiality, and has entered into the spiritual or eternal life. Having finished the work in limitation, he has passed in understanding to the limitless, the Holy Spirit, or Seventh Principle; this is Eternal rest. Our Sabbath day is a symbol of the above.

──────────────── *Oct. 9th.* ────────────────

Subject :—*Charity.*

Love and Charity are synonymous terms in scriptural language, as are wisdom and understanding. "Though I speak with the tongues of men, and of angels, and have not charity, I am become as sounding brass, or a tinkling cymbal." 1 Cor. xiii : 1. As the Omnipresent One is love, if we keep the commandments, we must be loving or charitable. Therefore to be unloving or uncharitable is not to keep the commandments, for *the law* is love, and may be fulfilled in one word, "Even this, thou shalt love thy neighbor as thyself," by seeing him as thyself. So it is written, the end of the commandment is charity; without love or charity there can not be a clear perception of truth, and without a clear perception of truth, love or charity is personal and limited in expression. Harmonious expression necessarily depends on the union of love, or charity, and truth. Therefore, be *love or charity*, and *truth*, and you will manifest what you perceive yourself to be.

Oct. 16th.

Subject :—" *The light of the Body is the eye.*"

" If therefore thine eye be single, thy whole body shall be full of light. But if thine eye be evil, thy whole body shall be full of darkness."

" If therefore the light that is in thee be darkness, how great is that darkness !"

The light of the soul is understanding. Therefore if thine understanding perceives that God is all, it is single to truth, and thy consciousness is full of light.

But if thine understanding recognizes evil within, where the Spirit of God forever resides, thy consciousness shall be full of darkness. Therefore if the understanding that is in thee be darkness, how great is that darkness? Understanding cannot serve two masters; if it be single to Goodness, it hath attained Goodness.

Oct. 23d.

Subject :—*Bodies.*

Bodies are material organisms, forms, masks or external appearances. No external appearance is real, in that it is continually changing. The real consists solely in Spirit, and Spirit is ever the same. Forms are transient, they appear and disappear, and that which produces one produces all. But, you will ask, are psychical or celestial bodies real? There must ever be a certain unreality in form, for all that is made is subject to change. Appearance or that which is made, is ever subject to the thought of the maker. The maker changes not and is eternal.

Oct. 30th.

Subject :—*Souls.*

Souls are Divine Ideas, eternal in the heavens, *i. e.*, in Infinite Mind. And they are the means by and through which Infinite Mind works in creation, and every form in nature is an example or appearance representative of an idea, which is the soul manifesting the form. Therefore souls are in Infinite Mind before the beginning, and have eternal life in, and with God.

Pain and Suffering

Ed. note: While the following was given as an answer to the question of why animals suffer pain and disease, it nicely exposes part of Cramer's basic belief system.

All suffering results from the delusion arising from the five senses. To sense only, is not to understand what the things are that we sense—that is, to sense only, is limitation in thought and expressed consciousness ; therefore sense seeing, unillumined by truth, means belief of limitation, which belief includes fear, doubt, desire, selfishness and separateness. This belief and sense seeing are one. The delusion of the senses is due to the fact that thought is turned from its source, and is looking outward, or is projected into effects, and is for the time based on the sense plane. Thought thus based is sensible of objects ; in other words, a consciousness thus based by thought is an animal consciousness. Therefore, the sensation of the animal is its thought, which it senses, for that which it thinks is the range of its present consciousness. If it were above the sense plane, in the spiritual, it would be above suffering. The animal cognizes through the five senses; by seeing, hearing, tasting, smelling and feeling. It is sensible or conscious of the manifest world, and sense fears to lose that of which it is alone sensible or conscious, and also fears that its desire will not be gratified. Much could be said concerning the fear caused by the manner in which they are treated by human beings, so called, but it is not our purpose to do so at this time. Fear is suffering itself, for by it the mental harmony is disturbed and the expression of life marred, and in extreme cases it is cut off. Material things are continually changing, so a consciousness based therein, and limited thereto, must necessarily suffer from fear and doubt, and from desire and want. When the visible universe and sensation are all that the thought cognizes, pain results therefrom through belief of limitation and fear   The thought of fear is the dis-ease which has its out picturing in what is called disease; the consciousness that is united with first cause, by understanding gained through adjusting every thought to its source, is free from the beliefs of limitation; and freedom is painless; reality is void of suffering.

"THE NEW ORDER."

An Occult Story.

BY

A ROSICRUCIAN.

Preface.

IT has been known to the author for some time past that a new order of teachers was becoming manifest on this planet; an order whose teaching and methods would be different from those of the Brethren of Eulis or any other school of Occultism; whose teachings would surpass those of past orders, and in surpassing explain them; for the time is at hand when this may be done with wisdom. It is apparent to the world at large that from several quarters in recent years have issued forth revelations of mysteries that had previously been occult. The names of many Theosophists and Rosicrucians, who have been thus labouring, will readily occur to the reader.

The religious movements at present being carried on throughout the world are a sign of a millennium on Earth, the spirit of which but few discern. All along the line of religious activity—amongst the Salvation Army, Missionaries, Churches, Evangelists, Theosophists, Metaphysicians—can be traced one purpose, which it is my aim in the following story to in part illustrate. The very literary and commercial signs of the times bear the mark of an era of progress in the world's history hitherto unattained. I am persuaded that notwithstanding all that has been and may be said on prehistoric civilization on this Earth, there has never been a time in the planet's unfoldment—which is its people's unfoldment—that has approached in true enlightenment the age into which the world is just entering. Under the teachings of The New Order the old world will pass away and all things will be beheld as new.

By no sense of perception can this Order be discovered. Each individual will discover The New Order for himself or herself, and receive the sign by which he or she shall at all times know those who have made a similar discovery. Initiations into The New Order are never conducted on the external plane; nor is the "Baptism" of a personal nature.

CHAPTER I

The Home.

It is fully seven years ago since those things happened which will be narrated in this chapter. At that time I was only thirteen years of age, and it will not be expected of so young a girl that she can remember things as they were then. But I will relate as well as possible what I remember of that time, with but little addition from what I have learned since awakening from my long sleep—and seven years is a long sleep, in this age, at any rate.

I suppose every one knows Bartone; it is a thriving town now, but seven years ago was only a small place of two or three thousand inhabitants. Situated at the foot of an inland running spur of the Sierras, it is a favourite resort for sportsmen and travellers on the look-out for the picturesque. Our house—we always call it " our house," though it is really only a small wooden cottage—is just the prettiest home, inside and out, in all Bartone; and is just what its name, " The Home," over the door indicates. Its two front windows look through two archways of vines on to the street and at the passers-by. How the boys and girls look at its two great eyes twinkling merrily in the sunshine! they seem to say, " I see you," and the little ones think, " I know you do." Then perhaps the front door opens like a great mouth, and out comes mother, and the whole face of our house seems to beam with sunny smiles; but not more so than Johnny's and Susan's do through the pickets, for they know by experience that all this preliminary means " grapes."

The window of my room is at the side of the house, looking out on to a little side garden with apple trees in.

It was in the winter of 1881—one day, I don't remember which—it was very wet, and I was sitting with my elbows on the window-ledge and face in my hands, watching the sparrows on the apple-trees chirping for some consolation; I was thinking how strange it was that my father, who had never been away from home for any length of time, should remain away so long these holidays. When he got his yearly holiday he would go off into the mountains with his fishing rod (which he might just as well have left, as he never caught anything,) and some provisions, but never remaining away more than about a week. But this time he had been away nearly two weeks, and his holiday was spent. To-morrow the other assistant—my father was an assistant in Mr. Purday's drug store—would want to take his holiday.

Just at this moment there was a knock at the front door, and I heard Mr. Purday say " Thank you," in a very solemn voice, in answer to my mother's cheerful welcome. Of course I went in to see what Mr. P. wanted. Mother never used to send me out of the room—like lots of girls I know, get sent off. As I entered my father's employer was saying—handing mother a letter at the same time—"What's the meaning of this, madam!" If he'd only said mam, instead of madam! I thought it would not have sounded so terrible. My mother read the letter as follows: "Dear Sir—You will probably be surprised " to receive this note conveying my intention to resign the position I have so " long held in your store. I was unable to give you earlier notice, as my " holiday was necessary to the completion of the plans I had in view. Be " kind enough to hand the enclosed note, which I have no other way of " sending, to my wife." There was a good deal more which I have forgotten, perhaps because Mr. P. made a suggestion that I should be out of the room while they talked matters over. But mother said, in her usual quiet way, "Go right on, Mr. Purday. We never have any secrets from Nellie."

"Well, madam," continued Mr. P., colouring a little under the mild rebuke—for next to nothing acts as a rebuke to one who is accustomed to be lord of his own way—"this extraordinary letter was put into my hands but a short time ago, and I'd like to know the meaning of it"—pulling out his watch as if he only gave mother a minute to answer in.

"Perhaps the letter addressed to me will explain it. Certainly I had no idea that Mr. Firth contemplated leaving his situation just now, although —— "

"Then you knew about it, too!" This discovery was evidently too much for the druggist, for without another word he got up and left, which I suppose was about the best thing he could have done. I remember but little more of these days; I know they made a tremendous impression upon me. I must not omit to relate the very last thing I remember, no matter if it do seem irrelevant just now; it was my mother's call. She was sitting by my bedside— it must have been late in the evening, and the lamp was burning low—her hands were clasped on an open bible, her eyes were closed. I shall never forget the calm expression on her face, nor the words that, scarcely audible, she uttered! "Come unto me, and I will give you rest." And I immediately thought of father. "Come unto me, and I will give you rest."

I remembered no more; but almost any one in Bartone could tell you the history of Nellie Firth, "the idiot girl," during the years succeeding the above.

. . . .

The law of nature is love in its harmonious and regular order of action, that by which God governs the universe.

To give alms before men to be seen of them, is to give for a vain and selfish motive or purpose, with desire for credit or praise; and if a gift be offered with such motive or purpose, the reward cannot be from the Spirit of Goodness, because the motive is not based therein. When the motive or purpose be like unto God, then God is manifest in it. "Verily all receive their reward."

. . . .

"THE NEW ORDER."

An Occult Story.

BY

A ROSICRUCIAN.

CHAPTER II.

A Revelation.

BY the morning after Mr. Purday's visit to Mrs. Firth, half the people in Bartone knew of her husband's " freak." And as much sensation as it was possible to weave into the simple facts was interwoven; so that by the time it reached Frank Fairchild—the schoolmaster—it had assumed alarming proportions. Master Frank, however, knew just about how little to believe, for he was intimately acquainted at " The Home," where he was treated as one of the family. He and Firth had many talks upon theosophical matters, and discussed together some of the important works upon such subjects, that had recently reached Bartone. But during the past year they had not studied together so frequently, for Firth had joined the Rosicrucians and was undergoing a year's "approbation" before final admission into the Order.

At this time Firth knew but little more than the mass of exoteric students, either of the purposes of occult study or of the acquirements of its representative students. To him an Adept was an expert in the production of phenomena—that might be called miracles—who, in order to accomplish the same, was forced to live in seclusion.

"Such a life seems to me," Fairchild would say, "to be one of selfishness, for the knowledge you speak of is just what the world wants; and one of ignorance, for the power you speak of being manifested in seclusion is just what I should imagine an enlightened teacher would manifest where the need for it is, and that is amongst the masses."

"Well, but it would be unwise to give such knowledge to the world."

"Very good; but do you mean to say that to obtain the knowledge of a Buddha or a Christ it is necessary to follow such instruction as is given in ' The Secret Pathway ' for instance?"

"It is no use discussing the subject further, as we will get on to the old ground of *discipline*, upon which we do not agree."

Thus their conversation generally ended now. But Frank Fairchild knew pretty well where his friend stood, and what his intentions were; so when the report reached him, that Mr. Firth was missing, he was not surprised. After school hours he walked over to "The Home," and there found Mrs. Firth apparently unmoved by anything that had happened; but Nellie seemed to be in a bad way—"expressing, what the doctors would call, typhoid fever," Mrs. Firth said.

"How is it nothing seems to put you out, Mrs. Firth ? Of course, when I think of your philosophy, my question is immediately answered; nevertheless I must say I admire the persistence with which you practice it. Would you like to call some doctor, just to see Nellie ?"

"No, thank you; I am quite sure that to be divided in belief or in practice is the weakest attitude any one can take. I know within myself that Nellie is all right, and no matter what the cause of her present expression, or what the result, all is for good."

"If I did not know you as I do, I should say you were a fatalist."

"A fatalist is certainly one who is ignorant of cause, and believes himself incapable of controlling effect, a belief I do not share in.   I am sure that every one controls their own effects, and I do not make any exception in Nellie's case."

"And so you are happy under all circumstances in the knowledge, that all cause is one and the same.   I can go very far with you; I can see this at least, that the causes that scientists speak of are really effects; and that effects cannot be causes—except in such a case as the formation of a river by the downfall of rain.   But this is merely a study of effects in relation to effects, not really of cause and effect.   But may I leave this subject, and ask if you have heard from Mr. Firth ?   For I hear that he has gone to live for a time among his mystic brethren."

"Yes, I have had a long letter from him, full of enthusiasm.   He says, that his year of approbation ended satisfactorily, and that he has been admitted into the Rosicrucian Sanctum, where his first expectations were more than satisfied.   It is a very long letter, I will read parts, that I think will interest you :

'I have seen but two Brothers, who are to be my associates, and are but beginners—though one of them has been here many years, having spent his five years' term of approbation in absolute silence.——There are many classes or grades of students, the distinction between each being the amount of knowledge each possesses.————All the affairs of the Lodge are directed by the Council, the members of which are chiefly men living and carrying on business as other men do in towns and cities.   The head of all, my associates tell me, is the greatest mystery of all, and is only known by the Adepts; adeptship is the possibility of every student who enters the Path.——The mountains here are very high, and the Caves in which we dwell are simply beautiful, and always lit up by electricity, produced without mechanical contrivances.—— There are students here whose knowledge of nature far surpasses anything the world knows about.———I cannot tell you how I got here, for I was blindfolded, but be not uneasy about my return, for I am assured that although the return is difficult, opportunity will be given me to return, if I so desire.———I can learn of no women students being here; probably the Queen, whose name is never mentioned by the Brothers, resides elsewhere.——Every Lodge has a password which admits into other lodges; my companions believe that some of the most important words have been lost.'——

"Of course they have been, for individuals in their descent for experience have lost understanding in Nature or Illusion.   The pass-words are not the spoken words of sense or Nature, but the real Word of understanding, which is the soul. It seems to me that, so long as men confine their consciousness in body, so long are they ignorant of any real word. But please proceed."

'One thing I find, that some of the lessons taught here are well known to the World, especially to metaphysical healers; for instance we are instructed to will one desirable result, at the same time steadily gazing at some particular object or subject. This is the attitude of imparting. To come into an attitude in which to receive, we are instructed that instead of retaining the activity of imparting one must relapse into the passivity of receiving, *still remaining positive in good* (which is the only magic).'

" I can see," said Mrs. Firth, " that we employ similar methods to those just mentioned. It would not at all surprise me to find that Metaphysicians are practicing openly what students of occultism are doing in secret. He goes on to say :

' I have been passed by the "Door," who is one of the advanced Brethren. There is no objection to my stating some of the preliminary exercises we have to go through for the purpose of obtaining will power and Illumination.'

" I cannot understand," broke in Mr. Fairchild, " any one sitting for will power and Illumination, as some occult students do. Mr. Firth and I talked this matter over some time ago, and this is the conclusion I arrived at: The illumination aimed for is that sense by which forms on the Astral or Etherial plane may be seen and communicated with, and which is similar to the physical senses; but the reason why people value it and make great efforts to obtain it is simply to gratify a morbid curiosity, and to be thought of as uncommonly wonderful persons. Why, the whole thing is nothing but a sensation, and the very people who seek it are the very ones who create the demand for sensational theatrical performances and notorious scandals. I never yet knew of any student who sat for 'will power and illumination' who was not full of predjudices, and thought a good deal more of his own personality than of the truth he pretended to seek. Such people's motives are very plain, they seek personal greatness through knowledge."

" But knowledge cannot be obtained in that way. I must remind you that you have made a great many unmetaphysical assertions about students of Occultism. I should like you to tell me more of their objects, if you can do so without holding them in the thought of ignorance you say they manifest, for I am quite in the dark about them."

" To many students occultism is a study of phenomena ; and their purpose in study is really summed up in three words—desire for sensation, although their avowed purpose is—desire for knowledge. To me knowledge means—knowledge of cause, and from it proceeds the understanding of effect; but to reverse this method and seek knowledge in effect—as most schools and universities on the earth do, and then to stamp mere knowledge of phenomena true knowledge—is ignorance, and an index of mental blindness. Well then, seeking knowledge in effects or phenomena on any plane, whether it be earth, astral or other planes, is a perverse method, which can only lead to bitter disappointment. The sensations induced by the methods employed to attain illumination by Old School Rosicrucians are in some respects similar to those induced by opium smoking and injection of morphine; though the consciousness is less blurred, and the after effects are not nearly so marked. But the thrills of joy that pervade the body, as a result of the processes adopted, leave on the individual a feeling of superiority over his neighbours which leads to a mental precipice of chaos. Often times these sensations take the form of intense love, which on account of its emotional character is easily distinguished from true and universal love. But I interrupted you in the reading of your letter, please read on."

"First, I want to ask you a question. You speak of an Old School of Rosicrucians—is there then a New School? And what have they to do with Theosophists?"

"You will perhaps be surprised to hear, that even amongst Rosicrucians and Theosophists few know of The New Order. In days gone by there were many different Orders of Secret Societies, some of which still exist; and each had in some way or other a distinction of its own; for instance, in the past Rosicrucians have had some practices to induce supreme illumination, which may have been known to some Phallic Worshippers, but of which Theosophists are ignorant. These practices, like the others we have been speaking of, were only sensational developments, and are fast sinking into disuse. But in The New Order all Secret Societies, without any distinction, become one. Theosophists, Rosicrucians and Magi of to-day have discarded old practices, except in a few instances, as a means to an end. Those who still go on in the old ways of occultism belong to a period thousands of years past."

"You make my husband's position seem quite appalling."

"It is in seeming only, Mrs. Firth," answered Frank, "for I know him to be in good hands. Although the School he is now in is an Old School, it is a New School also, into which he will finally graduate. You may be sure, that if he had joined an unprogressive Order, he would not have been allowed to make the disclosures he does."

"I am glad to hear you say so, it speaks well for the world at large. To proceed with the letter."

'I lie morning and evening in a dark cell with a magnet on my forehead, willing illumination, and breathing deeply, which produces a queer feeling of numbness, and lights begin to appear. Then once a day I breathe deeply and energetically, all the time looking at the end of my nose, and after continuing this five or ten minutes I lose consciousness of the body.——The Brothers say there are many here who can do with the body what they want to —making it disappear and reappear at will.——There is to be a work of special importance to the World undertaken shortly by this Order, but it is only revealed to me in mystic language, this is a part of the message : JEHOVAH HAS FOUND A SPECIAL CHANNEL THROUGH WHICH TO COMMUNICATE TO THE WORLD A CERTAIN KNOWLEDGE OF NEW SCIENCES, THE LOST SECRET, ETC., ETC.'

"I'd like to know what that means," said Mrs. Firth.

"Well, I'll tell you just why that revelation is given to Mr. Firth and to the World. The best experience he can have just now is one that will show him the nothingness of personality; and the revelations he will receive from time to time will bring that about most convincingly. And when he mixes with the world again he will not be misled by such like invitations to apparent greatness."

"That reminds me of what the Master of Nazareth said, prophesying that in the last days many would rise up saying—I am Christ."

"Undoubtedly, and if they do not use exactly those words, they speak and write to the effect that, Jehovah has found a special channel through ME; and they proceed to build up a great personality through promises of power and knowledge that will be given *them* to impart to *their* followers. Father forgive them, they know not what they do ! It's absolute ignorance, Mrs. Firth, absolute ignorance."

"Yes, yes; well, there's nothing more that would particularly interest you in the letter, except this, perhaps—that he asks particularly after Nellie ; and says he feels as if she were always with him, but cannot in any way account for the feeling. Maybe she is, poor girl, but I feel quite at ease about her, though to all appearances she is no better.

"I must tell you about my dream last night; I have felt doubly at ease about Nellie since. I seemed to be a warm golden light, looking down upon a blind man in a beautiful green valley. At first I could not understand myself as a light; I was everywhere in the valley. Then I seemed to think about the blind man, and saw there was not anyway for him to get out of the valley, which was shut in on all sides, except the way I went. And I immediately recognized that I was both in and out of the valley, and that as soon as the man could see me he would find his way out. Then two fine eagles came and settled one on each of his shoulders. And I heard Nellie say to my husband, ' Come unto me and I will give you rest.' And so, Mr. Fairchild, I am perfectly at ease about both Mr. Firth and Nellie."

" That was a very beautiful vision, and undoubtedly you interpret it correctly. To me it has a universal significance, and I am sure that the World is about to come out of the Valley by the recognition of One Light."

. . . .

"By Me the whole vast universe of things
Is spread abroad;—by Me, the Unmanifest;
In Me are all existences contained;
Not I in them!
          Yet they are not contained,
Those visible things! Receive and strive to embrace
The mystery majestical; My Being—
Creating all, sustaining all—still dwells
Outside of all!"

Song Celestial.

"THE NEW ORDER."

An Occult Story.

by

A ROSICRUCIAN.

CHAPTER III.

Invalids.

ALL people have practical experience of that phenomenon called Sleep. Most manifest it naturally, and take no thought about it; a few however have made it a study, and published the results thereof. Nevertheless there is but little literature upon the subject, that presents sound reasoning; and such as does answer this requirement is so mystical as to be beyond the comprehension of the many.

This subject had been engaging Mrs. Firth's attention considerably of late owing to an experience she has had with Nellie; or as most would say — owing to a dream about her. Since her illness Nellie had never seemed herself; she looked bright and healthy, but seemed to have lost control of her body to such an extent, that she spoke but little, and scarcely seemed to notice what was going on about her.

"I feel as if I ought to say somewhat about the child," said one of Mrs. Firth's patients one day—for Mrs. Firth in her ministry of truth had her calls to make just as a physician does—"but the fact is you have cured me after the doctors had given me up; and I feel that the same power that cured me can cure Nellie, else I would ask—Why do not you let a doctor try and get her well? since she has been so long like this. I have that feeling, as I said, and yet something tells me that feeling is not right."

"My good sister, the child but sleeps, she will wake again. And what matters it if the whole town do cry 'shame' on me, because of my persistence in my own way! I do not blame them. They are judging that I *should* do what they *would* do under similar circumstances; which is alright. And so long as they do not seek to coerce me in any way I have no reason to feel affected. You see we can each maintain our freedom, if we do not allow our conduct to be affected by our neighbour's thoughts; if we take the stand, that they are entitled to their opinions, and we to ours. How ridiculous it is to feel affected by opinions; does it not show how much we seek favour of man, or to imitate another—Society's ideal, perhaps?"

" I suppose it does; but there's a something strange about your talk, that makes me feel lost. It sounds simple, but I cannot follow you."

" Well, I mean simply this: we each judge from our own experience, do we not ?"

" Certainly. We have nothing else to go by."

" Truly, then we see ourselves in whatever we judge."

" That's where I get lost."

" Not at all, sister; but listen. No one can recognize what they are not conscious of."

" That is plain; and that is our experience or education, is it not ?"

" Yes. Then, whatever you pass judgment upon, you do it from your point of view of a similar experience. That is, you judge others by yourself."

" I must be pretty bad then ; for as I see I judge."

" But you will cease to judge in that way, after all the lessons we have had together; for the truth you cannot see, and it is that which has healed you. But if what you see be the truth, you would have to admit that it was changeable, subject to decay and old age, and ultimate extinction or alteration."

" Still we are told to judge a tree by its fruit."

" True; to judge the nature of a tree, whether it be good or bad, or what kind of tree it is; but we are not told to judge the *life, essence* or *truth* of the tree by its fruit. Do you see the distinction ?"

" I think so; but how should we judge, when we see corrupt fruit ?"

" In the same way that I judged you, when you judged yourself sick. It was by thoughts of truth or health that you were made whole. But if we judge one another by appearances we shall affirm as true what we see, and there is no greater injustice."

" I am detaining you over long this morning, Mrs. Firth, but you have no idea how I enjoy your treatments. If you have time, I would like to ask you one other question. What did Jesus mean by his apparently contradictory statements, that he did not come to judge the world, yet that he did come to judge, saying that all judgment was given to the Son ?"

" He meant this—that he did not come to judge in the sense his listeners understood judgment, which was by appearances; but in the sense of presenting truth, in the light of which men would see that their state of consciousness was but as darkness; and seeing this they would ultimately strive to attain the light."

" Then the way you treated me was by showing me the Light you have; the presence of which brought me into a recognition of that for want of which I suffered! Then I healed myself ?"

"Thy faith, dear sister, hath made thee whole. And now I must proceed on my rounds: Peace be with you."

In this way Mrs. Firth directed her patient's attention from Nellie and from any thought of sickness or sorrow. She was indeed the heavenly physician of Bartone. But to return to her meditation on Sleep and subjective states; her thoughts ran thus — — Now, if I consider myself as my senses reveal me, I know that I am engaged during the day in more or less intense outward examination of phenomena; but at night the senses, that have thus been intensely engaged, rest; and others are brought into use, for I see and converse during my sleep. And what I perceive in sleep is often similar to what I perceive when awake; although my perceptions are sometimes so much more profound, and sometimes so much more rdiculons than I am accustomed to, when awake, that they seem to be unreal fancies. Now that's the point — "unreal fancies"; why, I do really think that the land of dreams is the land of our fancies or thoughts, and possibly more real than the land of our wide-awake hours; for everything we see on earth— even the earth itself—has been thought out first. Yes, it certainly does. seem to me that our dreams are perceptions of thoughts. Then, when I am awake I am engaged in the intellectual study of symbols of thought; and this looking out at things that of themselves are lifeless, causes a sensation of weariness, and makes rest or retirement to a plane, where the tired senses are not required, a necessity. And so we see that children, who are unused to intellectual pursuits, require much rest; and that generally speaking grown people, who are used to looking upon appearances of thought, require less rest. Yes, this most certainly does seem to be a solution of the sleep question, and it seems to harmonize with the universal method also; for periods of activity and rest are apparent everywhere. Death itself is nothing but a passing of the consciousness into rest. The disintegration of a Planet then, should teach us that its Soul has entered into its day of rest; and sleep as applied to the whole Material Universe — or rather to the Universal Soul—must be the Sabbath of the Lord in which no manner of work or manifestation takes place in Matter; and this is what mystic philosophers must mean, when they speak of 'God's rest' and 'Brahm's sleep'; the great and general day of rest when all external appearances from the least to the greatest will cease to appear. And now I am in a fair way to understand last night's experience with Nellie. I must write to Mr. Fairchild to come and give me his opinion.

And Mrs. Firth forthwith directed and posted a note to the Schoolmaster.

. . . .

Judge Not.

———

" JUDGE not that ye be not judged: for with what judgment ye judge, ye shall be judged." Matt. vii, 1, 2. "For wherein thou judgest another, thou condemnest thyself; for thou that judgest doest the same things."

It is our thought and consciousness which is manifest, when we judge or condemn; and they are our condemnation. What we think is our own, begotten of our understanding, or misunderstanding. If we have aught against another, the first attention should be given to the mote that is in our own eye; not until we forgive, do we have truthful thought. In forgiving we receive forgiveness; in condemning we are condemned.

"Speak not evil one of another, brethren. He that speaketh evil of his brother, and judgeth his brother, speaketh evil of the law, and judgeth the law; but if thou judge the law thou art not a doer of the law." "The judgment of God is according to truth." When we speak the truth we do well. To be a doer of the law and not a judge, is to think of others and of self, as one with all good; which we are in being. To be a judge of the law—or of another, and not a doer, is to think of others, and of self, as one with appearance or expression, which is temporary.

. . . .

———

"THE NEW ORDER."

An Occult Story.

BY

A ROSICRUCIAN.

———

CHAPTER IV.

The Double Existence.

———

" CERTAINLY, I agree with what you say, Mrs. Firth," said Mr. Fairchild, on the occasion of his visit to "The Home," in response to the invitation and just as communication by word is the method appropriate to this material plane, so communication by thought is naturally the method appropriate to the astral plane or in dreamland, and the reason why we are more or less unconscious of the thought world during the day is, as you say, because our attention is taken up with words; similarly during sleep we are more or less unconscious of the word world, because our attention is upon thoughts. The only thing unusual about your experience was that notwithstanding you were engaged in the thought world you were conscious in the body of what you were doing out of the body. And I don't mean by this that you are anything that can get out of one body into another, but what I mean agrees thoroughly with your teachings, namely, that although you pervade all bodies equally you concentrate upon those centres of personality, both the material body and astral body, in which you as an individual seek experience. But the astral plane being the pattern of all things we see here, you were no doubt surprised how accurately every thought is registered there."

" Yes. And I must tell you as far as I can remember, what I saw. After Nellie had explained to me how that her earthly condition was brought about by too intense anxiety about her father, which I no doubt intensified, she pointed out many persons, who are called insane, criminal, etc., whose insanity and vice were owing either to an absence of attention to or centering in their physical consciousness, or to a presence within their physical consciousness of some erroneous idea held to chiefly through obstinacy. These persons were in Asylums or Gaols; but I could foresee with perfect certainty that such cases will in the near future be handed to competent metaphysicians for treatment. But what a beautiful land of thought we live in and know little or nothing about! a world of magnificent cities, full of busy people—most of them much further advanced than we appear to be; let me tell you of one. It is a City built of White Marble ornamented with the most brilliant jewels; I seemed to know the City well, yet to my physical senses it was all wonderfully new, and I asked the name of the City, and I was told Salem. The Streets were all laid out with perfect regularity; here and there were public gardens, the trees and herbs and flowers were most exquisite. In them I saw many creatures, pure white, the like of which I had never seen before, and I understood they were the forms of 'elemental spirits' Now and again I perceived people who are my friends on Earth; one gentleman I particularly remember, he was seeking lodgings in Salem, and was speaking to the landlady at her door; she was telling him that Salem was a City of Metaphysicians; and he was telling her that we had a great many Metaphysicians on Earth, and that he knew something of the Science; after which he made this remark, ' O what a cross dog! (referring to an angry looking little white dog the land-lady held under her arm). 'You must not say that,' said the landlady, ' treat it, he is not cross.' This little incident caused me to ask Nellie if there were any sick people in Salem, and she said that there were but very few and that they were never attended to as sick 'Things here are carried on just about opposite to what they are on earth', said a bystander, who either overheard my question or saw my thoughts, I do not know which. ' Hospitals are bet-ter calculated to make well people sick than the sick well, and prisons are little else than nurseries of vice. Here, if any one meditates crime he nat-urally seeks the companionship of the purest citizen with much the same motive as a sick man on Earth seeks some physician '. I asked the speaker if he had been long here (in Salem); his answer taught me such a lesson, that I will repeat it—' My sister, you are evidently now speaking to me after the manner of a child of Earth; you are questioning me as if I were the object you see before you. I perceive you understand me. Indeed I have this body, and also an earthly body—even as you have; but neither you nor I are either of our bodies. This City you so much admire is but a reflection of thought—the thought of us, its citizens." Later on I learned that not all cities on this ideal and real Earth are inhabited by metaphysicians; but that there are many different ones corresponding in thought to such as we see expressed on this material plane that we generally call Earth. Indeed I visited many cities, that I have forgotten the names of now. One I particularly remember because of its luminou' appearance at a distance, but when we approached it, it looked so dull and cold. It was inhabited, I was told, by such people as were making extraordinary efforts on Earth to be recognized as great persons; I could see that among them were sundry ' discoverers of knowledge ', monop-olists, possessors of mysteries, influential patrons and their followers. Close to this City is another, somewhat similar in appearance, but not so false-shin-ing, and in it dwelt those who allow others to do them homage, together with their homage-payers. Here I was surprised to see so many eminently ' respect-able ' and philanthropic people; leading teachers and preachers in every department. During our return to Salem I noticed that different methods of travelling were adopted; those, such as aerial machines driven by etheric force, will shortly be used by the inhabitants of Earth. I asked how such a useful invention might be discovered to the people; and was told—" By the right living of the people; all progress comes as a result of goodness."

" Well, did you see Mr. Firth in your travels ? " Asked Mr. Fairchild.

" Yes. And it seems that Nellie is always with him. He dwells in a city near to Salem, the peculiarity of which is that it seems dark without, but light within; it is just the opposite of the falsely-shining city I spoke about awhile ago. Nellie told me that it was not so very long ago since Mr. Firth gave up the life of Personality for one of extreme Humility, which seems to characterize the dwellers in his city."

"Then, from what you have said, it would seem that you, at any rate, have no doubt about double existences; this you have witnessed through your senses, just as I suppose all seers have witnessed the same phenomena. And I can corroborate what you have said from quite another standpoint: for in principle it must be that for every ultimate expression—such as the earth and all upon it—there is a pre-existing pattern. We know that it would be impossible even to write a letter unless the thoughts corresponding to the words written pre-existed. So I know that there is a corruptible body and an incorruptible body, a word-world and a thought-world. But that lesson upon the absolute unimportance of any body, is one we all need so much to learn and to live."

"I can assure you I am thankful to my unknown friend for his lesson. But for a long time past, while reflecting upon such subjects, I have seen how erroneous it is to attach importance to the body. Although you say truly indeed, that there is a corruptible body and an incorruptible body, still no matter which body we consider, it will be forever body—a mere symbol of being; it may be a more or less glorious symbol, but symbol it will remain forever. How mistaken is the conclusion that the symbol is the real, or that matter is spirit!"

"There is one part of your experience with Nellie, that I hope to hear a great deal more about before long; I mean in the City of Salem. And I shall want to hear all about the City itself, its laws, both moral, social and political; for as you know, I am somewhat of a radical on these subjects. As I have considerable to prepare for my school to-morrow I must say farewell till some future opportunity offers me more of your interesting descriptions."

———————

. . . .

UNITY.

The Spirit of Goodness is alike for all.   It knows not limitation, hence it places none upon us.   Truth knows not error, therefore when spoken, peace and harmony is imaged and expressed.

That which is made—Spirit—makes; it acknowledges and sustains all. They who serve the Spirit with truthful thought and love, Spirit is manifest in them.   They are in the Spirit, and the Spirit is in them.

. . . .

"THE NEW ORDER."

AN OCCULT STORY.

BY

A ·ROSICRUCIAN.

CHAPTER V.

The Master and the Retreat.

A S Mr. Fairchild, one Sunday morning, was walking musingly through a part of the woods close to Bartone, he suddenly became aware that he was being watched very intently by a young man somewhat of his own age, but of slighter appearance.   His sharp eye fixedly gazing on him, seemed to bid the schoolmaster to a discourse; to which silent request he assented forthwith by simply following out aloud the train of thought that he was indulging in before he came up with the stranger.

" If all these beautiful sights, the woods, the sighing breezes, the flowers, the murmuring streams, the birds, their songs, and all created things with all their varied voices, colour, form, be any reality, they must be God."

This was the thought that the very presence of the stranger helped the schoolmaster to express. Neither did he endeavour to stop the flow of words that followed.——" For if not, then are all these glorious and beautiful things in some way an existence without reality, a mere fancy, the very seeing of which is fancy. But yet if they be real, even then they are a changing show; the beauties of to-day, are faded on the morrow, and the next day brings oblivion of the past. This living and this dead, this slayer and this slain, this voice of joy and farewell sigh, are these indeed, the God that yesterday, to-day and forever is unchanging? It cannot be that, that which changes is also the unchanging; neither is the dead, the life. Tell me stranger,—for I perceive with you a presence of deep knowledge—what of this fancy and of God."

" The eyes are blind that see me not in all that fancy sees, yet I am not what fancy sees. Subtle is the glance that penetrates the real, and gives to NOTHING its appropriate name. From the unchanging do all changes come, yet I am all and change not. From the stillness all actions proceed, yet I move not; but in time and place, my thoughts will come and go, producing nature's fancies, that fancies only see."

" One thing surprises me" pursued Fairchild, with unusual absence of timidity or sensitiveness, for to carry on any conversation with one whom he perceived to be his superior in unfoldment was usually a task of some diffi- culty. " One thing surprises me, to find you a master here, so far from the outside world. I am taking it for granted, that you belong to the Retreat of Sages somewhere in these parts."

" There is not a heart that beats with love or fear, but I am there. There is not a prayer inbreathed, but upon my ear it fails. Did I not say the eyes are blind that see me not in everything? But I invite you to a sight that passes fancies, to a hearing that few ears are strained to hear. For this cause do we meet. But follow me to the Retreat of Sages, and there shall you learn of the outside world, its illusion and its use."

Soon the stranger and his pupil were within the walls of one of the mon- asteries belonging to an order, the members of which have sought seclusion from the sin and contamination of the world. They occupy themselves in meditation, thinking that by rigourous devotion to the rosary of their order, they will finally obtain remission of their sins and purification from evil influences.   Here the schoolmaster's eyes were opened, and he saw a city occupying the grounds of this monastic order, inhabited by people given over to selfish pursuits.   And he heard a voice say, Distance is illusion, and like is found with like; the fruit and the tree are always together.   Then he perceived other cities, where solitude was supposed to be; but those of the cities knew nothing of the solitude, and those of the solitude knew nothing of the cities; thus was each living self deluded; a veil of prejudice seemed to separate each from the other; nevertheless there was no separation.

After this they saw another city, and were attracted to an entertainment that was being given there in honour of a certain nobleman, who had parted with all his possessions, and devoted the proceeds to the poor, and whose time was also being spent in an endeavour to elevate humanity in general. After much had been said by his entertainers in appreciation of his example and noble sacrifice, the young nobleman arose and said: " A widow had two sons, the elder of which went into a distant land.   After many years word reached the mother and younger brother, that the elder was wasting his substance in riotous living.   Then said the mother—son, I perceive that thy brother which is lost, seeks again to return to his home, I will send you therefore to show him the way of return; trouble not because you must leave me.   Fear nothing, my Son, for on thy return with thy brother, surely our joy will be full.   After a long journey the younger brother reached the distant land of his brother, where he was entertained with great show, because that he had left all to save his brother.   Hereupon he arose and said—what workman receives the master's praise instead of the master, because of the beauty of some work!   He who carries out the Will is not greater than him whose will is done.   Remember then, the mother whom you have not seen, and whose will I do; if I am worthy of so great an entertainment at your hands, what honour may he receive, whose workman I am.

Then said the stranger, turning to Mr. Fairchild, " All these scenes are within the Retreat of the Sages, wherein also is your friend.   From these you may learn the reality of life, and the unreality of life's expression; the one is absolute, without limit and unchanging, the other is apparent by reason of limit and changing; the one is, the other is not—that is, it appears; and know that in the city is the solitude, in the solitude is the city to him who seeks.   Shun not either, but in each find me continually."

. . . .

DIVINE LAW IS LOVE.

" He that loveth knoweth God, for God is love," the same is obedient to the law of his being. Thought is the first expression of the thinker, or is the action of being; hence the expression or thought must be obedient to the law Love, if *its* expressions be harmonious. The Sons of God love all life and all things ; they are like the Sun, that shines equally upon the evil and upon the good and like the rain, that comes to the just and unjust alike. To be a Son is to do what the Father doeth. The awakened know what they possess, and their purpose is to continually give, in order that the law may be fulfilled.

. . . .

"THE NEW ORDER."

An Occult Story.

BY

A ROSICRUCIAN.

CHAPTER VI.

Training in Occultism.

THIS was the subject of the Master's address on the afternoon of which I am now writing. The occasion was understood as one of special importance. Assembled in the Great Hall of the Retreat were students of all Stages in unfoldment, and representatives from many centres of occultism. Although it was but a little after mid-day, the Hall was brilliantly lighted with electricity. All had been sitting in silent meditation for some minutes when the Master, who occupied no conspicuous place, arose, saying: "At all times in the World there have been students of occultism, for at all times in the world have there been individuals seeking for hidden pearls of truth. The wise Creator having endowed his children with a certain independence called free-will, and the desire to discover, it naturally follows that each will seek these pearls in his own way; hence there are many

different Schools of Occultism, and in no one school do any two students
walk the same path. Amongst the friends of Eulis at the present day are to
be found students of so ancient a school as that of Pythagoras; and the
discipline of Plato's academy is not by any means unknown in this Retreat. These as well as other centres of thought continue their beneficial
influence upon the Earth. But that which has hereto marked the distinc-
tions between all these different Schools is fast being withdrawn, and consequently we see here to-day, what has never before been seen on earth, a
great gathering of representatives from all these schools. But mark how this
meeting has been called, how we all have been gathered together; not by invitation, either by note or by bell, not by the sound of trumpet nor impression, not by freak nor accident; but by communion in Spirit and common
association of idea; so that it has simply come to pass that out of all the
many different Retreats, of which the Earth itself is but one, we find ourselves all one in that New Order of Truth, to-day for the first time manifest in Harmony and such numbers on Earth.

As I see amongst you many who by most would not be called Occultists, it occurs to me to speak of the world's misunderstanding of the term;
to it an occultist is one who hides (what it calls) himself in order to find
(what we call) himself. To the ignorant truth is hidden or occult, and not
so much as perceived as Being. These are the occultists that the sign-seek-
ing world pronounces wise, and following whom as a sign-post they remain sign-post conscious. But this day the many schools, and their many
Philosophies, are one School and one Philosophy; so that to the understanding of the New Order there is no such Truth as occultism. To whomsoever Truth is Being, to him is the priceless pearl disclosed; and he is freed
from sense attractions and attachments to his acts. I see among you
priests and laymen, professors and private individuals, gnostics and agnos-
tics, which latter term has for you no significance. In the variety of
thought represented there are none present but know that all variety is
the orderly expression of the mind, which we are; and this is the recognition that has providentially brought us together to-day. With good reason
I make use of the term providentially, for it is by the foresight of the Deity
and not by any chance that we thus meet.

Happily in one important respect our meaning is different from those that
occur outside these Walls of Truth; on earth we continually meet and as often
part, but in Truth we meet to part no more. And all who are assembled
here together to-day will remain in harmonious association forever. And

in returning to our respective occupations in the world let us carry that consciousness which to-day we make manifest to our friends in the world, that they, too, seeing our harmony may seek entrance to The Retreat.

As we look back along the seemingly endless path of our progress, we see how every experience has been our training in occultism—each has been a step deeper into the Kingdom of the soul where lies that pearl of so great price Eternal Life. Passing through the two kingdoms of Body and Soul we finally reach the Kingdom of Heaven, then to know that we have been wandering among resemblances, in pleasures of sense, amid phantoms of the mind. At first lost almost beyond the probability of reclamation, we struggled despondently in the meshes of our own laying, seeking this way then that, ever progressing in the face of all difficulties. So, forced through every stress of necessity, we have throughout all our experience unfolded almost perfect concentration and reached—or are within reach of—the goal of highest attainment on Earth. For which we continuously give thanks to our Heavenly Father, whose providence has been the guiding hand out of every perplexity and trouble. There have been schools, there are still schools, and through them each of us has passed, wherein years have been spent in the suppression of appetites and desires, in the development of the will, in education of the fine arts, in the demonstration of magic lore. And what lessons have we learned therefrom? We have learned that what has been suppressed has to be outgrown; that what has been developed has to be exchanged; that the garden of education has to be digged below the surface; and that magic is a fire that burns whoever handles it, but to him who handles it without a burn the magic has departed. This rehearsal is appropriate; for, remembering how through times and times of arduous work and travel we sought to climb the Hill of Knowledge, now we can valuable instruction give to those who seek it. I myself was present with Pythagoras and remember well that sage's strict adherence to his discipline of food and conduct, of thought and conversation, of meditation and arithmetic. Still, neither he nor his disciples reached that goal of happiness, which to-day they and we by simpler methods have attained. And yet without the discipline of past experience we could not know the Knowledge of to-day.

The end of my address is this, that in the world is not one soul misplaced; and in his place and the performance with contentment of whatever duty is his share, each one will find the straight and narrow path that leads the shortest way to that which each one seeks."

The Master having thus spoken, others followed, saying how simplest things are easiest overlooked; and that the veil of mystery that some held to so persistently, was but a form of that last enemy to be overcome—death or personality. And just as it is true that the end is the attainment of life, so it is equally true that the end is the overcoming of death. And there is no more death, neither sorrow nor crying, neither is there any more pain, for the former things are passed away now.

CHAPTER VII.

An Unexpected Visit.

———————

WILL any one be found to deny the steady increase, during the last few years especially, of all sorts of literature? I scarcely think so. And perhaps the most noteworthy increase has taken place in newspapers and periodicals.

Amongst the numbers of monthly publications issued in the United States in the year 1887, was one called "The Inner Voice," devoted, as its prospectus stated, to the development of the intuition, the study of the hidden forces in nature and the betterment of humanity. It was openly stated that the Editor of this Journal, whose name was Martin Pond, was a man who had travelled much, had studied occultism under adept masters, and gained knowledge of unknown forces and how to use them to produce phenomena more astounding than any the world had ever seen.

Martin Pond arrived a complete stranger at Chicago, but it was not long before his mysterious power became common conversation among Spiritualists, Metaphysicians and others; and in a lecture on "The New Life" he was enabled to bring before a large audience his view of Philosophy and his intentions with respect to founding a College and establishing a Magazine. After which everything looked so promising, that during the following month the first number of "The Inner Voice" appeared; and by the end of the year the subscription list was said to contain one thousand names. In each number now was printed a list of donors and the amount of their gifts to the College of The New Life. Each donor becoming a member of The Society of The New Life, the association grew and grew, and every thing went on prosperously. By the time "The Inner Voice" had completed its first year other Journals belonging to rival Societies began to make adverse comments on "The Inner Voice," with the result that its subscription list was soon doubled; and in its columns began to appear mysterious articles on Black-magic, Witchcraft, etc. etc. The Society of The New Life were not at all slow to concur in the new sentiment of their magazine, and shortly bitter complaints were made about the unwholesome influences of their opposition; and friends began to grow very learned on the subject of Elementals and Elementaries. Indeed there was so much interest evoked on these subjects that their President, Martin Pond, found himself obliged to write a book upon the subject which the Society kindly but firmly insisted on paying for. The result being a handsome volume of several hundred pages entitled "Intelligence Unveiled." It must be admitted that this work proved a complete failure.

Hitherto Mr. Pond had encountered no rebuffs; all had been more than successful; his followers, which numbered some even outside the Society of The New Life, were extravagant in his praises; he had more than satisfied his new found friends. But now "Intelligence Unveiled" came like water upon a fire, and people began for the first time to ask themselves—if they had not been a little unwise to bestow so many confidences upon a complete stranger. And old maids who had pledged their all to the New Life movement in general, began to think they had done a very foolish thing, and that at any rate they would go no deeper into these plans, but make ready for a complete withdrawal. So that before these matters were really spoken of publicly, and in the midst of his chagrin about the book, Mr. Pond was constantly receiving anonymous letters, which added considerably to his cares.

It must here be stated that sample copies of "The Inner Voice" frequently found their way to The Home in Bartone; and their contents often were subjects of conversation between Mrs. Firth and Mr. Fairchild. In a late number of the Journal had appeared an announcement that the Brotherhood of Adept Masters who superintended the entire New Life movements, had intimated to their agent, Martin Pond, the advisability of establishing the New Life College amongst the Sierras. And for the purpose of seeking out a suitable location the agent intended to make his way to Bartone almost immediately.

There are other reasons that decided Mr. Pond to take this trip at once. He wanted to get away from the atmosphere of suspicion that surrounded him in Chicago; he felt sure that in his absence all unpleasantness would die out; and that on his return all would proceed with added enthusiasm; which his report on the College scheme would stir up. Therefore he set out in fairly good spirits, full of plans to be consummated and wonders of how Bartone would look to him after an absence of so many years, and with the certainty that none of his most intimate friends could recognize him. Martin Pond presented a somewhat remarkable appearance, not that in his face there was anything peculiar; but he carried hinself with a swing of importance, his long hair brushing with every stride a short black cloak that covered his shoulders.

During the last few years Bartone had grown out of all recognition; old landmarks had disappeared, the town presented quite a new appearance to Martin Pond as he walked slowly through the streets seeking remembered places, but finding few. Having transacted some little business, and made inquiries as to the whereabouts of certain property holders with whom he had already corresponded, he returned to his hotel to prepare for an evening visit to The Home.

Mrs. Firth was working in the front room as usual, expecting that the school master would pay her a visit this evening. She had been her usual rounds during the morning, and in the afternoon had been instructing a class in the practice of Healing. Frank Fairchild made his appearance as expected, and was opening the pages of the last number of "The Inner Voice", which had arrived at The Home a few days ago, but no one there had had leisure to open it, when a knock came at the door. Mr. Fairchild, who opened the door, received the card of

MARTIN POND,
Editor of "The Inner Voice,"

and invited the Editor into the room where Mrs. Firth was working. There he introduced himself, apologizing at the same time for making his visit by evening instead of by day.

Certainly, he thought as he took his seat, my occult training has not been of no avail; I am master of myself to-day.

CHAPTER VIII.
Illumination.

"I AM master of myself to-day," thought Martin Pond, as he—unrecognized— took a seat opposite his unsuspecting wife, and friend, the schoolmaster. "The hours of steady discipline in suppression of the self have not been useless; the heart-beat is steady, the eye comfortably fixed, the muscles under control. I really wonder at myself." Amused with such thoughts as these, that occupied but a flash of time in the thinking, the editor felt a glow of satisfaction vibrate from head to foot and became perfectly at home.

As may be supposed it was not very long before the conversation turned upon the object of Mr. Pond's visit. "Before I called this evening, I had been seeing several friends of the cause with reference to a suitable locality for our college; and should like to hear if you are interested in it; and if so, will you give me the benefit of your opinions?"

"I understand," said Mr. Fairchild, "that you have more than one offer of property in the neighbouring hills, but I am not in any position to offer an opinion as to a suitable site for such a college as you require."

" What do you think of our prospects and objects ?"

" Well, really I don't know," admitted Master Frank, fairly perplexed by the question; because being without sympathy for the movement he nevertheless did not wish to impart his sentiment to one so interested in it as was Mr. Pond. But the editor himself had felt that these two at any rate would be supporters of this glorious plan; and the coolness with which his first advances were met, only made him bring upon himself more of the same treatment. Was it possible that these two could treat with indifference anything that came from him! Ah, perhaps it was because of his undisclosed identity! If they knew who he was, they would certainly be overjoyed. Should he unmask himself? No, not yet. He would seek his wife, and find her opinion.

" Do you get 'The Inner Voice' regularly, Mrs. Firth?" asked he. "Yes," answered the lady, "and I have speculated somewhat on how it came to be sent here."

" How do you like it?" returned the editor, ignoring the latter part of her answer.

"Well I must say frankly," replied Mrs. Firth, "that I have read little of it as a student would. Occasionally I glance through it. In the numbers of journals that are issued now-a-days, Mr. Pond, I see that all are doing a good work. The number of your subscribers is proof that you are supplying a considerable demand. Have you many students in your college?"

While the editor of " The Inner Voice" was striving to get some definite word or recognition for his journal, his friends were as steadily striving to evade any such recognition; and Mr. Pond very soon saw that "The Inner Voice" did not carry to "The Home" the conviction he had hoped it would. His thoughts began to make him feel uncomfortable. He certainly should not reveal himself as Mr. Firth now. But if they could not accept his New Astrology as given for the first time to the world in his pages, they must be much further in the dark than he had thought. But rememberimg that he himself had unfolded so much since he was last here, he felt a little comfort. But even of this he was deprived by Mr. Fairchild's next remark.

"Having had considerable experience in schools of the Secret Brotherhood, as I understand you have had"—

Well he should think he had; he did not say anything however, but the schoolmaster's tone was as if he had superior experience—his ignorance, of course.

"Having had considerable experience in schools of the Secret Brotherhood, as I understand you have had," said the schoolmaster, "you will undoubtedly have found its illusory nature."

"What do you mean?" enquired Mr. Pond, somewhat amused and astonished.

"Why I mean this; taking for example the discipline for illumination, that when through the breathing exercises and the bath, at the time of desires, a feeling which is called illumination, is brought about, lasting but for a limited time; but passing away it leaves the neophyte or student either in despondency or in an affected exhilaration, kept up by thoughts of its repetition—sensuous repetition, and when this fails there is nothing for the student but either to give it up altogether or resort to opium or hasheesh. I tell you, Mr. Pond, the methods adopted for inducing illumination are nothing but a snare into which the unwary aspirant falls. And except that it is an experience from which one may learn to shun it for all future, it is useless. So you see I place the Occult School, such as some of your correspondents would have you establish, alongside the saloons and snares of any city."

"I simply think," returned the editor, still feeling master of himself, but not so much master of his subject; for in his old friend the schoolmaster, he could not help seeing a familiarity with the subject, that he little expected to find. "I simply think that you have jumped at a great many conclusions. But I should like to know how you have gained the knowledge you have."

"I have never related my experiences, because I don't approve of such relations. But because I believe you to be doing what you honestly think to be the best for humanity, I will relate them to you, for you will perceive a better plan. I was always what I am; but in looking upon the vast universe it seemed that I must meditate upon myself. Choosing a spot in the etherial realms near the great sun, Aldebaren, I built for myself a cave or little world, which being subjected to the law of gravity traveled in its orbit around one centre, then another, according to my desire. On entering my cave I was supplied with a book containing all the information about the starry universe; how it was constructed, and why and by whom; and I placed upon myself this condition, that I would not leave the cave until I had mastered the contents of the book; for the Supreme God had given it to me for wisdom's sake.

Just as vessels navigate the seas, so my world navigates the air; ever moving on its course, attracted hither and thither, to this world and that, as experience dictates. But without light I could not read in the pages of my book of wisdom, and sometimes the interior of my little world seemed destitute of light; yet I was carrying out the instructions of the good book to the very letter; and it described such methods of study as may be found in many books here on earth. As I thus studied I found my aerial home drifted like a helmless bark on the stormy ocean. And it was not until I discovered that illumination, not sensation, is of the spirit, that I again got control over my world. Millions of years seem not to cover the time of all my experiences, but I am coming to the end of my voyage now; the cave is still a cave, but no longer darkened by inexperience. We are sailing on the same ocean my friend, with no other storms than our desires; and when we come to an end of seeking anything for self, the law of gravity will cease to hold our bark, all things will be to us an open book, and we shall be at home again in the harbour of perfection—through experience.''

Let the reader construe for himself the meaning of Mr. Pond's silence that followed this narrative. How did the schoolmaster know so exactly what to say! With what invisible magic was it accompanied! No words can describe illumination; but Mr. Pond, alias Mr. Firth, returned to his hotel this night full of distress and joy; joy and distress. Which was joy and which was sorrow he could not say; but if he accomplished no more in Bartone than this one night's work, with all its repentance, fast flowing tears, new thoughts, new life, he would have nothing to regret.

What a difference a few moments make, was exemplified in the coming and the going of the Chicago editor. When we think we are master of ourselves how near we surely are to some unseen precipice! But we are blessed in our falls, how great soever they may be.

"I see more and more every day the necessity of keeping a patient's thoughts concentrated upon some subject while giving treatments," remarked Mrs. Firth as the schoolmaster left The Home. She had learned a lesson from Mr. Fairchild's treatment of the editor. Although a good deal more transpired between the trio than what is above related, the light that dawned upon the unrecognized husband and his wife during the relation of the simple experiences, made it—that is, the relation—appear important; and formed the link that rejoined husband and wife. For is it not natural that the wife should associate the strange editor with her realizations, and that the husband should think of his wife in the New Light. Truly, Silence is the seed that brings forth the good fruit.

"THE NEW ORDER."

An Occult Story.

BY

A ROSICRUCIAN.

CHAPTER IX.

Metaphysicians.

IN time many changes are effected in things. During the six years that have elapsed since the opening incidents of this story, as much change has taken place within and about "The Home," as has taken place within and about Bartone itself. "The Home" that Mr. Firth (now known as Mr. Pond) left six years ago, was a simple, cottage home; that which he found on his short visit was a Metaphysical retreat. Before he left on the memorable evening mentioned in the last chapter, he had been made acquainted with a great deal that went on within these walls. He learned that the room in which they sat was used as a class room during the week; on Sundays a children's Bible class met there. Every Wednesday evening it was occupied by whomsoever cared to come and join in the consideration of some subject for Meditation. The Metaphysical books on the shelves to the right were for the use of the students and those who joined in the Wednesday meditations. Two sunny rooms at the back were set apart for poor patients.

Thus much Mr. Pond learned. Also some of the methods adopted in teaching and healing, which were new to him. The next evening was Wednesday, and before leaving he received an earnest invitation to be present and join the meeting in considering " What must I do to save." This meeting however he did not attend.

The meeting, which commenced at eight o'clock, was fairly well attended; a majority of those present were metaphysicians. The usual formalities attendant on meetings were absent; each person sat where he or she could conveniently talk with or listen to any other; each person was as much a president or other officer as another. As all present at these meetings met not to air some belief or prejudice, but simply to learn from one another—for all recognized that each could learn from another, order was kept as a natural consequence.

"If," said one of those present, "the subject for meditation this evening had been ' What must I do to be saved?' which question was addressed by the jailor to Paul, it seems to me we should have to consider the question of salvation from the standpoint of one who was in need of salvation; but as the subject is "What must I do to save?" we should consider it from the standpoint of one who brings salvation. In any case it must first be ascertained what salvation is; and I think this may be found in the simple statement of Jesus, that ' The truth will make you free.' For I know of nothing to be saved from but bondage to untruth, which is one's appetites and desires. But, some might say, although to be released from untruth may be to receive forgiveness of sins, there are other things to be freed from, for example, disease. To them I would say, there are sins seen besides sins unseen; an uneasy conscience is evidence of sin unseen, but disease is sin seen. And if the sin be forgiven it shall be no more seen. To me the answer to this evening's question, ' What must I do to save?' is contained in one word—*forgive.* I pray my heavenly Father, that we may become perfect in forgiving. To me there is nothing any man can receive but forgiveness, for has not each received his talent—the Spirit of God ! What is the world doing with its talent ? Let us forgive once and forever all that is remiss."

"I quite agree that one should forgive all, for only in so doing can all be forgiven. And that this is to save and be saved, I also think. And in order that this perception may be appropriately demonstrated to the masses; or rather perhaps, in order that the masses may be interested to seek this perception, I know of nothing better than open meetings such as these, and centres where metaphysical literature may be borrowed."

"The last speaker," said a visitor, " speaks of open meetings and borrowing literature, indicating that teaching and healing should be free. I would like to ask her if she does not think the labourer is worthy of his hire; and that better results are obtained when the receiver gives an adequate return for what she receives. I think people only value what they have to pay for."

"If the standard of what one has to pay is determined by the requirements to keep up a certain style or position, then is the standard false, the motive false, and the results false. Truth is simple, without requirements or style; and whoever bears undivided witness to truth will be like truth. I find that people value what they want; what they pay for it seems to me of secondary consideration. Of course I agree with you that the labourer is worthy of his hire; but who shall judge his worth, the master or the servant? This is precisely the question that troubles the world; and it is a trouble because each tries to get most of this world's goods. But such a 'because' has no metaphysical stand. How much money one should receive for teaching his neighbour to love his God, is a question that is entirely outside of metaphysics."

After some further conversation on this subject, Mr. Fairchild remarked that salvation was a perception or knowledge, for that nothing but God was free. "To know God is to be free. The first step to freedom is to believe that God is knowable. The second step is to perceive that he that knows is no different from what he knows. The third step is to perceive that he and the Father are one. All that then remains to be done by the individual who has taken this third step is to prove his perception by demonstration. What must I do to save? I must perceive what I am, and distinctly realize that you and I are one and the same—whoever in all the world *you* may be. I must be and do what I perceive. Thus by realizing that I am you will I save you."

" Well, certainly," said one, "that would be to love your neighbour as yourself; and your reason for so loving him is, because he is yourself. It just now occurs to me, that if people perceived that what they denounce, find fault with, etc., were their own shortcomings, the world would come under an entirely new rule, and each man would be his nation's ruler. This must surely come to pass; and then there will be peace on Earth. When anyone hates another, it is because he sees in that other what he hates in himself ; and he may perhaps punish that other with a punishment he deems himself worthy of suffering. It seems to me that repentance must precede salvation, for no one will seek except for that which is lost. To lose sight of Truth is to be in darkness, which must be productive of sorrow. Needs must be that all shall sorrow because of darkness, and seek the truth because it alone is light. And all men are sorry for the evils and sufferings of others, but as soon as they see that these evils and sufferings are theirs, then does repentance truly begin for them. To judge justly, to love one's neighbour as one's self, and to forgive, seem to me to be but different expressions with one meaning. The words that have fallen from many lips to-night but bring nearer to me with fuller reality the teachings of Jesus."

The meeting which commenced punctually, also closed punctually. At half past nine all prepared to depart, as far as the word depart can be used with reference to the movements of such a congregation.

These gatherings at " The Home" became more and more generally recognized in Bartone as of the highest educational value; the attendance from time to time increases.

"THE NEW ORDER."

An Occult Story.

BY

A ROSICRUCIAN.

CHAPTER X.

Occultism Unveiled.

AN old-fashioned belief amongst medical men is that the body goes through a complete change in seven years. As Martin Pond wended his way to the Sierra Retreat he was thinking of this belief.

Yes, it is just upon seven years since I first made my way over this ground, and now I return in person over the same conditions that I have so often returned in thought. How we walk upon our thoughts to our ideals; and when we arrive there the charm has vanished to some other ideal, after which we then journey! We are continually following one shadow then another; always reaching after something ahead, and repeatedly wearying we sigh for rests that continue to evade us.

Seven years! And what has become of the great things I was to do. The best that now remains for me is to return to Chicago, give up my trust, and declare the fabrication I have built up unsound. And then return to my wife and declare that my seven years absence was needed to teach me to know her.

Thus does the prodigal return home stripped of all personality—and even of separate individuality. With a thankful heart, however, I can give up every wish, want and worship; and go and teach my neighbor how much he has to be thankful for because he is allowed to give up what he has once thought desirable, saying : There was a certain rich man had a labourer who envied him all his riches and enjoyments. And one day conversing with the rich man the labourer told him he could conceive of no higher enjoyment than to be possessor of such grounds and wealth as he had. But the rich man said, I have had experience in those things and can tell you that such pleasure as you imagine is not to be had here. And as you are so intensely envious of these things, which I am heartily sick of, I will give them all to you on one condition. Then the labourer declared his readiness to be bound by any condition. The condition is this, said the rich man, that you shall in no wise be able to part with these things, nor sacrifice them ; nor even in the hour of your most earnest supplication to be allowed so to do. And so it came to pass that the rich man left for a far country, and the labourer entering into the rich man's possessions took to himself a wife, and spent his time in seeking out all the pleasures that the earth could produce   And there was nothing that his wealth did not enable him to procure. But as time elapsed the labourer sighed that he might discover some one to envy or something that he could not procure, for he had now nothing to wish for on earth, and yet was as hungry as the beggar that came starving to his door. Then came the rich man in the garb of a beggar, and the labourer prayed him that he would take back half of his goods; but the rich man said, I have no further use for such things, keep them according to the agreement, and he went away again. But after a long time the rich man again returned. Then the labourer going on his knees besought him most sincerely that he would take back the whole of his goods ; and if he would not do so much as that, at least that he would take from him his good health that he might die. Then said the rich man, insomuch as the health that you would part with you can never part with, remain therefore in possession of the things you do not possess until you discover that which you do possess.

And when I have told this story, I will ask my neighbor :   What think you the labourer will say to the rich man when he discovers his true possessions ? I tell you he will thank him with tears.

With such thoughts as these, Martin Pond arrived at the Retreat ; but on seeking entrance he was told that no one could be admitted into the Retreat that was not as worthy as the doorkeeper ; and that if he wished to enter he would have to prove himself a worthy doorkeeper first. This he was willing to do.   Then there came to the door asking entrance many old acquaintances that had followed him on the way, saying : Even as you have followed your ideal, so we have followed you, we pray you let us in.   But he answered, they that follow a shadow are but shadows, but they that lead leave all their shadows behind ; the Light alone can enter here, upon which he shut the door and heard no more their supplications.

Then the Master of the Retreat sent word that he should enter ; and when he was come he welcomed him with much gladness.   And calling an attendant he bade him take Martin Pond to the Supper Hall and provide him with all things that should be put before a distinguished traveler.   Then there was put before him a sumptuous repast, and many friends were in waiting to greet and congratulate him on his success, and help to pass away the supper time pleasantly for him. But he put all these aside saying, "The food of meats and flattery are without nourishment, go tell the Master that my food is to do the will of my Father and partake of His thoughts, and thus we shall together sit at the Supper of the Lamb."

In what way will the reader associate the foregoing with the unveiling of occultism ! Yet thoughts are things, and it is of things we partake for food. These things of which we partake, whether psychical or physical, are the veil that hides what all—rich and poor, high and low, good and bad—are seeking. And the only way to obtain that which is behind the veil is to refuse the veil.

In other words, each thought we have is a form, imbued with life so long as we give it life ; imbued with power to the extent that we give it power. But to know that we are the life and the power, is to control all things. He that loves rules, and he that rules rests.

"THE NEW ORDER."

AN OCCULT STORY.

BY

A ROSICRUCIAN.

CHAPTER XI.

United.

IN these days Nellie Firth completely regained her health; she had been gradually improving for some time past—leaving off first one prop and then another; but now she was quite able to go about with her mother in her house to house visitations. Amongst their older acquaintances it was a matter for a good deal of conversation; and those who were sceptic upon the subject of Metaphysics said, Well, she's been long enough recovering anyway; whereas those who were deeper grounded in the Truth rejoiced, saying, To God all things are possible.

Nellie remembered nothing of all these long days of sleep; neither will you, dear reader, remember what belongs to your days of sleep after you have arisen. Why should this last sentence be introduced here? Have you not discerned that the Story of The New Order is an allegory in which you are the character! Well, we will see.

The visit of Martin Pond; the excursion to The City of Salem; the goings on in Bartone were not remembered by Nellie. She now constantly spoke of her father as if he were with them at home again; she remembered nothing of his absence. Do you not think a time is at hand when we shall have such command over our thoughts that whatever we do not wish to entertain we may dismiss on the instant, and remember not? We shall arrive at that. But until we do we shall not be able to heal as the Masters of The Retreat heal—heal by forgiveness. For no one can remit a sin that they remember. One may successfully break certain conditions that seem to environ a patient; but there is no certainty of success unless you can control your own thoughts. Is it important that you should remember the number of the house you have left? Not in the least. Then you will soon forget it. Is it important that you recognize what is uncharitable, ungracious, unjust, unlovely? As soon as you have reduced these things to no importance, you can forgive them, but not before. Our years of sleep—like Nellie Firth's—are our years of personality and remembrance of what is unholy. But it is recorded in this story that Nellie was an idiot ! Truly, and so is every one who lives not by the Light of Truth.

At this time the Master of The Retreat and Martin Pond, or Mr. Firth, were speaking of the Redemption of the World and the value of Example ; the former was saying, Every effect has its efficient cause, so every good example proceeds from good ; and for those who cannot see the good it is well that they should follow the example ; for a good example will lead nowhere but to the good. But this at least we may say, that a time does come, when the good example remains no more in the world, having overcome it. So that if one wish to be an example to his neighbor he must overcome the world within sight of his neighbor. You will find many who sigh for instant perfection that they may be a Way to others ; these know not that on arrival of perfect manifestation the possibility of being the example they desire ceases. For every thing is in its proper place ; for those who are overcoming the earth, the earth is the proper place; for those who have overcome the earth, another place is proper. However, the desire to be a perfect example arises from looking to the effect rather than to the cause ; for whoever looks to the cause will find no imperfection. So it is a mistake for anyone to be wanting to be perfect ; it is only necessary that they recognize that they are perfect and hold to the recognition. Men will not always do good that they may become good ; they will not always heal that they may be healed ; they will not always comfort that they may be comforted. No, they will do good because they are goodness ; they will heal because they are health ; they will comfort because they are the comforter.

And so you are going back to the world to untie all ties. To be a true husband and father because you are free ; to be a true teacher, because The Spirit alone teaches ; to be a living example, because you no longer follow one. And as you go, teach as has been taught from the beginning, Repent, for the Kingdom of Heaven is at hand. For every one who perceives the right, perceives the Kingdom of Heaven ; and no one perceives the right without repenting the wrong. And peace be with you !

Thus did Firth receive his right to teach ; and then he left The Retreat. And on his way he taught and healed ; and many people marvelled, saying amongst themselves; Is not this the second coming of Christ ! But the teacher rebuked them severely, saying, "You know well that in the day of the second coming many false teachers shall arise performing wonders, and shall deceive many. And what do you think shall be done to the false shepherds who lead the flocks astray? And they who are led astray shall fall into the same condemnation because they have been warned beforehand but heeded not the warning. It is such as you that shall be deceived, because you are ready to follow signs and wonders, notwithstanding that you have been warned. Do you not understand why the second coming shall be like as a thief in the night? Yet you know well what to expect from a thief; for he will surely take from you those treasures upon which your hearts are set. So when Christ shall come again you will no more have your heart set upon worldly things. But you are looking for Him, else you would not question thus amongst yourselves. And I will show you how you shall find Him; by keeping His commandments, Love one another." But a follower of any teacher and not a doer of the commandment is seeking his own destruction.

And as the Teacher was journeying towards Bartone, news of his doings was published there. But when he arrived at "The Home," he was received with great joy, for this time he came as himself and not as a stranger. And so shall every one be received by their own. Hypocrites will hypocrites receive; but the righteous will the righteous receive. Let us then arise with the world as if we were alone in the world, for no one is a hypocrite by himself. And so doing shall we be of service to the world.

How to Love.

"To love God with all our heart and mind, and our neighbor as ourselves," is the only way out of selfishness and limitation; for they are the outgrowth of a belief in separateness from God, and from each other. If we believe that we are better than our neighbors, or superior to them, that belief is sense judgment, and must be put off as the corruptible before we can put on the truth, which is the incorruptible.

"THE NEW ORDER."

An Occult Story.

BY

A ROSICRUCIAN.

CHAPTER XII.

Conclusion.

READERS who have carefully followed this story from the beginning, will remember that I, the narrator, related it after a sleep of many years. That all that has been related occurred during my sleep. And now upon the return of my father to our home, I am entirely out of my apparently unconscious condition. I have given no hint during this narrative, that my story should conclude with a marriage. And yet stories generally end in this way, so perhaps my readers have foreseen that our devoted friend, the schoolmaster, would be the natural guardian of me, whom he has so studiously cared for during my long term of unconsciousness. This is indeed what has already taken place; and with this confession my story ends.

So much for the story, which is, as has already been said, an allegory in which you are the principal character. Let this allegory be somewhat unveiled, sufficient to show the reader that he, who is behind the veil, is the reader.

Whether Bartone ever existed or not is a matter of little or no importance. But one thing is certain, that every one has made his home in *matter*, near which are the mountains of wisdom. And every one will some day leave his earthly home for the mountains, and in wisdom will find his true home. But people, who look upon the earth in a literal way, frequently seek wisdom and happiness in the literal mountains of sense, amongst hills and valleys, amongst streams and flowers. But they, who ascend the mount of enthusiasm and sense enjoyments, surely descend into the valley of despair and sorrows. The earth is only a symbol, and disappointment awaits all who look upon it otherwise. But beside every home, even in the most desert regions, or in cities, is the mountain of wisdom in whose clear atmosphere of truth all may find what can never be found as belonging to the world. For the world is by nature a deception, and will forever remain so. However, let us not think that it is necessary to leave the world in order to get beyond its deception ; it is only necessary not to be deceived. Where better can the nature of deception be learned than amidst deception ! Or where can the untruth of appearances be learned, but in appearances ? Truly nowhere. Therefore regret not that you are in the world ; because thus only can you overcome it, and learn that the heaven of everlasting happiness is here, although no part of the earth. You can never find Heaven in any place ; although you will be manifesting in some place, when you find Heaven. The Kingdom of Heaven must be found within (in state); then wherever you go in manifestation, whether amongst the sick or the well, the good or the bad, you will be in the Kingdom of God.

Therefore let me warn you not to seek any Retreat upon earth ; for many will be provided for you. Let me tell you that in no Retreat upon earth can you find conditions so favourable to your unfoldment as in your natural place, at home and in business, in town or in country, according to which is natural ; neither is the kingdom of rightness to be found by dieting or through celibacy. But some will be found saying, Eat not this or that, and marry not. Be warned, however, lest you be snared into denouncing those things with which Truth has nothing to do. Follow no one, who has anything to denounce ; follow only the Spirit, who has everything to announce.

The individual in his descent into matter becomes mated to matter, or his own physical body. This marriage constitutes the fall, which is perpetuated in symbol—namely, in marriage between husband and wife. The offspring of such marriage is the child of earth. But the individual is not this earthly child, and in time comes to recognize it, and returning out of matter finishes its experience or story by the divine marriage.

The Firths—husband and wife—represent this. Their consciousness descends into matter, and Nellie represents it. The return of the consciousness to Spirit is expressed by the marriage with which the story concludes. To understand this, let it be perceived, that the Spirit or life of every body or form is man ; consequently every one is man. The body or form of every one is woman : consequently every form—male or female—is woman. When man becomes wedded to woman, he places his consciousness in material things. And when he becomes wedded to spirit, he returns his consciousness to its source. The bride of the consciousness wedded to matter is a corruptible body;

the bride of the same consciousness wedded to spirit is an incorruptible body. The wedding between the Firths will be dissolved in time, for the spirit (expressed by Mr. Firth) will surely seek and return to its source, after passing through all his experience in the created world. But Nellie, which represents Mr. Firth, will return to the true Master, when his long sleep in matter shall end.

In these few words is the plan of The New Order in part unveiled ; and from this much more may be discerned by each. The moral of this story may be summed up in the one word, Forgive. Forgiveness is the life of every perfect man. You shall forgive yourself all your imperfections, whether viewed in your own particular manifestation or in your neighbour's, when through association with their nature you shall discover their illusion. For you will never remember a delusion against anyone. You can forgive yourself and your neighbour in your dreams about yourself and him; your descent into matter, from Adam to Christ—from preface to conclusion of this story, has been a dream of the senses. All that men do upon earth is as a dream that will be forgotten, when they wake up. You remember earthly things now, but your rest is not in them ; be of good cheer for these shall be forgotten, that you may find your rest in heaven.

And lastly, this story is intended to convey a different idea of the true Rosicrucianism—-under which term may be included all occultism, whether of theosophists, phallicists, or any other. For the New Order of to-day is the fulfilment or fullness of the past, even as the law of Christ is the fulfilment of all law. Old methods must pass away in the new. The law of Christ which has not yet been adopted upon earth by the nations of the earth, is about to be adopted ; all revolutions necessary thereto are being brought about quietly. And there will be one Religion, and one Law, and one Nation. Behold the end is at hand ! The New Order shall be established upon the earth.

. . . .

HARMONY

Is Wisdom's Way of Presenting Her Expressions.

Vol. 4.   *OCTOBER, 1891.*   *No. 1.*

"And I heard a great voice out of Heaven saying, Behold, the tabernacle of God is with men."

"Nothing is there to come, and nothing past;
But an eternal *now* does ever last.":   *Cowley.*

At the present time, at this moment, do we in truth hear a great voice out of Heaven saying, that I, Infinite and Eternal Life in the fullness of my strength and perfection doth manifest and live in the living. In whatsoever I live or reside, with the same is my tabernacle.

My words shall not pass away, I, Life, which live in the living, am ever saying, Thy being is in Me, Eternal Life. "And this is Life Eternal, that they might know Thee the only true God, and Jesus Christ, whom Thou hast sent." In knowing this thou knowest all. He whom I have sent is My Word, now manifest and dwelling in your midst.

The way of Eternal Life, in which is no death, is demonstrated in living.

The way of Eternal Light, in which is no darknes,is demonstrated in knowing. I, Life, am not "the God of the dead, but of the living."

"Behold, the tabernacle of God is with men," now. "Nothing is there to come, and nothing past." At this moment, "a new and living way, which He hath new made for us, through the veil, that is to say, His flesh;" is by Me demonstrated in living and knowing. I hear a great voice saying, the word of Life which is the truth that frees, is nigh thee, even in thy mouth. Its speaking forth is faith's fruition. "Be ye Holy for I am Holy." Be what I am, and do as I do, and thus abide in Me as I abide in thee.

I will lead them in paths they have not known, I will make darkness light before them, and crooked things straight.—*Is.* 42: 16.

Legally wealth inherited or accumulated is mine, but morally it is simply a new opportunity for me to help forward the progress of humanity; for ethically I myself am not my own.—*Prof. Richard Ely.*

Ed. note: Although the first two volumes of *Harmony* Magazine included "Theosophy" and "Metaphysics" in the subtitle, Cramer immediately established how her ideas compared with other current schools of thought. The review of Hartmann's book came in the very first issue. Either Hartmann's book was enjoying such success that it needed to be dealt with immediately, or Cramer felt the need to clarify what she meant by "Theosophy." However, within only five months, she must have felt a great need to address Blavatsky's brand of theosophy; for Cramer's review of *The Secret Doctrine* totals nearly nine pages, much more than any review in the eighteen-year history of the magazine.

Hartmann merits some comment. According to the *Encyclopedia of Occultism and Parapsychology*, he was born November 22, 1838, in Bavaria where he became a physician. He "emigrated to America in 1865, traveling as a doctor to various cities and also visiting Indian tribes and studying their religious beliefs." While in America he became interested in Spiritualism and, also, corresponded with leading Theosophists. (He was associated with Blavatsky for a time.) After returning to Bavaria he "encountered a sect of secret Rosicrucians, from whom he acquired many mystical insights." He became President of the Theosophical Society in Germany, eventually resigning "in order to found independent societies." He died in Bavaria on August 7, 1912.

ROSICRUCIÆ.

" AN ADVENTURE AMONG THE ROSICRUCIANS."*

ALTHOUGH the above mentioned work was published in Boston last year, and is therefore no new book, we wish to present a short notice of it, as it contains some remarks valuable to students of Occultism.

Philosophers assert that there is but one Mind; still, to many students, there is an appearance of many minds, and most people are in the habit of speaking as if each individual had a "mind of his own," different from that of others. The fact is, that there is but one mind, which is the mind of each and all, and that the *apparent* multitude of minds is but different states of consciousness of that one mind. Which to state in another way is: That each individual soul has its own consciousness of the One Mind. Where is your mind? Look around you on this material plane, and whatever you perceive there is in your mind. Consider nature, the planets and the stars; whatever you perceive there is in your mind. Consider again, that which is invisible and cannot be perceived by the senses—truth, love, wisdom, justice—whatever you perceive there is in your mind. Is there anywhere, then, where this Perceiver—your mind— is not? And if this be your mind, shall you not further consider what you are?

With these preliminary remarks we return to F. Hartmann, who says: "We are all living in the sphere of each other's minds; and he in whom

* By Franz Hartmann.

the power of spiritual perception has been developed may at all times see the images created in the mind of another. The Adept creates his own images, the ordinary mortal lives in the product of the imagination of others, either in those of the imagination of nature, or in those which have been created by other minds. We live in the paradise of our own soul, and the objects which you behold exist in the realm of our soul; but the spheres of our souls are not narrow. They have expanded far beyond the limits of the visible bodies, and will continue to expand until they become one with the Universal Soul, and as large as the latter. * * * The power of imagination is yet too little known. If a man think a good or evil thought,that thought calls into existence a corresponding form within the sphere of the mind, which may assume density and become living, and which may continue to live long after the physical body of the man, who created it, has died. It will accompany his soul after death, because the creations are attracted to their creator."

From our preliminary remarks it will be clear that Mind in its true sense—and we submit that it should only be used in its true sense—is indivisible or impartible; that it is everywhere the same; that whatever is perceived by it is perceived by the whole of it. If it perceive an object, such object may be situated in some locality; but the Perceiver, or Mind, can not be said, therefore, to be situated in some locality; or present to some individuals and not to others. *It* is present to all alike, but as we said before, all have not the same consciousness of it. Accordingly, we do not interpret the following extract literally: "Inferior man, in whom the consciousness of his higher spiritual self has not awakened, cannot think without the aid of the physical brain ; he cannot experience a consciousness which he does not yet possess ; he cannot exercise a faculty which is merely latent within his organization. But the man who has awakened to the consciousness of his higher self, whose life has been concentrated unto his higher principles, which exist independently of the physical form, constitutes a spiritual centre of consciousness, which does not require the physical brain to think, any more than you require the use of your hands and feet for the purpose of thinking. Life, sensation and consciousness do not belong to the form ; they are functions of the invisible but real man, who forms a part of the invisible organism of nature ; whose mind is a part of the Universal Mind, and who, therefore, if he once realizes his true character, and learns to know his own powers, may concentrate his consciousness in any place within or beyond his physical form and see, feel and understand what takes place in such a locality."

On the subject of concentration we would add shortly, that it is the secret of individual success on all planes of thought. All failure s whether of a commercial, political or educational nature, are due to "not minding one's own business." In the School of Philosophy, understanding is only obtained by the soul by contemplating, meditating, concentrating her attention on what she wants to understand. Working from or at the circumference is diffusion; working from or at the centre is concentration. The highest unfoldment is gained by the contemplation of principle.

We consider the author most clear in his treatment of occult phenomena, as to which we refer our readers to Chapter III. of the work. The Law of Gravitation when stated intelligently, and of phenomenal appearances will be found identical ; the solution lies in Metaphysics, not in Physics.

As to forms we make the following extract: " Forms are nothing real; they are merely illusions or shapes of substance; a form without substance is unthinkable and cannot exist. But the only substance of which we know is the Universal Primordial element of matter, the A'Kasa. This element of matter is invisibly present everywhere; but only where it assumes a certain state of density, sufficient to resist the penetrating influence of the terrestrial light, does it come within reach of your sensual perception, and assume for you an objective shape. The universal power of Will penetrates all things. Guided by the spiritual intelligence of the Adept, whose consciousness pervades all his surroundings, it creates in the Universal Mind those shapes which the Adept imagines; for the sphere of the Universal Mind where he lives, is his own mind, and there is no difference between the latter and the former, as far as the latter extends."

Chapter IV contains 66 pages on Alchemy.

In conclusion, we say, that although "Adventures among the Rosicrucians " contains some very valuable thought, it is not a text book such as is "Black and White Magic" (by the same author). Now both of these books appeal to two opposite classes of readers—one class are the intellectual, who devour the scholastic learning, and get led away by the marvellous and remain in the symbol ; the other class are the intuitive, who, getting behind the form or symbol, simply understand. In reading such books the tendency is to place the consciousness in the external; we therefore advise our readers to take their stand in consciousness where they are in Being.

The Way of One is the way of All,
The Truth of One is the truth of All,
The Life of One is the life of All—
To wit, one Jesus.

A REVIEW OF THEOSOPHY AND "THE SECRET DOCTRINE *

FIRST NOTICE.

THEOSOPHY (as the term is generally understood) has come prominently before the World during the second half of this twentieth century; though its teachings have to a limited extent been introduced to English speaking peoples during centuries past. Nevertheless, English historians have not yet taken into full account the close association that exists between the political revolutions of the seventeenth century and the religious and scientific revivals of to-day, presaging a political, scientific and religious reunion in the not far distant future. We cannot see politics, science and religion in any way separate (we speak not of that which seems to be at the present day). In truth they are one; and a review of theosophy to some extent necessitates a history of those peoples or nations that have been prominent in the political world of recent times. We must go back in thought to the seventeenth century; and we shall see that England was the centre upon which the chief interest of the world was focussed, and from which has emanated elements, both discordant and peaceful, necessary to the ultimate settlement of the nations. The disturbances in England during the turbulent reign of James I, Charles I, and the Commonwealth were introduced, not immediately but surely, by a recognition amongst the masses of a higher justice than then existed, which was evidenced by the agitations on the labour question, coinage, liberty of speech, etc., characterising some of the preceding reigns.

The intrigues in the years preceding the departure of the Pilgrim Fathers in the May Flower, about the year 1620, to the shores of North America, and during the reigns of James and Charles, between England and other nations— and markedly France, Spain, Portugal, Holland, Africa and India—and which finally led to the peopling of N. America by the race which has in part led to national unity; we say these intrigues were but a prelude to a higher civilization than that of the so called golden age of good Queen Bess.

Referring to the turbulent seventeenth century, Green, the English Historian, remarks that science, rationalism and secularism sprang for the first time into vivid life in their protest against the forced concentration of human thought on the single topic of religion, and against the effort to prison religion in a system of dogma, and to narrow humanity with all its varied interests

---

* The Secret Doctrine—The Synthesis of Science, Religion and Philosophy. By H. P. Blavatsky (Published by the Theosophical Publishing Co., L'd.   Price for first 2 vols. $10 00).

within a contracted religious sphere. When we refer to The New Philosophy of Francis Bacon, of Galileo, of Isaac Newton; to the teachings of Bunyan; to the establishment of the Royal Society and Greenwich Observatory; to the proclamation of religious, social and political liberty, and to the short lived Commonwealth, that was the prophetic shadow of those passing events that have culminated in the United States in a government by the Common Will; when we refer to these we see the first fruits of a new recognition in every path of life of Divine Wisdom, that is, of Theosophy.

It will also be remembered how during the last three hundred years communications by sea, by land, by telegraph, have increased, and continue to increase, bringing into familiarity strange and distant peoples and lands, uniting new and old worlds both materially and psychically. Not the least important amongst these reunions is that of India to England; and if the East India Co. and Clive are to be credited as laying the foundation for their national marriage, Theosophy and Theosophists of to-day shall surely be accredited as laying the foundation for the marriage of Christianity and Buddhism. In making this statement we do not overlook or underestimate the work of Christian Missionaries; and will supplement it with this statement, that just as Christian Missionaries have introduced Christianity into India, so Theosophists have introduced Buddhism into England. Still we see in the work of the Theosophists this further importance, that they have not merely introduced Buddhism, they have to some extent affiliated or united it to Christianity as part of Religion; it still remains for the Christian Missionaries to embrace the truth in the religions of India within Christianity.

It is difficult to overestimate the importance of Theosophy in England and Christianity in India. It is the beginning of one religion (Truth) for the world; of Confucianism for the non-Confucian world, and of the Truth for China; of Zoroastrianism for the non-Zoroastrian world, of the Truth for Persia; of Mohammedanism for the non-Mohammedan world, and of Truth for Mohammedans; in short, of Truth for Europe, Asia, Africa, America and Australasia. It is the commencement of a permanent federation in which all differences will die a natural death, and all unity will be every where manifest. And the most significant commencement of this approaching 'millenium' is to be found in the events hereinbefore touched upon or at that period of renaissance. If we take Truth as the standard to which to attain, we immediately gain a correct meaning of the often used term 'Universal.' Truth is Universal. And the more truth men and women have, the less prejudice they have, and the more Universal they become. The recent movements in

Theosophy tend to Universalize or liberalize the thoughts of mankind; they assist in bringing them out of some particular or narrow conception of the Truth; they suggest that the attainment of Truth should be the only aim of mankind, and not to uphold some individual idea *about* truth, or some particular dogma. We do not by any means say that Theosophy as it is now taught is a perfect science; but what we do say about Theosophy as it is now taught is, that it does immense good in that it enlarges our views, expands our thoughts. As it is taught now it is decidedly an intellectual philosophy, and this the world at present makes great demands for. It is not the Science of Spirit or Christ, which is intuitive philosophy, but is readily interpreted by it. We will make this point clearer; an intellectual philosophy is one which deals with facts as facts; an intuitive philosophy deals with facts as expressions of cause. The former endeavours to understand cause by expressions, or expressions by expressions; the latter to understand expressions by cause. Material science is acknowledged by Scientists as an Intellectual philosophy, for they are aware of it; but Theosophy of to-day is not so acknowledged by theosophists—though equally intellectual—for they think it a philosophy of cause. We are speaking of theosophists in general; but it would be no more just to judge true theosophy by theosophists than true christianity by christians. Christianity, or the Science of Spirit or Christ, is Divine Wisdom or Theosophy; and if you would have one name for all, that name would be TRUTH, under which all will ultimately be united.

The Song Celestial, The Light of Asia, Black and White Magic, Light on the Path, Esoteric Buddhism, and the *Theosophist* (magazine), are amongst the best works recently published on or connected with Indian Theosophy. This list may be supplemented by the works of Max Muller and Mohin[i] Chatterji, and the early volumes of the Hibbert Lectures. All these are amongst the foremost contributors of recent times to religious progress.

A REVIEW OF THEOSOPHY AND "THE SECRET DOCTRINE."*

SECOND NOTICE.

NOW, to speak of " The Secret Doctrine." The two large volumes before us, comprising in all some 1600 pages, promise to be but half of the complete work; two other volumes—it is stated, are almost ready for the publisher. Volume I treats of Cosmogenesis; Volume II of Anthropogenesis. We learn from the preface that " The Secret Doctrine " is not a re-writing of " Isis Unveiled," and that in its pages are but few extracts from the same author's earlier work; that it is a collection of truths that may be found scattered throughout thousands of volumes. In the following extract the Author sets forth what she claims for her new work.

" That it has many shortcomings the writer is fully aware; all that she claims for it is that, romantic as it may seem to many, its logical coherence and consistency entitle this new Genesis to rank, at any rate, on a level with the ' working hypothesis ' so freely accepted by Modern Science. Further it claims consideration, not by reason of any appeal to dogmatic authority, but because it closely adheres to Nature, and follows the laws of uniformity and analogy.— — The aim of this work may be thus stated: to show that Nature is not ' a fortuitous concurrence of atoms,' and to assign to man his rightful place in the scheme of the Universe; to rescue from degradation the archaic truths which are the basis of all religions; and to uncover to some extent the fundamental unity from which they all spring; finally, to show that the occult side of Nature has never been approached by the science of modern civilization."

As to these aims, and judging from the first two volumes, we should say that the work will show that Nature is not a fortuitous concurrence of atoms; and likewise it will show that there are forces in Nature at present unknown to the Scientists of modern civilization; but we are not prepared to admit the possibility of any truth whatever falling into degradation; and as to truth being the basis of religion—as if religion were something built upon but separate from truth—we consider truth the whole of religion, and religion the whole of truth. We cannot endorse the claim that the Author has assigned to man his rightful place in the Scheme of the Universe, nor that much has been presented that will of itself tend to unity. Indeed we have rarely met with any work, so learned and with so much research, having withal so little knowledge. We recognize the Author's broad good will to humanity at large that has prompted her wonderful effort; yet if we accept her own criticism of her own book, she is the severest possible critic of it. In a few words, this is the ground of her philosophy; there is One Infinite God, who is all knowledge, but absolutely unknowable.--From any philosopher who voluntarily takes such a position as this, what *knowledge* is to be gained! Such philosophy is its own severest condemnation. We say " her philosophy ," for although "The Secret Doctrine " is not presented as containing any more than a collection of sundry truths, still it is really (so far as Vols. I and II go) the Author's interpretation of those truths, and must be accepted as hers and not the theosophy of ancient philosophers.

SOURCE:—In the Introduction great stress is laid on the importance of recovering ancient books, which are spoken of as the Sources of Knowledge. This is an example of what we meant in our First Notice by an intellectual philosophy; books are never Sources of Knowledge, but Knowledge is the Source of books. Now the real reason why these have been hidden from the world is the inability of the World to understand them; the requisite now is rather to get that understanding than the books.

GOD AND MATTER:—On page 10 of the Proem we come again at a cause of many theosphists' confusion. — — " The Occultist accepts revelation as coming from divine yet still finite beings, the manifested lives, never from the Unmanifested One Life." — — Here we read of a life as being outside of the one life or being. This comes about by an intellectual comprehension of life; intellect sees many lives and many gods, and personality generally; whereas reason or intuition sees but one life, but one God, and personality as merely expression of consciousness or character. And if we accept revelation as if from other sources than the One and only Source, then we are setting up other gods before the one; and exactly this is idolatry or personality. Further on in the book we come to another source of confusion — " The seven cosmical elements are simply conditional modifications and respects of the One and only Element. This latter is not ether, not even A'kasa, but the Source of these. — — For occultists, however, both ether and the Primordial Substance are a reality. To put it plainly—Ether is the Astral Light, the Up-adhi of Divine Thought. In modern language the latter would be better named *cosmic ideation—Spirit*; the former *cosmic Substance—matter*. These, the Alpha and Omega of Being, are but two facets of the One Absolute Existence. — — All who sought to give a name to the incognizable Principle have simply degraded it. Even to speak of Cosmic Ideation, save in its phenomenal aspect, is like trying to bottle up primordial Chaos, or to put a printed label on Eternity."

What does such a Statement mean? It means that matter is a condition of God: it means that material things are the Creator itself. And how does it come about that such statements are made? It comes about by trying to intellectually explain away that which seems to the senses to be a reality; it comes about by trying to explain God by what we see; it comes about by not realizing that God is one Spirit or only cause, and that matter is appearance or only effect. With all love we say that so many pages on the Secret Doctrine is only possible by trying to explain false premises; the gifted author doubtless thinks the work one of love in cause, whereas it is a work of effect in effect; the intention is all goodness, but the execution is entirely in the letter and not in the Spirit.

Throughout the work under review it is manifest that the " Unknowable God " of " The Secret Doctrine " is a Material God, notwithstanding that the God of the ancient books quoted therein is exactly the opposite—a spiritual, impersonal God; showing how very little these " Sources of Knowledge" have been understood, and showing above all the necessity of seeking knowledge within instead of without. Pantheism does not teach, that God is all that *appears;* it does teach God is all that *is.* It is in trying to explain away appearances, that good and earnest students are very apt to run into the path of conjectures, that leads from bewilderment to bewilderment; and lost in the deserts of language and book learning the cry of despair goes up—"Alas! there is no God—or none for me, for He is unknowable; I am lost, lost! " Not lost, friend—" Come unto Me, and I will give you rest; My yoke is easy, and My burden is light." We would not say, do not read " The Secret Doctrine "; we do not say refrain from travelling any path of experience you may think necessary; we say read it, travel your path, have your experience, but be guided by reason—God is Reason, not Matter or A'kasa, not even the Soul, but the creator of all these. He is with you throughout all your anxieties, but despair is so loud, so intense, and the presence you seek is so silent, so still. Listen not, friend, for the audible inner voice of a Master, not even of a Dhyan Choan, but seek only the absolute silence, without which you would not be, and with which you are always one. Then shall you realize that God is one Spirit and is All; and that matter, A'kasa and all bodies are appearances only.

The following is the Author's statement of Being; there is " an omnipresent external, boundless and immortal principle on which all speculation is impossible, since it transcends the power of human conception and could only be dwarfed by any expression or similitude. It is beyond the range and reach of thought, unthinkable and unspeakable [Vol. I, p. 14]. — — Hence while it [A'kasa or the Astral Light or Universal Soul] is the *Universal Cause* in its unmanifested unity and infinity, it becomes with regard to mankind, simply the effects of the causes produced by men in their sinful lives [Vol. II. p. 511.] — — Thus then, the first fundamental axiom of " The Secret Doctrine " is this Metaphysical One Absolute Be-ness, symbolized by finite intelgence as the theological Trinity." The erroneous interpretation of the fundamental axiom is, as we have shown, the false premises upon which " The Secret Doctrine " insecurely stands. As to the concluding sentence of the above quotation, we will simply say that the true perception that the One Absolute Be-ness is a Trinity in Unity, is conclusive evidence of infinite intelligence; The One Be-ness is alone able to truly perceive this one fundamental axiom; and all who perceive it are consciously at one with Be-ness.

MAN:—Man is not assigned his rightful place in the scheme of the universe by any other position than that taken by Jesus of Nazareth—"I and the Father are one." And this position we state will only be perceived by those who—having worked their way by thought beyond the deserts of materialism—being pure in heart, perceive God or Goodness as it is. Then indeed will all nature, matter, A'kasa, or light be truly beautiful as a manifestation or representation of that Be-ness which is "in heaven" or impersonal. Then indeed, and only then, will the whole material universe, with all its inhabited planets enchained around their inhabited Suns, with all its interstellar spaces full of the myriad forms of that one Life which pervades and is the reality of all, be understood and appreciated, and the infinity of the perceiver be recognized. Is the Infinite rejoiced at the recognition? Imagine the joy of great Peace; then ask the quiet student, who has perceived truth; ask the gentle Master who has stood face to face with Principle; ask the loving Chela, who has found the silence, and each will answer you from a source that is not books, from a centre that is not bound, from a heart that knows no limitation—" Friend, my Peace is yours."

MIND:—We desire to make a few short extracts on the subject of Mind. "Mind is a name given to the sum of the states of consciousness grouped under Thought, Will and Feeling. During deep sleep ideation ceases on the physical, and memory is in abeyance; thus for the time being 'Mind is not', because the organ through which the Ego manifests ideation and memory on the material plane has temporarily ceased to function. — — During the long night of rest called Pralaya, when all the existencies are dissolved, the universal mind remains as a permanent possibility of mental action, or that abstract absolute thought, of which mind is the concrete relative manifestation." Then if mind be a possibility of mental action, it must be the effect of which mental action is the cause; and of course this would make mind concrete, dependent on memory, etc. But what caused mental action? What causes thought? Surely the thinker; that is, the Mind. Hence mind is Being, or Abstract, not mental action or Concrete. And mind or being is all; human mind or human being is divine mind or divine being—else God or Being is not infinite. Such a question as is asked on p. 81, Vol. II, shows a deplorable tangle—" What is human mind in its highest aspect; whence comes it, if it is not a portion of the essence—and in some rare cases of reincarnation, the very essence—of a higher Being; one from a higher and divine plane?" To Mind or God there is no higher or lower. God does not judge by appearances, and to him the writer of " The Secret Doctrine " is as much as the least insect or greatest Dhyan Choan; and neither more nor less. Being, like a mathematical point, has neither parts nor physical magnitude; it cannot be portioned—so much to one, and so much to another; but each is all, and conscious of it in Being, though we do not say sensible of it in manifestation. To all who have conception of goodness the idea of it being divisible or portionable is unthinkable.

In conclusion, we hail the " revival of Theosophy," and rejoice at the beginnings with which the name of Madam Blavatsky will remain associated; also at the success which is attending the Theosophical Society throughout the world in its efforts to universalize thought and spread the tenets of Understanding. But before Theosophy is understood " The Secret Doctrine ", and kindred thought, must with kindly hands be laid on the shelf of oblivion as unreliable guides. — — There let it rest!

164

We are not "sent into the world" to take on and struggle with and overcome all the human beliefs and opinions that are seemingly in the world. We are here to bear witness of the truth. Our personal, bodily presence bears witness of the truth of our being. We are here because God is here, and our work is to do the works of God. We miss the mark of our high calling in Christ and as Christ, when we think "we are sent here" to deal with error. The truth is, we in our being are God expressing Himself; so each one can say: I am here always and expressing myself perfectly; I am bearing witness of the truth without ceasing.

Is Divine Science Theosophy or Christian Science?

A STUDENT writes : "I would like to state that twice in my experience, I had to fight for the integrity of the book—Lessons in Science and Healing—and of Mrs. Cramer's right to the claim of originality. The point was raised, first, that the book was only a copy of Mrs. Eddy's work, and to prove it, my attention was called to the fact that in the book itself it said, "The names Theosophy and Christian Science, when given their *true* and *universal* interpretation, cover the same ground as does the Science of Infinite Spirit."

Another time, I was asked if I taught Theosophy. I said, "No, my teaching does not touch Theosophy at any point. There is nothing in common with it and the Oriental religion." "Then, said the man, you do not follow in the steps of your leader, Mrs. Cramer, for she distinctly says in her book that Divine Science and Theosophy are one and the same thing."

Of course, it was useless to say anything about "*true* and *universal* interpretation" to either of the parties. * * * There must be some way of getting at this thing so that people will know where Divine Scientists stand. They want the Truth, but they do not want all that has been thrown at them for the last ten years under the guise of Science, which has been any old thing that the teacher himself happened to think of.

I have learned a number of lessons while out teaching, and one was that the old teaching is dead; by that, I mean the heterogeneous mass that has been masquerading as Science. The statements must be clean-cut, and so plain that there can be no mistaking them."

This very suggestive letter affords the opportunity of explaining more explicitly these points than was necessary at the time of writing LESSONS IN SCIENCE AND HEALING, or than has seemed necessary hitherto.

The intentional interpretation of the names Christian Science and Theosophy was just as I stated, *true and universal.* Christian Science did not mean to me Eddyism, for I was not a student of Mrs. Eddy's, neither had I read a single chapter in her book, "Science and Health," at that time. It had not been my privilege to do so, though I had thought many times I would set aside my work and devote my time to it until I had read every word of the book, but invariably everything would combine to completely occupy my time. And now I can see wisd m in it all, for many times have I met with the same accusation: "It is only a copy of Mrs. Eddy's book," and the very next statement would be, "It is mortal error." They seem to be utterly oblivious of the reflection they cast upon her book by the latter statement. The main points of her teaching first came to me from members of Christian Science classes, but not until my Primary and Normal Lessons were formulated, and I was before the public as a teacher.

In formulating Divine Science I had no books before me, no human authority in mind, but I did have in consciousness, as a basic principle, the infinitude and omnipresence of God as Spirit or Mind, which was all knowledge and all power. The all in all is God, and God manifest, was the only basis from which to think and to write. In this principle of oneness each statement of every lesson was based. This Truth I did not get from any book, but it was spiritually perceived, and intuitively realized, and this before I had read any book upon the Science. My definition of the name Christian Science, instead of meaning Eddyism, meant the universal knowledge of God, and the universality of the living Christ. It was raised in my consciousness to the plane of Divine Science, the Truth which proves that the inner and the outer— the Spirit and the body—are one according to Christ's teaching.

The word Theosophy did not, nor does it mean any of the theories of evolution, or of personal reimbodiment, or of physical causation taught under the name Theosophy. My understanding of the word Theosophy was, and is, Divine Wisdom, or wise in the things of God.

Students who have not been accurately taught, and who have not analyzed from the plane of pure being, do not distinguish the difference between Divine Science, which teaches that there is no physical causation, and that God is the only Source and Cause of all, and the theories based in a supposed physical causation, which claims that effects become causes, and that creatures make creatures. These students are frequently heard saying, when speaking of teachings just the reverse of each other, "They are all one and the same thing." They seem to think that unity—the at-one-ment of the whole—has no deeper meaning than their efforts to practice charity by saying that all

opposing theories are one with Science. "They are all good; they have their
place in the world; they are all stepping stones."

Mental teaching and healing, and evolution from a lower to a higher
plane in all its phases; the Theosophists Karma and reimbodiment, based in
the supposition that there are physical causes; Christian Science and Divine
Science are all classed in the same teaching. This is saying "Peace, where
there is no peace." A mathematician might as well attempt to instruct his
class by practicing charity with it when laboring with wrong statements and
miscalculation. He might as well say: "It is all one, and if you look for the
good only, you will find it in every phase of statement; the miscalculation is
a step in your progress toward principle," as for a student to undertake to
adjust theories based in the claim of physical causation unto God, or unto
the Truth of Divine Science.

Divine Science teaches the direct expression in creation of all that God
implies. True charity to any person or class, consists in revealing the principle or Truth that each one may demonstrate it for himself. True unity and
oneness is found in principle and nowhere else. Life is principle and is God;
it is also Supreme Law, which demonstrates itself perfectly, and never imperfectly. In Science we are not working toward principle, but from principle.

One Sunday morning, after church, when I had spoken on the subject,
"God Incarnation versus personal Reincarnation and Karma," a lady who
had been waiting some time to speak to me, said: "I have been attending
lectures on Evolution and Reincarnation, and have thought for several years
I would come to your College and take a course of lessons in Divine Science.
I think they are all trying to *attain* the same thing, and by looking for the
good everywhere, I find it in them all." To this I replied, "There is a great
difference between the teaching of those who are trying to attain to Truth, or
to evolve from a lower to a higher condition, and the teaching of those who
know Truth and are enjoying the reality of Being, and demonstrating the
same." My friend then said: "If the evolutionists have not attained to the
Truth, they are very near it, and the only difference between you and myself
is, that I am more charitable than you are. I believe in saying that all of
these theories are good, and I find good in them." My reply was, "The evolutionists who are striving to become or attain are not so near comprehending
Being but that they miss the Truth of it altogether. There is no true charity
in saying that "it is all the same." The true charity and love to humanity
demands that we speak Truth, for there is no other way to solve life's problem,
and we cannot instruct others in the solution of their problem by holding that
their mistakes—unprincipled statements—are just the same as the true solution based in principle. Therefore, while Divine Scientists have no thought

of antagonism in showing why theories and beliefs based in effect and supposed physical causation fall short of Truth, we cannot say that they are all one and the same. "For when that which is perfect is come, that which is in part is done away."

Such sentiments as these are so frequently indulged, and called Science, that nothing but a thorough spiritual education, one based in the Truth of God and Him manifest, and God manifesting in creation at this time, will ever make scientists. No one who knows the Truth of Being, the reality of God and man, can fail to see that these theories are not Divine Science, and do not stand for Truth. Divine Scientists hold all people, of every nation, in consciousness of the unity of life, the everywhere present spirit, but do not accept their varied theories wrought for the salvation of man.

It is true, as the writer of the above letter has said : "The old teaching is dead," for people frequently write, and come to us in person, with the same thing. The following conversation with a lady will serve to give the substance of what they all say along this line : "I first studied Christian Science, but I was not satisfied because I could not ascertain who I am, and what I am. I never knew where to place my patients when treating them. The theory of our being a reflection, does not satisfy me ; and having to say there is no body, brought no light or power. I thought I would attend meetings elsewhere, thinking I would get more light, so I have been going two years, regularly, to 'the Home.' I got so mixed up that I could neither help myself nor any one else. I found great difficulty in understanding the different teachers who spoke there, because they differed so widely in their teachings, and I found that they taught more from the plane of personal experience than from principle. There is no underlying principle to it. I have listened to you a few times, and am reading your books, and I see that you have a great universal principle underlying every statement, and by which you account for visibility, and prove its spirituality. I can understand myself and my relationship to God through your teaching."

Others express themselves very much as a lady did who called at Home College a few days since from one of our western cities : "There are so many writing and teaching who are merely giving their opinions about Science. They have read promiscuously, are all mixed up, do not know where they stand, and are giving their opinions of what they have read."

There is nothing that will straighten out this mixed up condition of affairs but for them to study Divine Science. When its principles are embraced they will know Science, and have no opinion about it.

Divine Science is not a heterogeneous mass of statements, it is the Truth of God, and God expressing Himself in creation at this time.

Divine Science is not sentiment or theory; it is not evolution from a lower to a higher plane; it is not any belief based in thought or mentality. Its practice is not from the mental plane, hence the name Mental Science does not represent Divine Science.

The Theosophical teachings, so-called, based in physical causes, do not touch the true definition of Theosophy at any point ; therefore, Divine Science does not touch Theosophical teaching at any point. While Divine Science includes Divine Wisdom concerning the things of God, it does not touch any theories based in mental or physical causes in any of their tenets. It has never been claimed that Divine Science is Mrs. Mary B. Eddy's teaching, for Divine Science teaches the Law of Expression, which law I spiritually perceived when writing my first Lessons, before I had read a word in her books.

By this law Divine Science accounts for the body and the visible universe and proves the at-one-ment of man with God; while in Christian Science no Law of Expression is taught, and visibility is not accounted for but is claimed to be mortal mind and is, therefore, denied.

In Divine Science our Lord Jesus Christ is God manifest in form ; "the Word, which is God made flesh." Everyone who has experienced the direct manifestation of God within himself or herself, will grant that the same experience and realization is possible to each and all. If one does not see this possible, it proves that he does not realize the true light that lighteth every man, and the one who has the true light will see that his light, which is life, lights or lives every man that comes into the world. So my work has been to teach the Truth or God manifest in creation, and who or what man is in Being. There is no true originality but what is based in the origin all of things ; all teaching thus based is original. Those who are seeking it elsewhere will fail to find it.　　　　　　　　　　　M. E. CRAMER.

God Incarnation Versus Personal Re-Incarnation
Evolution and Karma

GOD

We are debtors, not to the flesh, to live after the flesh. (Rom. 8:12)
For by grace are ye saved, through faith; and that not of yourselves, it is the gift of God. (Eph. 2:8)

The freedom and power of DIVINE SCIENCE is a shining light penetrating and warming the entire world with the "life more abundant," which Life is ever enjoyed with the consciousness of what Being IS. The entire religious world is undergoing a mental change, preparatory to perfect adjustment to true Theology, the science of God in creation. In DIVINE SCIENCE is taught the relationship that creatures hold to the Creator — that living forms hold to Supreme Being. Truth is now leavening the whole lump and is revealing anew the absolute idea of the Christ and primitive Christianity in its original God-given glory and power of healing.

No expression can be superior in quality or greater in quantity than the Expressor. No effect can be higher in its nature than its source and cause; this is a basic principle to be adhered to in the study of truth, hence, the principle of equality lies at the bottom of the essay.

INCARNATION

The word *incarnate* means *to clothe or embody with flesh; to form.* The theological definition is, the act of taking a human body and the nature of man — **as the incarnation of the Son of God.** The basic truth of the declaration made by St. John in his account of creation is, that the word that is with God and is God becomes flesh and dwells among us.

As the NOW can never **cease** but continues of all time, we know that what has been, is **now** and what is **now** will continue to be; the first thing to grasp is **that I am spirit or mind, the Expressor of bodily existence,** for nothing can be expressed that is not. Thus is it self-evident that I am one with God, the Father; I therefore lovingly accept the position of source and cause of my expression and abide as the consciousness of its perfection — knowing this is the way to include it within myself as life and love, with sincerity and faith.

The record of the word that is with God and is God, becoming flesh, testifies of self-expression; Jesus' words were infinite mind revealing itself unto itself. In true incarnation, we are clothed with spirit (not unclothed), but clothed upon in the same sense that Jesus referred, when he said, *That which is begotten of Spirit is spirit;* creation is expression.

RE-INCARNATION

The theory of personal re-incarnation before the world today is based in the assumption that the Infinite source and cause of form (and of all the manifested universe) expresses itself imperfectly. The current theory assumes that the imperfect expression, by continued re-incarnation or embodiment, is to perfect itself. Thus (according to this theory), through efforts made by the imperfect expression, it eventually accomplishes what God the perfect, fails to accomplish in the beginning.

The claim is that individuality is built up and rounded out through experience; hence, every experience that one can possibly have is considered necessary to the completion of individual life and the rounding out of character (the purpose of which is to eventually become as gods — separate individual entities).

It is to be understood that theosophy teaches that the first incarnation, or expression of form, is by Infinite Cause, of God, and that all re-incarnation takes place because of worldly love and desires. It is claimed that as soon as there is a desire for any visible thing (for any form or shape), there is Karma, and that Karma — the basis of which is desire — is called *material-love.* So, re-incarnation (according to theosophy) is based in personal desire and takes place without God. It is, therefore, a doctrine based in illusive imagination, in which its adherents ignorantly worship, and of whom it can be said, "Ye worship ye know not what."

The highest claim made for personal re-incarnation is discipline, gained from experience; but it is not that discipline which comes from divine knowledge, which is eternal self-knowledge. The very fact that its adherents expect to overcome desire or love of the material (which causes them to re-embody) proves that when they do overcome, then all the experience gained through what desire and material-love have been the basis of, will come to naught.

There is no overcoming but that of coming-over from this and similar theories unto the truth of God, the only creative Cause. In that mind, it is said, "What is made is Mine." "I and My Father are One." "All Things are Mine" in atonement. Verily, "When that which is perfect is come, that which is in part is done away."

There is nothing Godly but what is like God; there is nothing ungodly but what is unlike God. The Creator does not begin His work with view of its becoming more perfect through experience than He has made it. Rather, it is ever intended that man should rely upon his innate power and possibility — his present perfection of life, substance, intelligence and power.

The "beginning" spoken of in all the spiritual records of creation is *creative action;* it is the expressing and speaking forth of what the *I am* is.

The commencement of the theory of re-incarnation is just the reverse; it begins not in God, but in material-love and desire (something that is to be overcome) — with view of the imperfect, becoming perfect. Its beginning is not that of speaking forth the truth of what *Being is*, the perfection that *I am*; but instead, it supposes that through much experience the imperfect is made to approximate the Absolute and the Real and is caused to become what it is not.

According to this theory, God has incarnated in us in the first expression; then comes re-incarnation and evolution (resulting from desire), which — it is claimed — will perfect and complete our existence.

The following is from the pen of M.J. Barnett and sets forth the claims of personal re-incarnation in theosophical language:—

"When we say that we do not desire to live again on earth, how little we know of our desires and of their influence upon our destiny. As little as we think we want a repetition of our present life, it is the very strength of our desires as related to material existence, that brings us here again and again. Are we through with material life when there are so many physical experiences that we have never had and that we desire, and so many kinds of intellectual and artistic culture that we are just beginning, as well as thousands of other kinds that we long for, but the ability to acquire which is now only latent within us, and would it not necessitate hundreds of lives in the future to accomplish that which we feel might, under favorable conditions, be possible to us?

"If we, at the close of life, are pursuing an art or a science, have we reached our final aim in regard to it? If we aspire to become noble in character, have we yet conquered every selfish propensity? If it is for all these kinds of experience (as well as many more) that we are brought here on the physical plane to struggle our way upward in our relation to matter — with all the trials and discipline that such relation involves — if such is divine intention (as it certainly appears, if there is any aim or intention in it), then would it not be farcical to give us only the fleeting moment of one life in which to accomplish the stupendous work that lies before us?

"Who does not desire to do more than he has yet done even in his own little line of work? Who does not desire further opportunity and better conditions in some department of life's activities? We should not have such desires if there were not sometime and somewhere a response to them. They constitute the very attractive force that will bring us back into material life."

Dharmapala, the Buddhist priest, said to a San Francisco audience, "You can be free from Karma at any time you choose, by being based right." It is only in Divine Science that we learn what self-hood is and where it is based and that we are free from worldly theories only in truth.

EVOLUTION

The Darwinian account of evolution consists of a theory of the evolution of form, or of reproduction, the higher forms evolving from the lower. According to this theory, the variety of form, color, etc. is produced by what is called natural selection — Nature's choice. Here is the notion that the origin of species is caused by circumstances (not a fixed law). Here is the notion that the inter-mixing of certain types, or forms, produces the different species, hence the variety of form.

This theory of evolution is one based wholly in form and observation. It is asserted that beginning with the simplest known form, every succeeding form is due to and is the result of the preceding form; that is, **forms make forms,** or the source of form is form, i.e., the more complex has evolved from the more simple one.

This theory claims form to be both cause and effect, the cause being inferior to the effect; hence, the result is considered to be superior to its cause. Yet it can be truthfully said that no law is known by which an effect or expression can be greater than its source and cause.

ESOTERIC BUDDHISM

The theory set forth in Esoteric Buddhism, by Mr. Sinnett, differs from the Darwinian theory only in that it is a more interior process. It regards what is termed the evolution of the soul; its starting point is in Cosmic light, primal expression of spirit. This theory may be stated as follows:

> *The beginning of evolution of soul commences with an expression of Infinite Spirit, called Cosmic light. It is to be noted here that the reasoning begins in the expression or effect, instead of the Expressor or Cause; this effect, cosmic light, finally evolves the soul of a planet, then produces from this soul, in regular order, the souls of all things manifested upon the planet; beginning with the soul of the mineral, which soul embodies for ages in one form of mineral; thence passing to a higher form of mineral, and still higher, until it passes through the entire mineral kingdom to the vegetable kingdom embodying repeatedly in the different species of the vegetable kingdom until it reaches the highest form. Then it passes to the animal kingdom, beginning its embodiment in the lowest order and going through the same detail in every animal form, thence to man, continuing to incarnate until the highest consciousness in the human form is reached. This is called attaining to the sixth principle, or human soul.*
>
> *The claim or outgrowth of this theory is, that the human soul, then, continues to embody upon the earth evolving higher and higher until material-love or desire is satisfied or overcome. It is claimed that this process is to give the soul a permanent individuality, a lasting and ever abiding consciousness of being, built up through experience. It is*

*claimed that then the soul (through wisdom gained from the experience
of re-incarnating) becomes a planetary spirit — "the Atma consciousness or spiritual soul."*
   *The difficulty is that in the process it must overcome material-love and
desire, the very source and cause of its re-incarnation — and therefore
of its experience. This theory has been largely considered by many who
are striving "to rend the veil of sense and pass into the realization of
things which lie above and beyond this shadowland."*

The origin of man (the true conception and birth of his body) is not
found in any of these theories. Sinnett's theory is essentially the same as
the Darwinian, in that it deals with the evolution of form — the one form
being physical and visible to the natural eye and the other form being psychical and invisible to the natural eye.

Darwin states a theory of the evolution of all known physical form,
from the lowest to the highest. Sinnett states a theory of the evolution of
all psychical form, from the lowest to the highest. Darwin calls form **body,**
and Sinnett calls form **soul.** They both claim that the lower form is on its
way to the higher; that the lower is the cause for the higher; that the higher
form is always the outgrowth of the lower. Hence, in both theories,**effect**
is presented as being superior to cause; the expression or unfoldment is
claimed to be greater than its source.

Yet to all true reasoning, the adage is true that a stream cannot rise
higher than its source. The expression of a source and cause can never be
superior in quality or greater in quantity than that which has given it
expression. The unfoldment can never become superior to the unfolder;
nor can the unfoldment overcome and set at naught its source and cause.

Now let us consider the words of Jesus — "That which is born of
flesh is flesh." All theories having form as a source and cause by which to
account for creation *profiteth nothing*; they constitute *the flesh that profiteth nothing,* of which it is said: "If ye live after the flesh, ye shall die; but
if ye through the Spirit do mortify the deeds of the body, ye shall live."

We are not the debtors to the body that we should make it the source
and cause of being — of our individuality and character, of our immortality and spirit-consciousness.

St. Paul's advice to the Ephesians is good for us to follow, i.e. "Put off
the former conversation," *the old man,* which is corrupt, according to the
deceit of sense. If we do this we shall set aside all theories based in a supposed physical causation.

False conclusions are what Paul refers to as **deeds** of the body that we
are to mortify. He speaks of *false conversation* which is no more than
erroneous belief. This is to be done that we may prove that "By grace are
we saved, and that not of ourselves, it is the gift of God." Hence to live

after the Spirit here and now is to recognize and know that there is no other causation.

There is nothing born of the flesh that profiteth anything, for that which is born of flesh is nothing more than what is included in the supposition that there is physical causation. This is what Paul referred to in the first chapter of Romans: *When they knew God, they glorified* **him** *not as God, neither were thankful, but became vain in their imaginations * * * who changed the truth of God into a lie and worshiped and served the creature rather than the Creator....*

This worshiping and serving the creature is believing that our forms are the product of lower forms or of other forms, or that creatures are the source and cause of creatures. Let us conclude that all these theories and conditions that are born of flesh are idolatrous and profit nothing.

GENESIS

Verily, we need to revive and to realize, each for himself, the grand old record of the Genesis of creation. We need to come, every man and every woman of us, to the Edenic order and law of our being. It is folly to suppose that the lines of investigation and discovery of truth end with a knowledge of construction of form. The individual refuses to rest content with the claim that the substance and reality underlying both ideal and visible phenomena, is unknowable. The mere recognition of an infinite and eternal energy from whence all things proceed — compels men to try to find out something of the nature of that energy. Consequently, while not discarding the old records (the spiritual statements made of God manifest in the world) but working in direct harmony (along the lines whence the fathers gathered the material for their conclusions), we would be led to ask, what will come of it?

We cannot be dogmatic in our answer as to the outcome, but will say that every new discovery tends to affirm both the oldest and the newest statements of unity. If, in the language of natural science, there is "an Infinite and Eternal Energy from whence all things proceed," the record is true (though stated in different language) that *in the beginning was the Word, and the Word was with God, and was God, and without it was not anything made that was made.* Also does "the one Eternal Energy, from which all things proceed" sustain the statements that *as it was it is now, and evermore shall be* and that *in God we live, are moved, and are?*

The record also sustains the statement from *The Song Celestial:*
"Never the spirit was born; the spirit shall cease to be never;
Never was time it was not; End and Beginning are dreams!
Birthless and deathless and changeless remaineth the spirit for ever;
Death hath not touched it at all, dead though the house of it seems!"
The oneness of substance also sustains the record of the Genesis of
Creation: that there is only God and His word; that the Fatherhood of God
includes the brotherhood of man. This is what the consciousness that there
is one source brings out; it does away with all dual doctrine, hence with all
dual results and sense limitation.

That which fills all space being spirit, all things are found to be in a
state of at-one-ment with their source and cause and with each other.
Spirit, therefore, carries within its infinitude of love the whole universe as
Itself expressed.

In *The Song Celestial* Arjuna says to Krishna:
Fain would I see, as thou Thyself declar'st it, Sovereign Lord!
The likeness of that glory of Thy Form
Wholly revealed. O Thou Divinest One!
If this can be, if I may bear the sight,
Make Thyself visible, Lord of all prayers!
Show me Thy very self, the Eternal God!

Krishna replies:
Gaze, then, thou Son of Pritha! I manifest for thee
Those hundred thousand thousand shapes that clothe my mystery:
I show thee all my semblances, infinite, rich, divine,
My changeful hues, my countless forms. See! in this face of mine,
Wonders unnumbered, Indian Prince! revealed to none save thee.
Behold! this is the Universe!—Look! what is live and dead
I gather all in one—in Me! Gaze, as thy lips have said,
On God Eternal, Very God! See Me! see what then prayest!

All theories in which created things are based in sensuous desire and
love, or judgment from observation, claim that unfoldment is greater than
its source; and greater importance is attached to effect than to cause.
Greater importance is attached to the creature than to the Creator. Greater
importance is attached to *becoming* in the future than to *being* in the present.

The theory of evolution and progression from a lower to a higher
plane (also of Karma) is that one effect becomes the source of another
effect; thus effect is worshiped and served instead of the ONE which produces the effect — the one holy Spirit of Mind, of Intelligence.

These theories ignore the creative power of the one Infinite Substance
everywhere present. The advocates of these theories have accepted effect

to be cause. Furthermore, they have accepted effect to have power over them, even to be the Creator and reality of being. So, their claim amounts to this, that we are made from many experiences resulting from action based in effect and a supposed physical cause.

All of these theories are a striving to become, and are void of the *realization of being.* Until their advocates see this and accept themselves to be the life which *was, is, and evermore shall be,* they will grope along mentally, around and around in a wheel of effect. It is not possible for one to be the cause of his experience if he is made by and is the result of his experience — particularly, if it is something to be overcome. The claim that we are the result of experience gives us no power whatever *to express being* or *to be the cause of our experience.*

There is nothing Godly but what is like him; he is not something that resulted from his works, neither does he evolve or progress from a lower to a higher plane. His knowledge is not gained from experience; but, instead, all his works are done in truth and are the product of knowledge of what he is. Is it any wonder that those who advocate personal re-incarnation should consider re-incarnation a punishment?

CHRIST CONSCIOUSNESS

Let us consider how free we are in truth, the glorious Gospel of Pure Being, lived and taught by the Christ. The word is **with** God **and is** God—is always God. This word which is God is incarnated (or expressed) in all living; nothing is made without it. It is manifested in form and dwells among us; of its fullness have ye all received. It is God who is the true light that lighteth heaven and earth and all things therein. Yes, He lights all visibility; this WORD *is the lamb that taketh away the sin of the world.*

There is never a time when the whole earth and all visible expression of life is not full of divine grace and truth. The word which is God —in the beginning and at this time — does not express itself according to the belief of physical causation. It is God who is expressing himself within himself and unto himself. Creation, therefore, is not of the will of the flesh, nor of man — but of God.

"The law was given by Moses, but grace and truth came by Jesus Christ." The very fact that there is but one substance proves that there is but one salvation, which lies in the truth of our being at one with the **One all** at this time.

We are to conclude that since there is but one God, there is but one supreme source and cause. Hence it is unsafe and unsound to believe in many causes; to have many conceptions is a state of confusion. To know the truth of our existence is to know that it is the living word, the word which is life to all our flesh. It is to know that our whole body is life, and we can say, "whatever flesh we bear, never again shall we take on its load." In truth our bodies are not burdens; we are not heavy-laden because of them. We should not consider them servants or slaves.

It is the Spirit that knows the things of the Spirit; there is no man that can know the things of God save the spirit of God within him. The brain is not the cause of true thinking; the brain and true thinking are both effects of one cause.

Since incarnation is God expressed in all the universe, at this time, is there any truth in personal re-incarnation, Darwin's theory of evolution, or Karma?

With the view of creation that "incarnation is God expressed," it is clear that God is expressing, incarnating, himself in an endless process; it is clear that in truth we are all living after the order of Melchizedek — as the son of the most high over his own house — co-existent and co-eternal with God. The conclusion is that Infinite power has always expressed itself perfectly in all, and it will never express itself otherwise.

The only true meaning of the word re-incarnation is REPETITION, a continuing of incarnation; hence, in using the word we should consider that God, being yesterday, to-day and forever the same, is ever creating. What he once did he is now doing, for God is the only source and cause anywhere present. There is no expression in bodily form apart from him, none that he is not the cause and life of.

The truth, therefore, that makes free is, that there is no form but the form of God. "Though being in the form of God he thought it not robbery to be equal with God." The Gospel of St. John and the Spiritual Monism, which natural scientists are accepting, are included in Divine Science, the direct expression of God in creation.

There is no truth in the theory that one person re-embodies in another; worldly love and desire are not the cause of our being here. There is no truth in the claim that the higher can be evolved from the lower, or that any effect can be superior to its cause, or that we are the result of our thoughts or experiences. These theories have other gods before Me — gods that are ever becoming greater than what they are — ever striving to attain something beyond their grasp, ever seeking to become something that they are not. Thus, through vain effort, they subject their existence to hope (which makes the heart sick) with vanity of personal effort.

When once it is seen that the all is one spirit and substance, there is no objective universe; the universe is seen to be within its source and cause. This is *transfiguration* and *translation of form*. It is now clear that man is the epitome of the universe, the microcosm of the macrocosm. It is also evident that the opinions and beliefs generally called "man" are not MAN. It is evident that there never was a man to God who was not his own image and likeness.

It is not by works that we are whole (lest any man should boast), for we (individually) are God's workmanship, created as sons and daughters unto all good things. In the knowledge of Divine Science we no longer see ourselves twain; there is not even a veil between the Holy Spirit and the body. We are one substance throughout. No commandments or ordinances are imposed upon us; we are free, forever free, in the glory of at-one-ment.

God-incarnation is Spirit expressed, and what is begotten of Spirit is spirit. Spirit expresses itself, not in time but in eternity; Spirit expresses itself, not in place but within Itself.

Personal re-incarnation is purely suppositional; there is no evidence that the claim is true. It is based in the theory that God is not eternally perfect, that it is possible for Him to express an imperfect creation, and that his creation through its own efforts must become perfect, only then returning to God its source. No person ever re-embodied as another person; to do so, would be to take the Creator's work out of God's hands. Re-incarnation of personality, evolution and Karma, are a network of theories without principle or God as a foundation, hence without any good whatsoever.

The consciousness of Truth, of God-and-God-manifest being the ALL is — in Reality — the Karma-less condition to which all believers in Karma hope to attain (at some future time in some far away place). Conversely, the Truth that this Karma-less state of being is "here and now" is rejected and a suppositional state "of ceaselessly becoming what they are not" is accepted. In these beliefs, the eternal Omniscience, Omnipotence, and Omnipresence of God is ignored.

To KNOWLEDGE these theories do not exist. Knowledge recognizes God to be the same at all times, KNOWLEDGE recognizes that the All is God the creator and his infinite creation.

There is no incarnation but God expressed.

Ed. note: Cramer exhibits a renewed vitality in the 1902-1903 Volume Fifteen, possibly because the entire nation-wide network seems to be thriving, despite the IDSA's demise. As the Cramers make plans for an extensive tour two years later, Charles comments that everything (arrangements for speaking and healing) are falling into place, for "the pioneer work is finished."

Acceptable Time.

Now is the accepted time.—II Cor., 6 : 2.

THEY who are engaged in fulfilling law are about the Father's business, and resist not.

A blessed new time—new and living way, is the never ending Now—always here in its fulness ; ever present. alike with all without respect to person ; always the same, yet ever showing an infinite variety of beauty in nature. He who does not indulge procrastination nor retrospection, but abides in the ever present can realize the fulness of Truth, even

> Faith unwavering, walking in light ;
> Life never failing, happy and bright.
> Love ever perfect, knowing no fear,
> Which insures each one an endless New Year.

The old Italian god, Janus—the supposed deity with two faces, one looking into the past at what has been the other looking into the future at what is to be—caused men to call the first month of the year January. In Divine Science, father time has no place but in the Father-hood of God. The unfailing presence of God and the ever abiding now are one.

In the blessed now we, sons and daughters of infinity, are looking to the truth as it is in the present. What has man eternal, as endless life or unlimited soul, to do with past or future ? Who are we that we should be thought subject to time, to the calendar, to days or to years ? Who is man—male and female—that he should be the user of time and yet be its subject ? Friends, it is a mistake to suppose that we are subject to time and must succumb to what we are capable of intelligently calculating. Let us begin where all things begin, in God, and calculate according to the ever new now, and have no regrets for what has been and no longings for what is to be, but make the most of what is at the present time. Know this, that what was and what shall be is *now*, and that we are free with the liberty of all that is self-existing.

Now is the accepted time : this is true to the creator, to you, to me, and to all people. A thing accepted is a thing admitted or received to be true. Now we admit and receive it to be true, that there is no time but the now.

In the wonderful record of Genesis, seven days are used to indicate the truth of all time ; the week stands for a continuation and constant repetition of the eternal now. With the ending of the seventh day, the first begins without the slightest cessation of the endless now. So the week instead of extending over certain ages of time, "glacial periods," etc., stands for all time. What occurred in the past, according to the Genesis of creation, is taking place now and shall ever continue to take place. It is God who creates heaven and earth, who says let there be light, who sees the light, who calls it day ; who sees the darkness on the face and calls it night. It is God who says let there be a firmament, who says let it divide the waters from the waters, who makes the firmament and divides the waters, and calls the firmament heaven : who says let the waters be gathered together into one place and let the dry land appear. It is God who calls the gathering together of the waters seas, and the dry land earth, etc. It is God who sees that all this is so—His word is Truth—and pronounces it good. So, when we call living things good and very good, it is God speaking. Our pronouncing are his words : such are the words that are "life to those who find them and health to all their flesh."

Twelve months is another symbol of the all time Now, that is used in the Scriptures. The tree of Life in the midst of the garden of God is Life itself in the midst of all created things. This Tree of Life is spoken of in Revelations as bearing all manner of fruit, twelve months in the year; this means that life bears fruit in creation continually. We are building the body anew constantly; we appropriate from the food of which we partake, from the air we breathe, from the atmosphere in which we live, and we express from the spirit of God in whom we have being, to make new blood, new tissue, muscles and bones ; we are growing new nails and hair all the time, and our bodies are ever new, ever young, ever composed of indestructible substance, animated and lived by the light of pure intelligence : if we do not see them so, then our eyes are not single to truth ; the thing for us to do in this case is to single them to truth so that we can see the body full of light—that true light, which is life, spoken of in the first chapter of St. John as being with God and as being God.

Glorious age ! this eternal *now ;* happy are we who are alive to see it. More blessed this glorious era than the past or the future. Now is a true jubilee time ; it contains what has been and what will be.

Since ever man lived, reasoned and thought,
   Now for action and now for rest,
   Brings forth within him the strongest and best,
And causes him to find the good he has sought.

This is faith in the All as sure and true. Come! Now is the accepted time, to-day is salvation ours. Let us endeavor to think with the eternal and live the blessed now spiritually, in the springtime, with the re-birth of all things; the summer and full fruitage; the fall upon the ingathering; and the winter in sweet comfort and rest. What a fulness of comfort is ours. "I am come not to destroy but to fulfill"—fill full all things now.

All hail thou Now that's apparelled so bright;
   Thou spring'st like a youth from eternity's breast,
Richest gift of God! abiding presence of light,
   Thy full acceptance is our unfailing health.

Let us in this blessed time of our Lord (Life) know with Ruskin, "There is no wealth but Life,—including all its power of love and joy, admiration and progress; that man is richest, having projected the functions of his own life to the utmost, exerts the most powerful influence—and still lives on." Blessed words, no wealth but life, without it what? Nothing.

Literally speaking, this HARMONY represents the last of the first quarter of our glad new year of 1903, but it is the middle or end of the sixth month of the HARMONY year. Let every reader realize that now is the only time that they can enjoy the full measure of the HARMONY taught in its pages.

We cannot live where the All Good is not, where Life is not, where Love is not, where Holiness is not, where the One All is not.

"This is a blessed day!
I am fired and inspired with the glory of the Omnipresent One.
I am included in the Great Method and Plan of the Universe.
The Past and the Present have melted into the Blessed Now!
My soul fills and thrills with the Eternal Spirit!
My heart pulsates with Love and Joy!
My mind is cool, calm and serene.
I am with God and His people!
Blessed day!"
Now is the accepted time.
Now the grace of God is not received in vain, and we approve ourselves in all things Now as the ministers of the All Good.

In this " new and living way " which has dawned alike for us all, let us be a unit in the realization that we now live in the great forever. During the past year we have had ample opportunity to give true expression to our Being, and to render true service to each other. The principle of unity has been so deeply appreciated, so earnestly cherished in our hearts as Divine Scientists, that I am encouraged to persevere in the ongoing of our great work with renewed energy.

I am able to look abroad over the great kingdom containing God's humanity and to see in many hearts the gratitude felt for the light that has dawned to them from living their knowledge of Divine Science. All who are truly interested in Science feel that their lives have been made brighter, their yoke easier and burdens lighter from their knowledge of Being.

Through living the law of unity we are able to experience the working of Divine Love unto victory in overcoming seeming weakness and unfaithfulness. We feel to-day that as Divine Science stands for the unity of the whole it is the fulfilling of all law and prophecy for humanity. Therefore, wherever it gets a foothold, it is there to stay. The awakened alone can realize its depth and power ; for it is coming forth from within into the hearts of the people.

I feel the heartbeat of sympathy and love from all who are interested in our glorious cause, who desire to uphold and help its spread throughout the land. We have done our best, considering we have been looking backward and forward, and have forgotten the present, to extend " The glad tidings of great joy ;" but the acknowledgment of our united effort is helpful to all and is far reaching in its influence for good.

It is possible for each Divine Scientist to experience more of the all-powerful omnipresent good, and this will be done through our remaining conscious of the solidarity of our knowledge of truth and our love for the support of the cause of Science.

We would speak the word now for those who need to recognize their good and to make practical their truth, that it may enter their hearts from the inner side and express the spirit of truth. Our words for them may not be for what they think they need, but they will be for the fulfilment of every necessity. Lift up your heads, Oh, children of God, and behold the beauty and goodness there is everywhere for you. An inheritance which is God, think of it ! Wonderful, wonderful. A Father or Parent source that is all in all, nothing higher, over or above, or that can subject it in any way, and such a state of being is our inheritance.

Let us freely use our inheritance ; that is, think, speak and act as if it were ours now. When we think the days round out into weeks, and weeks into months, and months into years, we should pause and remember the accepted time, the day of salvation.

Now is the time to remain young, to appear so, to show out health and happiness and to show out the spirit of unity.

BROTHERHOOD.

"A river went out of Eden to water the garden.

DEEP DOWN within the being of every one is a well, whose spring is the Eternal Principle of self-demonstration, so that all manifest good is an out-flow of what is potential therein, and not an inflowing ; and whenever we will, we may drink of its pure, vital water, and cease to thirst ; letting the innate goodness of eternal self-hood flow out in our relations to one another, will quench thirst for righteousness. All have drank, but if some remain thirsty and parched, they have had but a sup of this water of Life, and need to know that as many times as they come to this well to *draw* and *drink*, they will *thirst again.*

The woman of Samaria, ignorant of what constitutes the gift of God, said : " Sir, thou hast nothing to draw with, and the well is deep ; from whence, then, hast thou this living water ?" True, Jesus, the Christ, the son of the living God, has nothing to draw with, and the well is deep, and those of us who have sought to approach the depth of Infinite and Omnipresent Life from time to time, and draw from it, have thirsted again.

Jesus answered and said unto her : " Whosoever drinketh of this water, shall thirst again." The individual can no more draw from the Infinite God, or Good, to satisfy his thirst after righteousness, than can he command God to obey, and compel His service. Of a truth, none of us have any power whatever, with which to draw from the well of living waters.

" Blessed are they which do hunger and thirst after righteousness, for they shall be filled." So to-day we come to the well of living waters, not believing that we can drink of its waters by drawing upon them, but that we may demonstrate something of the true way of Life, of which Jesus would have each one know—I Am. In this heavenly place are we assembled, seeking not some transitory condition, that has no destiny but to progress toward the Eternal.

"For whosoever drinketh of this water, shall thirst again." But instead, thereof, are we seeking to demonstrate the Truth of our eternal self-hood in God ; to let that which is the power and possibility of Eternal Life spring up within our hearts and thoughts into everlasting life, and flow out in every word and deed.

"Whosoever shall drink of the water that *I shall give him*, shall never thirst ;" and why ? This drinking is self-revealment, the out-flow of a self-hood which is God-hood—the Supreme. What is this water, this principle of self-demonstration ? Is it not Love ? And Love is with God, and is God. This fountain of Love is what each one wants to find, though he knows it not.

"But the water that I shall give him, shall be *in* him a well of water." So it is to be understood that what is given comes forth of that which shall be ever within us, and not from without. Now let us consider the matter of the " I " a little further ; Jesus said : "If thou knewest the gift of God, and who it is that saith unto thee : ' Give me to drink,' thou wouldst have asked of him, and he would have given thee living water." To know the gift of God, is to know Eternal Life, and to know the Christ, is to know that I am life, and am the one who speaks. He who knows this Truth has the well of living water within himself.

Christ said : "Give me to drink," for the purpose of opening the conversation that followed, that he might instruct the woman of Samaria in the Truth of Being ; and show her that it is right for us to have dealings with each other, and that drawing unto one's self, and partaking of that which is believed to have been drawn, is a *material act*, and satisfies not—the effect is temporal ; but would we worship in Spirit, and in Truth, and enjoy the out-flow of the Truth of Being, whose nature is Love, we must abide therein. Being is before doing. The query in the thoughts of many at the present time is, that " if we cannot draw upon the Infinite, and use God, or if He does not serve us, how is it that we have life, intelligence, and power ?" Such do not recognize the truth of the gift of God for themselves, and that " As the Father hath Life in Himself, just so has *He given* to the *Son* to have Life in himself ; and " Because I—the Christ—live, ye shall live also."

The idea that we can draw to ourselves from God, and " from every Source, whatsoever," would make Him subject to desire, which is, virtually, a claim that there is materiality which can draw to itself spirituality ; for if that which expects to draw from a Spiritual Source is not spiritual, it is attempting to draw from a Source that is foreign to, and unlike itself ; and if it is spiritual, it is already at-one with, and like the Source it would draw from, and is, therefore, under no necessity of drawing. Know this, that you can truly say : " I am Eternal Life."

Love is sought in father and mother, and in children, and is found and enjoyed because it is there ; but they who find love alone in their kinfolk, have the first practical lessons of love. For the home is the center from which God's loving work is done for the world, and the relationship and ties of the home must be extended to the whole race of mankind, as we learn to worship in Spirit, and in Truth. This is the actualization of the principle of Brotherhood, based in the Fatherhood of God.

Let each and every mother know that all generations shall call " me " blessed, for with her motherhood found in Being, and mother heart, has she blessed the race. Nothing shall block the avenue of her love for the people of God. This is not the old, but the new view of the true and ever-living mother. Those who have learned the truth of their own God-nature, let them not wait, or sigh for a higher realization, but proclaim what a blessed thing it is for us to dwell together in the unity of the Spirit, having but one Father, and but one abiding-place; One, in whom all have Being, from whom flows "peace like a river."

In brotherhood based in the Fatherhood of God, is perfect equality, in which we learn what is meant by the words : " He that loveth father or mother more than Me, is not worthy of Me." Here a chord is touched within, that to the ordinary sense of things has not hitherto freely vibrated, and the first query is : shall this love that has been almost all-absorbing, be changed into indifference and neglect ? Such queries arise with every presentation of Truth that is fuller than what has been previously accepted. On the other hand, the love for father and mother is to be more deeply rooted, and filled with the understanding of reality and equality. The "Me" is the Christ of God, the Eternal Life of father, mother, sister, and brother—of every creature. All are commanded to love God with all their heart, and their neighbor as themselves; not more, but just the same. So father and mother are to be loved as " The Me," and not more. To exalt them in thought above " Me," is to depreciate Eternal Life, and the Law of the Lord, which is equality.

The Christ love, which springs up in us as a well of living, vitalizing water, equalizes and harmonizes all things. It is not less than personal love, but is that Self-love which includes all of the individual and personal demonstrations of itself toward father and mother, and friends. It thinks only of what is right in the sight of the Truth of the Infinitude of God, for all who are embraced, with never a thought of using them as instruments of pleasure or indulgence ; but to give them that living water that shall be in them, springing up into everlasting Life. This is the principle of true brotherhood, the full liberty to act out the Holiness of Being, knowing that in freedom alone doth God direct.

We seek not to establish a new brotherhood, but seek rather to unveil and make known the one, to all people, that is already established in truth, and that there is no brotherhood that is not already within God—the Omnipresent. Blessed love is that which space cannot deprive of the privilege of bestowing blessings and blessings upon humanity. This is the holy love that will reveal itself within all. It is, to-day, partially understood in all countries ; not fully grasped, for some are asking for more light, seeking still to know the basis that is so apparent to Divine Scientists.

A mighty wave of light, or life, the nature of which is Love, is sweeping through the mentality of humanity, and those who fall into the stream will rise, and be made to sail above the waters of emotion, or abide in the consciousness of Infinite Being. Then will they know that they are as the son over his own house ; that they are the well of water. In other words, they are Eternal Being, which is self-manifesting. They draw from no Source beyond themselves, for their Being is in God. "And I, if I be lifted up from the earth will draw all unto me."

Conclusion.

What is the highest and only true conception of the only principle of Brotherhood ? Friends, it is the Fatherhood of God ; it is more than the love of humanity, as that phrase is generally understood.

In giving alms, aiding the organizations formed for the alleviation of undesired conditions, studying the ways and means of advancing the cause of Truth, we do well, for they all testify of the Love of God in our hearts ; but the Love which makes us a brotherhood, and is God, warms and lights the person from within. This Love can find companionship with God in every living creature. It can make each one know its own Divinity. This Love of God radiated in full in Jesus, the Christ, when he looked upon the multitude, and was moved with compassion. What a depth of meaning in a single word—Compassion !

In this love for the multitude, there are no lines of separation because of wealth, education, worldly position, and reputation ; no recognition of sex, no distinction made between the people of God. Love has compassion for the multitude. This principle of Love being manifest of God in each one of us, is the light that lighteth all. This great, selfless Love banishes all claims of sin, sickness, or death, and reveals Heaven on earth. It is the realization of the union of Father and son, and knowing all life to be one. It is knowing "I am not a servant, but the son," radiating the light, and glorifying the life of the Infinite One. It is being the One who is filled with love for all. Let us stand firm and immovable in the Truth that "I and my Father are one," and that the great principle of the brotherhood of man is inherent within us, and be the perfect idea of God : The Eden, out of which flows the river to water the garden.

Office of Thought and Flaming Sword.

WE MUST ever bless the name of Him who said : "I am Truth and I am Life ;" for that declaration was made for each one of us ; that each one might speak the same for himself.

Jesus the Christ is universal, or it would not have been said He is the "First born of every creature," and that there is "No other name under heaven by which men can be saved." Also " of whom the whole family in heaven and earth are named."

To understand the office of thought, it is essential that one's identity be placed aright ; identity means reality, or Being that is self-existing. Thought will always be afloat ; that is, what is usually called thought, will be uncontrolled until the unchanging principle of Being is made the basis and standard of thought. Why should one think death instead of life ; think sickness instead of health ; think misery instead of happiness ; think poverty instead of supply ; think desire instead of fulfilment ; or discord instead of harmony ? But for the erroneous belief of separation from the All Good, which includes these things, and the supposition that there are two powers the reverse of each other, to which we are subject.

" Where your treasure is there will your heart be also." The treasure of our existence, the abundant wealth always in store for us, is our Being, the true nature of what the I is. This is the treasure that is laid up in heaven, " where neither moth nor rust doth corrupt ; where thieves (taking of others instead of being) do not break through nor steal." So, the true value is placed upon Being; its wealth is revealed, and there the heart is also. Henceforth there is no conflict between wealth and poverty, health and disease, for the treasure house of all good things is yourself.

" The light of the body is the eye ; if therefore thine eye be single, the whole body shall be full of light. But if thine eye be evil, thy whole body shall be full of darkness." The eye being the light of the body, is a symbol of the Truth that the I which is single is the true light which Jesus said I am, and which he told His disciples they were. So, we have only to be thankful that our I is single, and is the true light of mentality, and our bodily existence. " If thine eye be evil (if the I be double or dual) thy whole body shall be full of darkness." Therefore, as long as we claim that our Being is identical with good and evil, we are claiming that it is double, which is false to the truth that it is single, and is the reverse of light or pure intelligence. The supposition that our being is identical with God and devil, or good and evil, is trying to serve God and mammon ; we cannot serve two masters, no more could we be identical with two sources.

Claiming to think from without in, is placing one's self separate from the Creator and creation. It is claiming to be body and to stand alone as personality, which means hoping to become Life eternal, Spirit immortal, Being unlimited, at some future time. From this supposed identity, thought reasons about becoming by and by ; about evolving from a lower to a higher consciousness ; and progressing onward and upward forever toward a source that can never be attained, and which always eludes its grasp. These theories are not satisfying. They are not comforting, because they are not the Spirit of Truth.

Hope deferred makes the heart sick. Postponement impairs circulation and bodily activity. A desire to go toward a source that cannot be obtained, gives a sense of weakness. Longing to be what always eludes our grasp, causes a feeling of helplessness. Believing that unfoldment is higher than the unfolder, or that which is evolved in thought, consciousness, or body, is superior to what it is evolved from, is the pride of egotism, which has no existence in Truth. It is clear, therefore, that this basis is not the rock-foundation of principle from which to evolve or reveal the singleness and totality of the I am, which knows " Beside me there is none other."

They who reason from the above standpoint are habitually " taking thought for their life, what they shall eat and what they shall drink." Thinking to make life by what is taken in at the mouth. Thus do they overlook the fact that Life has made the body and all the food of which we partake, and that the Law of Expression works from within out ; also that " man does not live by bread alone, but by every word that proceedeth out of the mouth of God." To suppose that one can prolong Life, sustain Life by food, or that it can be made or marred by thought, is to misconceive the nature of

Life. There is no life that is not eternal ; no Life in which there is death ; none but what has expressed the universe of form, and that holds it in its loving embrace, knowing it to be good and very good. Let us love the statement, "I am Life."

There is another position from which some make an effort to think truthfully, which is the medium ground, or number two, in the Law of Expression. They look within, to the silent, invisible omnipresence, and conceive of its unchangeableness ; that in its nature there are no degrees, variations nor moods ; that it is without limitation or environment. Then they look without and judge from observation, observing change and variety, and see no connection whatever between the invisible and the visible ; the silence and the oral word, or the Spirit and body. So, they in thought, deny the body and all visibility ; hence, with them there is always a separation or suppositional belief, that there are two minds that are the reverse of each other ; hence, two sources, and either can be a basis for thinking and outward demonstration. This double-faced attitude can only reason about the within and about the without ; so, they who place their identity in the medium plane, do not claim to be either the within or the without. They say you cannot be God, for that would be sacrilege ; and you cannot be the visible, for it is mortal, sinful, and is not of God. It is evident that this position is not a rock foundation of unchangeable Being, from which to evolve true thought, pure philosophy, or Divine Science. In the above methods of reasoning, on account of the position in which they have placed man, they are naturally troubled in thought, and are seeking numerous methods by which they hope to control thought, gain concentration and self-poise.

In Divine Science there is but one view-point from which to see the truth of Being, the truth of thought and word ; that view-point is Being itself. Being is self-existing, has always been, is now, and will always be. One who refuses to identify himself with error of belief, either in Spirit, soul or body, or in Being, doing or result, and identifies himself wholly as one God, acting and producing a result, has singled his I to truth. He then knows that he is the thinker, and that what he thinks does not make him ; but his thought testifies of the truth of what he is, and that he is Life. The question, therefore, has been wisely asked : "Is not the Life more than meat, and the body than raiment ?"

In the light of pure intelligence, the knowledge of Divine Science, one may ask : "Which of you by taking thought (for your life) can add one cubit to his stature ?" Therefore, we take no thought, what shall we eat or what shall we drink, thinking to make, sustain or prolong life. The gentiles (those not recognizing life as eternal or Being as self-existing) reason as if Life was made by doing, and controlled by thought. We have sought the kingdom of God and his righteousness, and have found ; and in our finding all things that our Father knows we have need of are added.

Being or Life is first in order in the three-fold nature of the One All.

The following diagram illustrates the order of the Law of Expression :

1. Creator	= Being	= Spirit	= Mind.
2. Creative action	= Doing	= Soul	= Mentality.
3. Creation	= Result	= Body	= Visibility.

As the law of God works from within out, it is inherent in Number One, its action is Number Two, and the result of its action is Number Three. Number Two or Number Three cannot work to produce an expression from the visible to the invisible. Expression takes place always and everywhere in the above order. Therefore, neither thought nor word can make nor mar Life or Being.

You naturally ask at this point if the above is true, how can healing be done by the power of thought, or how can people help themselves by thinking true thoughts, the reverse of error ? We can heal by the power that we put into thought, and demonstrate by means of thought because it is that by which we image forth the perfection of Being ; that by which we bear witness of the Truth of the very nature of the I that is single. The I that is Number One in the diagram being Infinite, it does all when it gives expression to Itself in thought and word, or in mentality and visible form. As sure as one thinks from the standpoint of Being, he thinks that which embodies his nature, and his thought finds an outward expression in form because the law works from within out. He no longer thinks about the within and about the without, but he thinks himself, the innermost, into expression, which is called the outermost. This is the order by which Divine Science healing is done ; this order is universal and will work for any one who will take the right position and maintain it, and hold his own thought and word in their divine order and relationship to himself ; or by seeing the inseparability of the above Trinity.

We think life because we are Life ; we think truth because we are Truth; we think wholeness because we are Whole ; we think love because we are Love ; just so do we think health because we are Health. Health is just as unchangeable, just as unfailing, and as incapable of diminishing as is Life. To realize this we must let it be so to us in thought. Our knowledge is our realization, therefore the reader of this should say: I realize, because I know. I now realize the truth of Being, and the unity of the whole is my freedom.

FLAMING SWORD.

"And the Lord God said, Behold, the man is become as one of us, to know good and evil." "One of us" does not mean the unity of God; it means division, based in the habit of identifying self with good and evil—with God, and with beliefs and opinions that fall short of what God is. "Now, lest he put forth his hand and take also of the tree of Life, and eat, and live forever;"

"Therefore the Lord God sent him forth from the Garden of Eden, to till the ground from whence he was taken."

Lest the suppositional man of belief and opinion who assumes two natures—one good and the other evil—eat of the tree of Life and live forever, that state of belief is not in the Garden of God, so the man who claims it is is put to work, as it were, to till the ground. The ground from whence he was taken is Totality, Supreme Being, God, the One All. All who believe in dualism must till this ground in order to live, or earn bread by the sweat of their brow, until they return to it. When they return to it they will enjoy the Christ-consciousness that I am the bread of life, and work all things together for good from the standpoint of the Truth that "I and my Father are One." They will know that all things are theirs, and of all that is theirs they can lose nothing. Then tilling, toiling and spinning cease. They take no thought for their Life, and are in a position to consider how the lilies grow.

Lord God, is God living in man. He is also man identical with God. He it is who drives out the suppositional self of dualism, and when he has done so he places Cherubims, or blessings, and a flaming sword, which is the word of Truth, at the east of the Garden of Eden. East of the Garden of Eden, means Being, or Life. Blessings are the expressions that are enjoyed by maintaining the idea of God as our Being. The Word of Truth which turns every way, to keep the way of the tree of Life, is speaking Truth always, regardless of conditions and circumstances.

The tree of Life is a symbol of Life itself. A tree is composed of roots, body and branches; the roots and ground represent our Being in God; the Body represents our mentality, through which our Being nourishes the outer; and the body composed of many members is symbolized in the branches.

In Divine Science we speak the Truth of our Being, of our mentality, and of our visible body, and admit of no error of belief in either. No belief of duality or separation can enter in, or in any way touch our Being. This Truth is the Flaming Sword that turns every way, to keep the way of the tree of Life. It keeps Being, mentality and visible form in a state of unity, and as one perfect whole.

We have returned to the ground, and are speaking from the standpoint of Supreme Being; and are in charge of our mentality and body. Hence, we know nothing but divine order.   M. E. CRAMER.

Spiritual Definitions.

THE following definitions are published for the purpose of aiding in the study of Divine Science :

Divine Science interprets God as the One All, beside whom there is none, before whom there is none ; in whom all creation lives and moves and has its being. The self-existing One, inclusive of Creator, creative action and creation. It teaches that God's Omnipresence proves that divine consciousness or intelligence, power or love, is equally everywhere in all things. There is no apartness, degrees or portions to the One All. It is unlimited, inseparable, absolutely everywhere in its fulness at all times. No more of Intelligence or power in one place than in another. This is realized only by being God and abiding in Him as the All. It is never to be realized by believing we are different in nature from Him, or by trying to be something beside the One All. God is not the Infinite without including creation. The Infinite is both Creator and creation. As God alone is before He creates, there is no intelligent attitude for man to take, but that he is before he is expressed in form, and is the " Word " that is with God and is God. There is no mortal being or evil power   There are no opposites to the Divine Attributes.

Adam :—The Hebrew word Ahdam—Adam, is not merely the name of one person, but, like the Greek Anthropos and the Latin Homo, it is the class name of a genus whose real nature it portrays.

The name of Adam was given to man—male and female ; in the day (pure consciousness) in which God created man, in the likeness of God made he him : male and female created he them ; and called their name Adam.— Genesis v : 1, 2.

The name Adam has three principal significations : They are all sourced in Being, as shown in our Genesis manuscript lessons. The meaning of each is at one with Adam, the image and likeness of God. It stands for man's being in God, and existing in His image and likeness. (See sixth manuscript lesson.) Jesus of Nazareth was in realization the second Adam. In Spirit and in Truth we are all Adam, the perfect image and likeness of a perfect God.

Beginning :—Means source, origin ; " I am " the source and origin of all things. So, " I am the beginning." Being acts and produces or images forth, within itself, what it contains.

Firmament :—Means heaven ; the real state of Being expressed in creative action and creation. It is that state in which there is no sorrow, crying nor pain. It is at hand. It is within you.

Day :—Means Light, Knowledge, Consciousness, Intelligence.

Night :—Means darkness, shadow, believing effect to be Cause.

Evening :—Means to mix, to mingle, to blend.

Morning :—Birth ; coming forth afresh.

Earth :—A name for form, " dry land;" what is seen with the eye, and is apparent to the senses.

One, or First Day :—Stands for Totality, the All.

Two, or Second Day :—Means to do, action, repetition, continuation of the same.

Three, or Third Day :—Is the rule by which everything is done that is done. It is "The Law of Expression." In Genesis it particularly speaks of result, creation, the realm of visibility.

Man, male and female :—God's image and likeness.

Image and Likeness :—Means God expressed in men and women, the fulness of His nature imaged forth in them. In Being, Man is like God ; he is wholly divine.

Dominion :—Dominion is oneness and equality with all that is ; with God as Creator, creative action and creation. That state where the Lion and Lamb lie down together and the child innocence leads them.

Beholding everything as good and very good, is knowing creation to be like and at one with God : even Himself expressed.

(*To be Continued.*)

What to Conquer.

I do not ask for any crown
But that which all may win :
Nor try to conquer any world
Except the one within.
Be Thou my guide until I find,
Led by a tender hand,
The happy kingdom in myself,
And dare to take command.

—*Louisa M. Alcott.*

Spiritual Definitions.

FOURTH DAY—Perfect existence. It means that as one, even the Christ, came forth, just so does everything come forth. Never a time when the one was not, and when there was other than one Divine law, order, or method. Christ has always been with us, and will ever be. Before Abraham was expressed, all that is or ever will be was. What is self-existing is the I Am. The outer helps, so-called, we use in general cultivation, if truly helps are ordered of the One All ; that is, they accord perfectly with Divine law or order. So all things are worked together for good in God.

FIFTH DAY—Means Law. "The waters" bringing forth abundantly. Life revealing its possibilities in all living things that have life.

SIXTH DAY—Fixed ; finished ; that which is so ; eternally the same : man, male and female, God's image and likeness. "No variation or shadow of turning." Jesus, the Christ—the annointed—the only begotten of God of every creature. The second Adam, so-called, just as the first who is God Himself revealed ; spotless and free.

SEVENTH DAY—Finished ; completed. It is Omnipresence ending all its work within itself where the work begins. There is no other place to end or finish any expression, to reveal any possibility ; or complete any undertaking. That this may be clearly seen and practically demonstrated, we should not forget that man is unlimited Mind, which is pure Consciousness and perfect Idea. So to work the law of Being, one must begin his every work within himself, proceed to a finish and retain it there, and thus maintain in consciousness the wholeness which he is. If he is anxiously concerned for the spiritual welfare of others, believing that their theories are inconsistent with their practice, thus giving people cause to think they are not living the Truth; the one so believing has departed from unity ; and in that regard is not attending to "the Father's business." It is not according to principle that we expect any good thing, except what is in us as Consciousness. When we begin to expect from others certain lines of mental conduct, wanting them to conform to certain rules in eating and sleeping, to bring them up to the standard which we claim people have a right to expect from them, we have forgotten that there are no others ; there is but One. It is our business to remember that to be God-like is to expect nothing but to demonstrate within ourselves, and to attend strictly to His business, which is attending to our own. Expectation, to be realized and appreciated, must be lived and proven within one's self and to his own consciousness.

We have no right, in Truth, to expect anything of others; we have the right only to expect that we will live the life and know the doctrine, and when we do we will cease setting up other gods made according to opinions and beliefs. We will know others as self, All as One.

GENESIS.

GENESIS in Latin and Greek, means to get; to be born. The Genesis of creation is the act of producing, giving birth or origin to anything; it means production; formation; origination.

The first book of the " Old Testament," so-called by the Greek translators from its containing the history of the creation of the world and mankind, is called Genesis.

Though some fragments claim a higher antiquity, Genesis is acknowledged to be the most ancient complete book in existence. Genesis, taken in connection with the four books that follow, is the foundation for a Theocracy based upon the idea of a single family—One God and one humanity.

There seems to be portions of more ancient narratives embodied by the writer in the book, as it now stands, whence some have supposed that the original narrative has been enlarged at various times : yet it is believed that the record in its present state is substantially that of Moses, with a few later additions made in the time of the monarchy.

Some commentators maintained that two quite distinct narratives have been interwoven together : the one, more ancient, in which the Deity is throughout designated by the general term Elohim—God ; while in the other He is called by the more mystic name of Jehovah—the Lord. The first is said to represent a general divine influence in the world ; the second, supernatural over-ruling power creating and directing it, and requiring admiration in return. These two portions are characterized as the Elohistic and Jehovistic ; the former teaching natural, the latter revealed religion.

There is, however, a unity throughout the Pentateuch, a unity which can only be ascribed satisfactorily to one writer. The literal record embodied in the entire book of Genesis is an account of events of over twenty-three hundred years.

" The general subject is creation, the decline of humanity through sin, and its capability of being reclaimed by communion with God, its maker. Hope and faith are kept alive by the example of a chosen few, who, through obedience to God, became heirs to the promised blessings which are continually postponed, with mercy to those who are sinful and a deepening of faith to those who are righteous."

Spiritually speaking, every creation of God must be seen to be good would we see truthfully ; for that is his way of seeing it. Man—Adam—male and female—so named in the day, or light, in which they are created, is to dress and keep the garden—the whole of creation—as God made it. He is to keep it, in his consciousness, as "good and very good." To do so means harmony in one's self and harmony with all surrounding things.

As all things were brought unto Adam, to see what he would call them, just so are all things brought unto each of us to see what he will call them, and each one must take the responsibility to himself or herself, not only of calling them by the names to which we are accustomed, but to call them "Good and very good," and pronounce nothing but the word of God for them : what we pronounce for another person or thing we proceed forth in, our words are our expressions, so, to be about our Father's business, we should affirm as does He.

Every person is supposed to know what is right to do, and what is right not to do ; from the standpoint of principle, the unity of spirit, the One All, we do know all things ; we are knowledge. So, we each are to keep the garden of creation in its generic good, its original and natural state of purity.

M. E. O.

A Consciousness of Unity.

Peace on earth is a consciousness of the wholeness, or oneness, of body (not our physical body only, but the body or "matter" of the universe) and Mind, or God. Every part of the material universe, and every part and organ of our own body is an instrument to express the thoughts of the Infinite Mind. God is manifest in every movement of the solar system and in every detail of our daily life. We are so much a part of the Whole Purpose that whatever operates elsewhere concerns us, and whatever we do affects all.

Herein lies the secret of harmonious conditions and of happiness, beauty and perfection. A consciousness of unity in the seeming diversity is the bond of completeness, and is the basis of love, and love is the fulfilling of the whole law of God.

GENESIS.

WHEN one is taught from childhood, or conceives later in life, that we are mortal now—nothing real at the present time, and cannot be while we remain in this world, it is apparent that true consciousness of Being—the Christ-consciousness—in which all know themselves to be Life eternal, is not acknowledged. They are indulging a belief that in Adam all die, and that all are under sin, and are indulging a mere hope that after death of the body all shall be made alive in Christ. This is the same old "Fall"— the fall from being wisdom, one with God, to becoming wise through partaking of good and evil, which means claiming one's self to be subject to opposing powers and taught by them. A sense of freedom could not result from this low mental attitude. Come up higher, "Come unto Me" we would say to all who read this, whoever you are, wherever you are, regardless of race, color or sex, irrespective of station in life.

The fourth chapter of Genesis is written in a manner to represent the dual belief of good and evil, and that God and man are separated and unlike each other in their nature.

When Eve bears Cain she believes she has gotten, or acquired a man from the Lord ; in this belief is the conception of separation.

When Adam and Eve, who stand for the whole race of mankind, have a desire to be made wise through contradictory experiences, they begin their effort to acquire wisdom, and therefore to acquire all that they are to have or possess. In so doing the mental method is inverted, and changed from that of being Divine dominion into that of acquiring it ; from that of being the "Life hid with Christ in God," into that of acquiring life, and getting a man from the Lord.

Cain, means ACQUIRED POSSESSION, and stands for the first begotten son of man. This is the first account we have of there being such a person as the son of man born of woman. Eve saying, " I have gotten a man from the Lord," or by the help of Jehovah, represents the general belief in separation from the Lord, and that all that we express or manifest, or in any way give birth to, we have acquired and gotten from a source outside of and beyond our selfhood. Cain is the son of man conceived of man, born of woman, but in some mysterious way " acquired or gotten of the Lord." He stands for all belief of acquired possession. *And she again bore his brother Abel.* Abel means meadow, breath. Breath stands for that which God breathes into man ; the expression of God in man. Meadow stands for the fact that he was an expressor of innate powers, a feeder of sheep. Spiritually speaking, to be a feeder of sheep, is to be the breath or life of the flock, the same is the good shepherd. Verily, there is but one life. To live and act this truth is to make the acceptable (Rom. xii : 1) offering unto the Lord. Cain was a tiller of the ground, just what the man was outside of the garden of Eden (Gen. iii : 23). "*And in the process of time* (Heb., at the end of days) *it came to pass that Cain brought of the fruit of the ground an offering unto the Lord.*

And Abel he also brought of the firstling of the flock (Heb., sheep or goats), *and of the fat thereof, and the Lord God had respect to Abel and his offering.*

But to Cain and his offering he had not respect."

Cain was, and is, a tiller of the ground, because of the belief that he was, and is, to get everything that he has, or is, in being, from some source outside of and foreign to himself. The tiller of the ground, in belief, is not the ground—Being—the seed sown (word spoken), nor the harvest reaped. He eats of that which is harvested (partakes of results), yet he claims not to be the harvest or results partaken of. He does not claim to be anything, not even the fruit of the ground, which he brings to the Lord for an offering. The idea is, although he acquires and owns the harvest, he does not place himself anywhere, or claim to be anything in bringing forth the harvest, but the tiller or laborer ; therefore his offering is outside of Being, as it were ; it it is not within the garden of Eden or the kingdom of God. This condition is a total denial of Being. Therefore the *Lord had no respect unto Cain and his offering.*

Abel brought the firstling of the flock, as it was, and is, in Being, in its first estate. *The fat thereof* is the fulness of Being. Faith is substance, and by faith Abel offered a more excellent sacrifice than Cain, shows that he made the offering, or offered the flock as the true substance of which it was composed. This is virtually offering the flock, or the entire creation, as the image of the invisible God (Col. i : 15). " Therefore unto Abel and to his offering the Lord had respect."

Be Ye Perfect.

WHEN we are children our desire is very strong to have our wants gratified ; we so feel our dependence upon our parents and friends that if they refuse to gratify our wants, or neglect to do so, we cry for the purpose of obtaining the thing wanted. As we grow older, and begin to wait upon ourselves, we feel ourselves less helpless, hence we cry less, yet at times we may beg of and tease our elders. As we develope manhood and womanhood, we take the responsibility of doing for ourselves and of making conditions in business that will provide for our wants ; thus we fulfil the desire for every necessity.

Spiritually speaking, under the old method of teaching, we have been taught to imitate the above ; we have been made to feel utterly helpless and to cry aloud to a God separate from ourselves for the good we desired. Then we have had the period, in belief, that it was necessary to beg or persuade God to have mercy upon us and to bestow upon us the good He alone possessed. In this state the belief is, " We must help ourselves as far as we can and God will do the rest." Now, in the true method of teaching, we realize that we must be men and women such as God creates, and no other kind ; then take the responsibility of acknowledging, claiming, receiving and enjoying our good, here and now. All things are good, therefore it means to enjoy all things. In this realization there is no crying, no beseeching, no begging ; the former beliefs and conditions have passed away and all things are new, and all things are ours. All things that are God's are ours, and all things that are ours are God's, for we are One.

This state of realization and affirmation is the one spoken of in Revelation where God " wipes away all tears from their eyes ; there is neither sorrow nor crying," poverty nor beseeching, for oneness is infinity and unlimited ability.

A short time ago I had a very clear dream just before waking in the morning, and while in a semi-conscious state. I saw twelve science workers sitting in a semi-circle on a platform in a public building. I was not conscious of an audience, except that I was listening to their expressions of desire. They commenced on the right end of the circle, and arose one at a time and gave expression to their hearts' desire of what they hoped or intended to demonstrate in the future. One said, " I hope to be able to demonstrate instant healing in all cases." Another desired " to be able to teach in such manner as to convict people of their false opinions and to convince them of the truth." The third one that arose said, "I want to demonstrate perfect health for myself before I attempt to do anything for others." The fourth one, filled with the power of holy spirit, eager for the opportunity to speak, and all aglow with the light of truth, said : "I will have nothing but perfect health now. I will have nothing but perfect demonstration." This seemed to be all that was essential to be spoken, so the meeting ended. Now, I personally know the parties who spoke ; they who were hoping are still hoping ; their hopes have not been actualized, while he who affirmed "I will have nothing else, there is nothing else to have," actualizes his affirmations daily ; he is the fulfilling of law and prophecy within himself, in his home and general work ; he is doing what he knows is right to do, and is leaving undone that which should not be done.

The above dream serves to illustrate the method of dressing and keeping the garden in our consciousness as good and very good ; and in actualizing our own heart's desire. We may affirm daily and hourly : "I hope to be well ;" "I hope to do instant healing ;" "I hope to teach in a manner to convict and convince ;" "I hope to realize that all is good and that all good is mine," but our affirmation will never work the law ; they are not the fulfiling of law ; they can never prove to be the fulfilling of law and prophecy. Why then subject your existence to postponement? Why make your body the target of the race habit of procrastinating? The Infinite One does not postpone its good ; it never makes future tense statements. Let us affirm : "Now I heal instantly ; now I teach truthfully and correctly ; now I demonstrate perfect health. Health is my real, true state ; it is manifest to me and I enjoy it perfectly." Then, let us be so true that we are always ready to think and say, "I have nothing else. I do not have the all good, plus evil ; success plus failure ; the fulness of what is plus an imaginary lack or want."

You are a man—you are a woman—whoever you are, and wherever you may be. You can exercise unlimited and unqualified possibilities, knowing that it is only the highest, so to speak, the absolute that evolves anything ; it evolves everything because it is all that truly is.

Would we have demonstrations in the now, we must be the demonstrator of them now, and be the thinker of true thoughts now, and be the speaker of true words and doer of right deeds.　　　　　　　　　M. E. C.

Divine Science, the World's True Regenerator.　　　W. J. COLVILLE.

| VOL. 10. | OCTOBER, 1897. | No. 1. |

In Earth as In Heaven.

*A*LL down through the ages it has been thought that the Kingdom of Heaven was a special place, located somewhere in space, where everything is beautiful, and everybody happy and satisfied. But now that Divine Science has proven the infinity and omnipresence of God, and we are conscious of His presence everywhere, we know that the special place where heaven is to be found is here, and the time for our enjoyment of it, is now. Now, the accepted time for the enjoyment of all that is good and real, can never be realized through postponement, for procrastination is the thief of time.

Jesus Christ—God with us—always has the right idea of heaven, that it is at hand, and that the son of man is in heaven; hence the instruction to all the disciples to pray," Thy will be (is) done in earth as it is in heaven." "And when ye pray, believe that ye receive and ye shall have," means believe that what you have prayed for is just as you have stated; that is, have the faith that what you have asked for is, and is included in the gift of God, Eternal Life.

The general idea of the conditions to be enjoyed in heaven, held by the christian world, is not to be discouraged, but should be understood, and if so, then understood because heaven is at hand and is with us here and now —wherever we are.

Jesus sent his disciples forth and instructed them to preach the gospel and heal the sick, saying the Kingdom of Heaven is at hand ; so it is self-evident that the Truth of Heaven at hand is within us here and now, to be preached and applied through instruction that makes whole. A heaven that we may possibly enter in some far-off to-morrow has in Divine Science given place to one in which we now experience within our being a state of supreme happiness, in which we daily and hourly commune with God, the everywhere present good; a state of at-one-ment so complete that self-communion is divine communion.

The nature of the general idea of heaven is that it is a place where it is perfect happiness to be; where all are free from every condition that tends to unhappiness. Free from death, sorrow, pain, disease, labor and want, this is all good, but is not all this the true state of our being? Reflect for a moment upon the depths of meaning hidden in the following statements, and our true nature will be revealed. " Without the word (that is with God, and is God), is not anything made that is made." " It made the world and all things therein." " It is the true Light that lighteth every man that cometh into the world." "God has nothing but his own perfect substance to make worlds (and all that they contain) out of." There is nothing for us to be but the Life-substance of the one living and true God. We are holy because He is Holy, we are spirit because He is Spirit, we are life because He is Life. We are heirs of God, and joint heirs with Christ. We inherit His Being and eternity. There is no other reality, identity or consciousness of Being, hence nothing else to be. In this the "hidden mystery is revealed." So the true state of our being is that of a little child.

Jesus said: " Suffer little children to come unto me, and forbid them not, for of such is the Kingdom of Heaven. To suffer children to come unto me, is to allow, and accept them to be just what Christ is—" the word made flesh," and educate them in the Truth of Being, so that they will know what they are, and just what their relation to their Father is, and that the God and Father of one is the God and Father of all. To forbid them not, is to draw no lines between them and Christ, and make no separation between Spirit and body. To come unto, is to be the same as. So we are not to prevent ourselves from claiming the Christ of God for all, and teach people that from Being they can truthfully make claims of equality with Jesus Christ.

The little child is a perfect example of the inhabitants of Heaven. It represents true meekness and lowliness of heart in being natural—just what God made it,—and not trying to become something different. It is trustful and happy now, and believes that what it wants it can have; that it has a right to have its natural wants supplied.

The child represents original purity and innocence. It is without human beliefs, opinions and claims about itself, and is in the same state that all things are that God creates or makes. So were we educated from childhood in the Truth of our Being, we would never make false statements, or say I, to anything but God ; we would claim and realize that which rightfully belongs to the child of God or Son of the most high. " For of such is the Kingdom of Heaven," means that little children are the Kingdom of Heaven. Within God, by the nature of law, power, are we begotten in His image and likeness, and little children stand for the whole of creation, and right here we are able to see and enjoy the divine love and protecting care of the " Holy One" in whom we live, whose will is done in earth as it is in heaven.

Let us accept little children in the name of Jesus Christ as Christ children, the only name for them, and suffer them to come unto *me* by so doing, knowing that anything that we ask for them in their true name *I* will give it, that God be glorified in them.

Thy will is done in earth as it is in heaven. Thanks be to God who has given us the victory in Jesus Christ our Lord, we are not twain, neither do we believe in duality, or any theory built upon a false claim of duality. Two are as one. That begotten of Spirit is. spirit. Heaven has come.

M. E. CRAMER.

Man in God.

THE Source and Cause of a thing must of necessity—always and everywhere—contain within itself the thing it produces or gives expression to. The thing produced or expressed must, therefore, be the embodiment of its Source, and in substance and nature be the same.

"Ye shall know them by their fruits." The only true estimate that can be placed upon the thing produced, is placed there by its source, for the value embodied therein is the nature of that producing it.

To be able to speak with knowledge, and to act in wisdom's way in all that we say and do, it is essential that we not only know what is, but that we know the nature, law, power, and possibility of that which is.

Holy Spirit or Divine Mind must be Infinite and everywhere present; hence, it would not be according to Truth or justice to suppose that it was more in one place than in another, or that to it the existence of one thing was more perfect than another. If God's infinitude was not everywhere present, it would be possible for us to be where the fullness of knowledge and power was not, and we would have foundation for beseeching Him to come more fully into our lives. "Be still, and know that I am God."

A very interesting and suggestive conclusion is now emerging from the work of natural Scientists. "It is practically established that the difference between the consciousness of man and that of the lowest forms of life, the single or unit cell form, is one of degree, and not of kind. That the lines of continuity run back from self-consciousness in man to the psychic life of micro-organisms, and if Haeckel, and Cope, and others of the world's great naturalists are right, the line cannot be drawn even at the beginning of organic life; we must go even back of the atoms and find consciousness in the ether. It is here that Cope finds the scientific warrant for the idea of God, and the hope of human immortality. He further suggests that mind is a mode of motion, or mode of wave force of the same substance as that which underlies visible phenomena."

The Genesis of Creation, and all the true statements of unity contained in the New Testament, and claims made by Jesus the Christ of us of at-one-ment with God are based in scientific Truth. For the Truth of unity and at-one-ment is the only Science of Being or Life. It must at once be seen that if there is but one Spirit or substance, the unity of this substance is maintained in all of its expressions. So, in the language of Calthrop, we say: "God has nothing but Himself to make His children out of. They are Spirit because He is Spirit. They live, because He lives." And here we understand the words of Jesus : " Because I live, ye shall live also." "As the Father hath life in Himself, just so is it given to the Son to have life in himself."

All scriptural statements of unity are found to be based upon the present scientific view of the unity of substance—one Omnipresent and Omnipotent reality, in which and of which all phenomena spring.

What a wonderful flood of light is here given by which to view the deep meaning of the sacramental occasion instituted by the man of Galilee: " This is my body which is given for you," with the injunction that we should partake of it until I come. But what is the self-revealed Truth when " I come ?" It is simply this, that *I am* it. Then it is that our life has appeared, and we appear with Him in glory, and with the brilliancy of pure intelligence we perceive the Truth of the words of Paul: " There is one Spirit and one body." " We are heirs of God and joint heirs with Christ." " To-day is the day of salvation." There is only one Mind and we are it, one Substance and we are it. Verily then in Him we have our being.

A God whom we may possibly approach in the future, and after death, or that we may progress toward throughout eternity but never attain, is in Divine Science among the things that have passed. "Old things have passed away, and all things have become new." And we know God as the one in whose bosom we rest, and whose life we live, and whose love we express, and daily and hourly reveal. " He who loveth knoweth God, for God is Love." " Behold, what manner of love the Father hath bestowed upon us," that we should be called the sons of God. God the absolute Truth, His at-one-ment the Omnipotent Power, Love the only law, makes the sure foundation on which all living rest. The general realization of the twentieth century will be what many Divine Scientists are enjoying at the present time, the Truth in simple language. God the ultimate Truth, or spirit, the absolute principle. That the God-head does not mean three originant principles, nor three transient phases, but three eternal inherencies of one Divine Mind. It will then be understood that what truly is, is God. The all in all will be known as SPIRIT, SOUL, INTELLIGENCE—as one Spirit; or MIND, IDEA, CONSCIOUSNESS, as one Mind.

The ultimate of freedom, power and happiness, is to be found in adjusting all our ways to the truth that God and his expression is all there is. So it will be generally understood that when Spirit or Mind expresses itself, it expresses its idea and consciousness; then no living form will be pronounced against, but all will be raised, a glorified, sanctified body. For that which is begotten of Spirit is spirit, and the body of spirit must be the expression of what spirit is. In other words, that which is begotten of Mind is mind, and the body of mind must be the expression of what it is.

A full consciousness of the oneness of substance must enable us to see that all conclusions arrived at from that basis must be the conclusions of God, and we can clearly see in it the light of the world, the true light that lighteth all, in which is no darkness. Great are the changes that are to take place in dissipating the world's way of thinking, and establishing a true conception of unity and at-one-ment.

So far my aim has been to prove the oneness of God and man, or in broader terms, the oneness of God the creator, with God his creation. Man, as the image and likeness of God, is perfect conception; "Jesus, the image of the Invisible God, the first-born of every creature," is perfect conception. There is one universal, holy, immaculate conception for all time, in which man ever exists as God with us. God's idea of man must be his idea of self, for the Infinite One being all, it could have no idea of another being; therefore, to make God-idea our idea of self, is the same as making our idea of God that of self; this finds us in the God-head and a unit throughout.

Would we do unto our source and cause as we would have it do unto us, it is essential for us to do just what we would have it do; so if we want God to include us within his being, will and law, we must include Him in our being, will and law.

That which fills all space being Spirit and one in nature, all things are found to be in a state of at-one-ment with and to exist within it, and to be itself made manifest. So Spirit carries within its infinitude of love all the worlds invisible and visible, and all things therein and thereon contained. Divine Science therefore, includes the ultimate spiritual principle, and teaches the unity of the whole, and blends all phenomena into pure being. So it must come to be seen by all, that to have a true conception of anything, we must start with God and reason from being; begin our reasoning at the top, as it were, or in the plane of source and cause, for it is self evident that the action and result of a source and cause cannot be understood except by its own knowledge, and this we can do, for I, intelligence or consciousness, am spirit. If man and God are one in spirit they are one in body, for what is potentially one is identically one when expressed.

Were we to reason from the standpoint of duality, or of separation from God, we could in no wise arrive at an understanding of the teachings of Jesus as applying to ourselves.

The estimate placed upon selfhood when reasoning from the supposition of innate sin, that there is a conception that falls short of Truth, and birth that misses the mark of equality with God, we would not be able to realize that we were created in righteousness and holiness of Truth.

In the new and living way of thinking, true theology and Science are brought into solidarity, for space is no longer thought of as vacant, but is really the divine presence of Supreme Being. This conception once grasped, we no longer wait, weary with hope deferred, for the good, the true, the real, for we find ourselves in a new world of power and beauty. It does away with the former conception of cause and effect, and establishes the true idea of it, which is that the effect is forever within the cause. God is seen to be the Truth, substance, intelligence and reality of all. So God comes to mean unto us all that is good, real, and eternal.

This view leaves no room whatever for death or dead matter, and no conception or claim of such a thing. The All in All is absolute Life. Let us decide scientifically upon the form of it, and determine correctly what it shall be to us. For the form is the word of Life that shall not pass away.

Let us, therefore, hold living forms in God consciousness and intelligence ; that is, know that they are there, and are divine substance, and act as if Truth was Truth. This will do away with the unsatisfactory practice of holding thoughts or words to bring things to pass. For it is not true motive to expect to change the substance, or to perfect it by such method, for it ignores the nature of the whole, and sets at naught the true conception of the body.

If the word is love or life that you have taken up, hold the body to be that word of life and love, and you will prove that my words are Truth, and they are life, for they are life to those who find them.

Principle or Opinion, Which ?

ONE of the subtlest temptations is that of basing our dealings with each other not on our highest conviction of what should be done, but upon what people think about us, and the work in which we are engaged. It is essential that we keep vigilant watch of our mental conduct, would we break the habit of acting upon the erroneous statements made as to what our motives are.

The feeling prevails among many, that if we are falsely accused as to the motives we have in our work, that we should so conduct our work as to make it impossible for them to so judge. To decide that we will pursue a certain course, or that we will discontinue certain methods because we have been wrongly accused of having motives that we have not had, is to act from the standpoint of these accusations ; they have been accepted as a premise for action.

A thoroughly original man or woman is one who acts from principle, from the real goodness of his true nature. Such an one is illumined with that light in which there is nothing but what is revealed, and he deals frankly with all with whom he has transactions. This is the light of pure knowledge and consciousness, in it all things are wisely done and divinely ordered.

There is in seeming a kind of so-called wisdom, the promptings of which would have us transfer our working basis from knowledge of Being, to what people say of our work ; this would be, as it were, dropping from knowledge to ignorance. It is in the same line with the habit of accepting pain or a sense of inharmony as a condition from which to draw conclusions, and make statements of ourselves. We all know that freedom of Truth can never be sensed by working from any premise or any point of view but Truth absolute.

Do not allow youself to cease working from principle for any one's opinion concerning you. God is Principle, and is your Life, and the same is Divine Judgment ; hold to it, therefore, with a divine steadfastness in unbroken faith of *being* it. There is no more subtle error, and no more disastrous blunder of ignorance, than to conclude " I will not do this or that because my motives (though theyare absolutely good and unselfish) are not understood."

To refuse to accept peoples' judgments of you, is to refuse to change your plans because of them. To deal with a man from principle, is to invite him to stand on that plane with you. "And I, if I be lifted up, will draw all unto Me." This has been proven many, many times in Divine Science; through trusting people, and believing in them, they have developed beautiful characters, and loving dispositions. This was most strikingly demonstrated by Seth Henshaw, a good Quaker and anti-slavery worker, who, when boys entered his yard or orchard to pluck ripe fruit, would place ladders against the trees, and invite them to help themselves. They soon felt that it was a shame to deal underhandedly in taking fruit from his orchard, and also felt a strong desire to deal frankly and justly with all. They would say, " I would not steal from Uncle Seth, no matter what my conditions were." It is true that like begets like, and like calls forth like, also like blends and communes with like. He was a man whom everybody felt it would be wrong to deceive or to take advantage of. There are men and women in every business community whom everybody feels it would be impossible to deceive or wrong in any way because they are so habitually loving, and just, and trusting. To go up into the high mountain of supreme consciousness of Being, is to know what is right. To be thus set, is to draw others unto us to the same elevation of knowledge and power.

Sow In Righteousness.

Sow to yourselves in righteousness, reap in mercy: break up your fallow ground, for it is time to seek the Lord till he come and rain Righteousness upon you.—Hosea x: 12.

TO seek is to find, and to find is to be where the treasure is for which we have sought. Divine Science, reveals that now all the wealth of God's Kingdom is contained in Being; all the spiritual gifts that are sought for are stored up in what "I Am." This is being where they are, and is seeking and finding. To break up the fallow ground is to sow unto self in righteousness and wholeness of Truth as does the Infinite Creator.

To sow unto ourselves in righteousness is to cultivate the ground of Being, and do the will of Him that sent us. This is working the Lord's method of raining righteousness.

During our recent work throughout the east, we met with not a few people becoming interested in Science who were claiming mental and bodily conditions over which they seemingly had no control, but it was found that in every case they had not been trained to demonstrate the law of expression from and by Being. They had no idea of what their own position should be to be a demonstrator of Truth. Some were feeling that true freedom was not for them to demonstrate or realize, for they had tried in every way they could, and were earnest and sincere.

No one can sow unto himself in righteousness without knowing who he is and what he is, and knowing the Law of Expression. To know this Truth is to know how to break up the fallow ground and sow righteousness unto ourselves.

When we know for ourselves what it means to be able to decree a thing, and see it established unto (within) us, then it is that such words as the following come home to us with depth of meaning: "I will be thy king; where is any other that may save thee in all thy cities?"

To break up fallow ground is to utterly destroy the non-productive habits and conditions that bear not fruit of righteousness or wholeness.

Lyman L. Palmer, of Chicago, writes of a recent class that he has taught. "I have had a wonderfully instructive session with my class. There is no comparative degree in Truth. It is all good."

Henry Wood is now engaged upon a new book which will shortly be published, and duly advertised and reviewed in HARMONY.

Questions and Answers

Ed. note: Almost every issue of *Harmony* Magazine contained a section of questions and answers, usually by Malinda Cramer; however, in a few instances, the answers came from Charles Cramer. This may prompt a question of what role Charles L. Carmer played in Divine Science. The answer seems to be that he played an extensive role.

Not only did he apparently fund much of the cost of *Harmony*, after 1894 he helped with the writing and editing of the magazine; however, he always signed his contributions. Malinda considered Charles as an essential part of her ministry; in the last fifteen years or so, he participated by jointly healing with Malinda in San Francisco and particularly on their various nation-wide tours.

In Volume 7 (p. 71) Malinda presented Charles to her readers as "our companion in life, who has silently co-operated with, and encouraged us in all our work in the cause of truth." She continued that it was obvious that she needed "someone connected with us who is in perfect accord with our understanding."

Q. WHAT is meant by going into the silence ?

A. It means to enter into a state of mental abstraction in which thought and attention is withdrawn from all external things, conditions, surroundings, time and place; but there are two ways of entering into this state, the one is positive and the other negative. When it is entered in the positive way the attention is withdrawn from the external and centered upon Being or God, the principle and substance, and reality of self, and all visible things, the purpose being to realize at-one-ment with God, and thereby commune with Him and self, and from this plane of consciousness express or demonstrate our inherent power and possibility, or in other words, express what we are.

When the silence is entered into in a negative way, the attention is withdrawn from the external the same as in the positive, but it is not fixed upon Being nor upon any definite purpose to be accomplished, hence it is an attitude of waiting for something to come, not knowing from whence it comes, but the conclusion is that the impressions received must come from God, because received in the silence, when the truth is that most, if not all, received in this negative state are simply impressions, and are just as liable to be received from one source as another, and as liable to be false as true. Going into the silence in this way is to become a medium for impressions, and is more apt to injure than benefit those who practice it. God expresses Himself, and is never impressed, and if we follow His method we shall express ourselves, and not place ourselves in an attitude to receive impressions.

The common practice with some, of holding in thought a word or words for the purpose of bringing about certain results, and not realizing that they are the reality of the word, can bring nothing but a sensuous response. To go into the silence understandingly, is to go into it for the purpose of speaking the positive words of the truth of what God is, which words testify of our at-one-ment with Him. These words do not result in a sensuous response, but make visible the truth of what God is.

Q. I have studied under a number of teachers of the "new thought," and have always been led to think that these higher truths should not be used on so low a plane as material prosperity, or business success. It was taught that we have a right to expect health and spiritual prosperity, but that it is wrong to use the Truth to further our financial interests.

I have gathered from the teaching that you not only approve of using Truth for prosperity, but teach that we may use science to promote material prosperity. Is this right? Is it according to the Bible?

A. If Truth is not to be used and made the basis for prosperity on this plane of existence, then there is nothing that can be used and made the basis of our dealings with each other but error. As long as we hold that there is both material and spiritual prosperity, we will hold one in Truth and the other in error, which is a dual theory not found in Truth. The moment we hold Truth for both they are seen to be one even as Truth is one—unit.

If it is wrong to use the Truth to further our financial interests, it is certainly right to set Truth aside and use error. They who have been thus instructed in the "higher thought," have not been taught unity of action and result, hence it is possible for them to suppose that Truth could be used for the well being of some, and to the detriment of others, but this is not possible.

One who reads the Bible and does not see that prosperity is God's law, does not read attentively, and all he needs to do to realize that God is His own success, is simply to behold the Truth of the visible universe spread abroad before us. Since God is successful, and is infinite, man's success is to be found within him, hence it is written, "No good thing will be withheld from them that walk uprightly." The righteous shall flourish like the palm tree, he shall grow like a cedar in Lebanon.

"Turn not to the right hand nor to the left, that thou mayest prosper whithersoever thou goest." And Jesus said: "It is the Father's good pleasure to give you the kingdom." Surely success must be a good thing, rightly understood, and being a *good* thing it is Godly ; so I would say : "First seek the Kingdom of God and His righteousness and all these things shall be added." In the Kingdom of God and His rightness there is food, raiment and shelter for all.

The belief of inequality and want has come about through misunderstanding of God's law, and through the belief that we are not to use the Truth in our business relations. To actualize the divine graces in the business world in our daily dealings one with another is the only practical thing to do.

Yes, it is right to use Truth to succeed in everything that we do; it is right to make it the basis of all our undertakings.

There is a difference between making it a basis for success and using it with view of acquiring whatever may be desired without regard to the law— Love and the Spirit of Justice. When Truth is made the basis the law is fulfilled, and Truth is demonstrated. When the intention is to acquire without regard to law, there is no realization of demonstrated Truth or law.

Give, and it shall be given unto you; good measure, pressed down and shaken together, and running over, shall men give into your bosom. For with the same measure that ye mete withal it is measured to you again. Can the blind lead the blind? Can anything but charity beget charity or call it forth in others, and relate one to all that charity implies? No, with what measure we mete withal it is measured to us, for the same is our act, our estimate of the Law of Being.

God uses the Truth in manifesting the so-called material universe, and if it is right for Him to use it in all that He does, it is certainly right for us to follow His example. The only wrong is in not using it.

Q. What are we to do if our boys form bad habits, shall we be anxious, and talk and plead, or shall we silently declare their perfection?

A. As we know that all that is in reality, is divine Life, we know that all living are manifest or brought forth in, and by that Life, and are therefore divine; and being divine are perfect and complete, the image and likeness of, or, like unto the source.

This being true we should silently, and by spoken word, affirm that our boys are born of God and are God's boys, and are not bad; nor are they subject to bad habits, but are masters of all habits. We should consider them companions and equals, and not endeavor to subject them to our opinions and desires. Perfect love should govern all our relations with our children. This will cast out all fear and establish perfect confidence; thus shall we be to them a living example of faith in the doctrine of wholeness and perfection. Anxiety is fear and doubt, and if we are anxious about our boys' habits, we believe them to be bad, and talking and pleading on that plane of thought is an example to them of our lack of faith in their divinity, perfection and goodness.

"Religion is the best armor a man can have, but it is the worst cloak."— *Bunyan.*

Cease, then, from striving to make the visible world produce true happiness for you—from seeking to make sensation a cause of real joy. Place not your heart, dear student, upon earthly things, or your consciousness upon the things of the past; but live in the presence and the present, for this is Life eternal.

. . . .

CORRESPONDENCE.

"YE ARE GODS."

PETALUMA, Nov. 26.

Dear Friends :

I am in the dark about " Ye are Gods " [subject for meditation for November 21st], as the quotation is from the Bible, and is so quoted as to carry an incorrect idea, so far as Bible authority is concerned. The *G* should have been a small letter [gods instead of Gods], which means a judge and in no way refers to deity. A following of the passage through the old and new testaments will show that in no case was such meaning attached as God—for in every instance a small "g" is used.

Yours, etc.,   C. W. O.

[We have had other similar enquiries to the above, to which the following answer will apply. So far as the Bible authority referred to is concerned, our correspondent is most likely correct; but the only necessary and true authority for the interpretation of Scripture is the spirit of understanding—or intuition—within each individual; there *is* no other real authority for any one, and the belief that another's knowledge is sufficient for any one does not by any means relieve that one from the necessity of gaining his own knowledge for himself *from* himself. " By *thy* words thou shalt be justified, and by *thy* words thou shalt be condemned."—Matt. xii. How the word *Gods* should be spelled is a mere matter of letters, what it means is a matter of spirit; questions pertaining to the letter may be settled by the intellect, but concerning the spirit all questions must be settled by the intuition, which is the Spirit of Truth or the Comforter within every individual. " Our sufficiency is of God, who also hath made us able ministers of the new testament ; not of the letter, but of the spirit; for the letter killeth, but the spirit giveth life."—II Cor. iii. Now the idea that "Gods" would immediately suggest to the intellect is "many (infinite) Gods," which the intuition immediately denies, saying—there can be but one Infinite. The intuition or Spirit of understanding would further say—but there may be many individuals—Sons of God—conscious of The One Infinite, and these may be called Gods. Furthermore, Understanding would affirm as follows—there is nothing permanent but God and His creation (Souls or Sons), hence if the term Gods have a true meaning in the absolute, and if it cannot be applied to the one Infinite, there only remains His creation to which it may be applied, hence " ye are Gods " means ye are those wise Souls or Sons, who are at one with the Father ; and this conclusion was the one suggested for thought on November 21st. Now if the word "god" means judge, then it must be in the sense indicated in John v, " the Father hath committed all judgment unto the Son;" thus the Son is the judge, and Sons are judges ; hence if the passage read "ye are judges," it would mean " ye are Gods or Sons."—Eds.]

Q. If we can bring things to pass by thought, will you please give us your interpretation of the 25th verse of the 12th chapter of Luke: " Which of you with taking thought can add to his stature one cubit ? "

A. Taking thought is very different from being thought. To take thought, is to think about things, and is to recognize nothing but the thought and the thing—the thinker is ignored ; hence the thinker, the thought, and the thing, appear to be separate, and it is believed that the appearance of the thing controls the thought, and that the thought controls the thinker.

But to *be* thought, is to be the thinker, which includes both the thought and the thing, and hence is the possessor of both, and instead of being subject to, is creator and controller of both.

This is creative thought, and is oneness with God, for it is His method of manifesting His will ; and is what Jesus meant, when in the 31st verse, he said, " But rather seek ye the kingdom of God, and all these things shall be added unto you." As the kingdom of God is within us, it is to seek the thinker within ourselves, and thus control thought, and bring things to pass.

Q. How can all things be spiritual ?

A. God being infinite, He is all; there is nothing but Him; if there were, He would not be infinite. Hence all things made are made by Him, and are Himself made manifest, and He being spirit, and all things being Himself manifest, they must also be spirit.

Q. What evidences have we that there is any intelligence, independent of the body ? I have never seen any valid reason that I, or any other person. possessed intelligence, independent of the body. What is a soul ?

A. These questions with the statement implies the following conclusion, viz: That you possess intelligence, but that it is co-existent with and dependent upon the body; and if that be true, if the body ceased to exist, the intelligence must of necessity cease with it.

Neither the statement nor such conclusion, as to the beginning or end of intelligence, is justified by a logical analysis of the question. No one will claim that the body is the cause of itself, but I think all will admit that it is the effect produced by some cause, and whatever that cause may be, it must have expressed itself in producing the effect; hence the effect, which is the body, is the cause expressed.

I think none will deny the self-evident fact that the body is the expression of intelligence, showing, as it does, in its construction and in all its intricate workings, the perfect adaptability of each and every part to the whole, it is of itself sufficient evidence of the intelligence of the power that formed it ; and if formed by intelligence, or an intelligent power, that power must have ante-dated that which it created or expressed, for cause must always precede the effect which it produces. Hence it is not dependent upon its production for being what it is, but the effect produced is always dependent upon the cause for being what it is. If, then, intelligence manifests the body, and is not dependent upon it before manifestation, neither is it after manifestation, or if manifestation ceases.

Now if you possess intelligence, you must certainly be intelligence, for it is impossible for you to possess a quality that is greater than yourself. We cannot conceive of intelligence being contained by or expressed in anything but mind, and, when expressed, is the expression of mind's idea ; hence idea is the soul of all forms expressed by intelligent mind. As nothing but life can contain or be either mind, idea, or intelligence, whatever is expressed of either, or all, is the expression of life and its idea in the form of living things. Idea, being the soul of things, it can neither be weighed nor measured, and salvation consists in the recognition that it eternally exists in intelligent mind or in infinite life. What is known of so-called physical law, is in perfect harmony with these ideas, for it is known that all visible form comes forth of the invisible element, or substance, which is in no way changed by the manifestation or formation of its possibilities ; it was the same substance before, that it is during, and continues to be after, manifestation, for it is eternal and indestructible, hence in *reality* must be unchanging, no matter in how many forms it may appear.

From the above views you will undoubtedly infer that we believe that the visible universe is a manifestation of intelligent mind. The difference between your position and our own on this question is this : you make form, or effect, the basis of your conclusions as to what intelligence is, while we conceive intelligent mind to be the source and cause of form, or effect.

ALL'S WELL.

Sweet-voiced hope, thy fine discourse
  Foretold not half life's good to me ;
Thy painter, fancy, hath not force
  To show how sweet it is to be.
    Thy witching dream
    And pictured scheme,
To match the fact, still wants the power ;
    Thy promise brave
    From birth to grave,
Life's boon may beggar in an hour.

"Ask and receive," 'tis sweetly said,
  Yet, what to ask for, know I not ;
For Wish is worsted, Hope outsped,
  And aye to thanks returns my thought.
    If I would pray,
    I've naught to say
But this, that God may be God still ;
    For Him to live
    Is still to give,
And sweeter than my wish, His will.

O wealth of life beyond all bound :
  Eternity each moment given :
What plummet may the present sound,
  Who promises a *future* heaven ?
    Or glad, or grieved,
    Oppressed, relieved,
In blackest night, or brightest day,
    Still pours the flood
    Of golden good,
And more than heart full fills me aye.

My wealth is common ; I possess
  No petty province, but the whole ;
What's mine alone, is mine far less
  Than treasure shared by every soul.
    Talk not of store,
    Millions or more
Of values whice the purse may hold ;
    But this divine—
    I own the mine
Whose grains outweigh a planet's gold.

I have a stake in every star,
  In every beam that fills the day ;
All hearts of men my coffers are,
  My ores arterial tides convey;
    The fields, the skies,
    And sweet replies
Of thought to thought are my gold dust—
    The oaks, the brooks,
    And speaking looks
Of lover's faith and friendship's trust.

Life's youngest tides joy-brimming flow
  For him who lives above all years ;
Who all immortal makes the Now,
  And is not taken in time's arrears,
    His life's a hymn
    The seraphim
Might hark to hear, or help to sing ;
    And to his soul
    The boundless whole
Its bounty all doth daily bring.

" All mine is thine," the sky-soul saith ;
  The wealth I am must thou become,
Richer and Richer, breath by breath,
  Immortal gain, immortal room.
    And since all his
    Mine also is,
Life's gifts outrun my fancies far,
    And drown the dream
    In larger stream,
As morning drinks the morning star.

Inspiration from Others

Ed. note: From the first issue of *Harmony*, Cramer included various examples of wisdom. The magazine regularly carried a section entitled "Bibles of the Ages" in which she quoted various scriptures and writings from throughout history as well as the King James Bible.

BIBLES OF THE AGES.

THE SMARAGDINE TABLE.

Firstly.—I speak not fictitious things but that which is certain and most true.

Secondly.—What is below is like that which is above; and what is above is like that which is below, to accomplish the miracle of one thing.

Thirdly.—And as all things were produced by the one Word of one Being, so all things were produced from this one thing by adaptation.

Fourthly.—Its father is the Sun, its mother is the Moon, the Wind carries it in its belly, its nurse is the Earth.

Fifthly.—It is the father of all perfection throughout the World.

Sixthly.—The power is vigourous, if it be changed into Earth.

Seventhly.—Separate the Earth from the Fire, the gross from the subtle, acting prudently and with judgment.

Eighthly.—Ascend with the greatest sagacity from the earth to the heaven, and then again descend, to the earth, and unite together the powers of things superior and things inferior. Thus you will obtain the glory of the whole world, and obscurity will fly from you.

Ninthly.—This has more fortitude than fortitude itself, because it conquers every subtle thing and can penetrate every solid.

Tenthly.—Thus was the World formed.

Eleventhly.—Hence proceed wonders which are here established.

Twelfthly.—Therefore I am called Hermes Trismegistus, having three parts of the philosophy of the whole World.

Thirteenthly.—That which I had to say concerning the operation of the Sun is completed.

[The above is extracted from the introduction to "The Divine Pymander."]

BIBLES OF THE AGES.

PLATO.

PRAYER—THE DIVINE NATURE—THE JUST MAN.

PRAYER is the ardent turning of the soul toward God; not to ask for any particular good, but for good itself; the universal, supreme good. We often mistake what is pernicious and dangerous for what is useful and desirable. Therefore remain silent before the gods till they remove the clouds from thine eyes, and enable thee to see by their light, not what appears good to thy self, but what is really good.

Whatever is beautiful is so merely by the participation of the Supreme Beauty. All other beauty may increase, decay, change, or perish, but this is the same through all time.

By raising our thoughts above all inferior beauties, we at length reach the Supreme beauty, which is simple, pure and immutable, without form, color, or human qualities. It is the splendor of the Divine image, it is Deity himself. Love of this Supreme Beauty renders a man divine.

God provides for all things, the least as well as the greatest. He is the original life and force of all things, in the ethereal regions, upon the earth. and under the earth. He is the Being, the Unity, the Good; the same in the world of intelligence that sun is in the visible world.

God is Truth, and light is his shadow. What light and sight are in this visible world, truth and intelligence are in the real, unchangeable world.

The end and aim of all things should be to attain to the first good; of whom the sun is the type, and the material world, with its host of ministering spirits, is but the manifestation and the shadow.

The perfectly just man would be he who should love justice for its own sake, not for the honor's or advantages that attend; who would be willing to pass for unjust while he practiced the most exact justice; who would not suffer himself to be moved by disgrace or distress, but would continue steadfast in the love of justice, not because it is pleasant, but because it is right.*

*Plato was born B. C. 429.

THE ANNIHILATION OF SELFHOOD.

Practical Buddhism may be thus summarized : It is, *To see, feel, speak, behave, live, act, think, and aspire rightly.* This is the absolute direction to attain to the absolute. We find the same rule poetically rendered in an ancient Hindu drama, as follows:—

" Be virtue, friends, your only store,
And restless appetite restrain ;
Beat meditation's drum, and sore
Your watch against each sense maintain.
The thief that still in ambush lies,
To make devotion's wealth his prize.

" Cast the five senses all away
That triumph o'er the virtuous will ;
The pride of self-importance slay,
And ignorance remorseless kill.
So shall you safe the body guard,
And heaven shall be your last reward.

Why shave the head, and mow the chin,
Whilst bristling follies choke the breast ?
Apply the knife to parts within,
And heed not how deformed the rest.
The heart of pride and passion weed,
And then the man is pure indeed."

—*Mystery of the Ages.*

(" The Toy Cart "—H. H. Wilson's translation.)

SPIRIT.

MASTER.   The Spirit of Man, whereby he strives,
           Flashes from star to star, if so it will,
           And—if it will—sleeps in the smallest drop
           Of the mid-most heart blood ;—Yama sayeth so.

DISCIPLE. Yet, * Pundit, this is hard to comprehend !
           How can it be that what hath plenitude
           To range from star to star should hide itself
           I' the hollow of a heart?

MASTER.   I answer thee
           Out of the great Upanishad, surnamed
           Khandogya ! Gather me up yon fruit
           Dropped by the parrots from the Banyan !
           What seest thou therein ?

DISCIPLE.   A scarlet fig
           Not larger than the Moulvie's praying bead !

MASTER.   Break it, and say again !

DISCIPLE.   I brake it, sir,
           And see, a hundred little yellow seeds !

MASTER.   Break it, and say again.

DISCIPLE.   I break a seed :
           It is as slight as though a silkworm's egg
           Were crushed ; and in the midst, a germ, a speck.

MASTER.   Break it and say again !

DISCIPLE.   The speck is gone
           In touching, † Guru.   There is nothing, now !

MASTER.   Yet, in that "nothing" lay (thou knowest well),
           The Nyagrodha tree, the Banyan tree,
           Comely and vast as it was formed to grow,
           With all its thousand downward-drooping stems,
           Waiting to fall from all its thousand boughs,
           And all its lakhs on lakhs of lustrous leaves,
           Waiting to push to sunlight, and to make
           New canopies of flower, and fruit, and shade,
           Where creatures of the field, fowls of the air,
           Monkey and squirrel-folk might find their home.

---

* Master.   † Master (i. e., Divine Soul.)

And man and cattle 'neath its ample roof,
Have shelter from the noon. This Forest-king
Of bulk to overspread a Raja's camp,
Was wrapped in what thou sayest passeth sight !
Art thou answered?

EDWIN ARNOLD.

ÔM.

" This word, so rightly breathed, signifieth Brahm,
And signifieth Brahma. GOD withdrawn,
And GOD manifest. Who knows this word,
With all its purports, what his heart would have
His heart possesseth. This of spoken speech
Is wisest, deepest, best, supremest! He
That speaketh it, and wotteth what he speaks
Is worshipped in the place of Brahm with Brahm!"

— EDWIN ARNOLD.

References from *Harmony* Magazine

Page	Title	Date Published	Vol./Page No.

By Malinda Elliott Cramer

Page	Title	Date Published	Vol./Page No.
4	Of the Soul	10/1888	1:21[1]*

* The second issue of Volume 1 was mistakenly numbered again beginning with page 1; the remaining portions of Volume 1 have correct pagination. ([1]denotes issue 1; [2]denotes issue 2.)

Page	Title	Date Published	Vol./Page No.
4	The Great Lesson To Be Learned	4/1889	1:202-203
	The Mystical		
21	Excerpt from Volume Seven	10/1894	7:9-11
22	Erroneous Teaching	7/1903	15:315
23	What I Have Seen	7/1903	15:307-309
25	The Second Birth	1/1892	4:132
26	Mathematics, or Truth	7/1889	1:289-291
	The Basics		
29	Perceiving the Presence	11/1888	1:1-4[2]
32	Oneness	3/1889	1:161
33	Misc. Thoughts	12/1888	1:66
34	The New Doctrine	3/1890	2:172-173
36	The Holy Temple and the Inner...	10/1889	2:1-3
38	Want, Love and Works	10/1888	1:15-16
40	The Law	11/1888	1:7[2]
41	"And With What Ye Measure..."	8/1889	1:321-322
43	Christmas	12/1888	1:67-71
47	For the New Year/Affirmations	10/1895	8:15
48	The Glory of God...Personality	3/1890	2:161-163
51	Perception or Consciousness	11/1888	1:10-12[2]
53	The Comforter	11/1888	1:12-15[2]
57	Re: Warren Felt Evans	12/1889	2:93
57	Metaphysical or Spiritual Healing	10/1888	1:17
58	Christmas Bells	11/1897	10:61
59	Meditation	pub. beginning 10/1888	thru 10/1889

Vol 1:3-6; 4-6[2]; 71-74; 100-104; 131-134; 162-166; 195-198; 227-231; 258-261; 292-295; 323-328; 354-359. Vol 2:3-4.

Page	Title	Date Published	Vol./Page No.
110	Pain and Suffering	9/1889	1:365-366
111	The New Order	pub. beginning 12/1888	thru 11/1889

Vol 1:75-77; 104-110; 142-144; 171-174; 204-206; 235-238; 267-269; 295 298; 331-333; 363-365. Vol 2:7-9: 42-44.

Page	Title	Date Published	Vol./Page No.
124	Judge Not	6/1889	1:257